How Computers REALLY Work

Milind S. Pandit

Osborne McGraw-Hill

Berkeley   New York   St. Louis   San Francisco   Auckland   Bogotá   Hamburg   London   Madrid   Mexico City
Milan   Montreal   New Delhi   Panama City   Paris   São Paulo   Singapore   Sydney   Tokyo   Toronto

ACQUISITIONS EDITOR
Jeffrey M. Pepper

ASSOCIATE EDITOR
Vicki Van Ausdall

TECHNICAL EDITOR
Nick DiMuria

PROJECT EDITOR
Janet Walden

PROOFREADER
Linda Medoff

COMPUTER DESIGNER
Stefany Otis

ILLUSTRATOR
Marla J. Shelasky

COVER DESIGN
Woods & Woods Design Communications

Osborne **McGraw-Hill**
2600 Tenth Street
Berkeley, California 94710
U.S.A.

For information on software, translations, or book distributors outside of the U.S.A., please write to Osborne McGraw-Hill at the above address.

How Computers REALLY Work

1234567890 DOC 99876543

ISBN 0-07-881936-9

To a profound idea that was conceived at the same time as this book.

CONTENTS

Acknowledgments

This book was made possible by the efforts of very special people:

Thanks to Marla Shelasky for illustrating it and to Janet Walden, Vicki Van Ausdall, Jeff Pepper, and the others at Osborne/McGraw-Hill for publishing it.

Thanks to the professors at the University of Michigan, Ann Arbor, who taught me most of what's in it.

Thanks to my fiancée, Sanjyot G. Kelkar, for inspiring me to finish it.

Thanks to my brother, Devavrat S. Pandit, for his practical advice on many matters.

Thanks to my father, Dr. Sudhakar M. Pandit, who first introduced me to computers.

And most importantly, thanks to my mother, Mrs. Maneesha S. Pandit, for believing in me no matter what.

Milind S. Pandit
13 June 1993

Introduction

This book is directed at a very large audience—those who are curious about how a computer operates. Unlike many computer books, it is not concerned with specific hardware or software. Rather, this book concentrates on how a computer processes data. The approach is unique, but the information is central to a firm understanding of computer operations and is something every computer professional should know. I have striven to make difficult topics extremely clear through use of analogies, avoidance of lingo, and *a lot* of planning to simplify the discussions.

Various parts of a computer work together to make the whole computer function. Within those parts, smaller parts work together to make the larger parts function, and so on. This book is written in the "bottom-up" style. This means that I talk about the smallest parts of a computer in detail first. Then, I show how those parts work together to form the next larger parts, and so on, until I show how the largest parts operate together to form an entire functioning computer.

To learn how a computer works, you need to know two things about each computer part:

- What it does

- How it does it

In each chapter, you will learn these two things about a part of the computer. After you finish the chapter, you don't have to worry about exactly *how* the part works. Try, however, to remember *what* the part does. This will help you understand the following chapter. Occasionally I will discuss a simple part in detail and then ask you to just imagine a more complicated part.

Those of you who have used a computer before may wonder what the first couple of chapters have to do with computers at all. To you I say, Be patient. As the book progresses, you will see how important these basic devices are to the function of an entire computer.

It is said that a picture is worth a thousand words, and I know that pictures always help me to understand unfamiliar or abstract ideas. That's why I've included many figures and illustrations in this book. At first glance, some of them may appear intimidating. If you read through, however, you will see that they truly help simplify the difficult concepts presented. You should look at the pictures and understand what they show.

I made my explanations in *How Computers REALLY Work* as simple as I could, so that anyone could understand them. Real computers aren't so simple, but if you understand my explanations, you will have a very good idea of how a computer works. I hope that readers will find my book interesting and extremely informative, and that it will serve as a launching point for future leaders of the computing world.

1

How Transistors Work

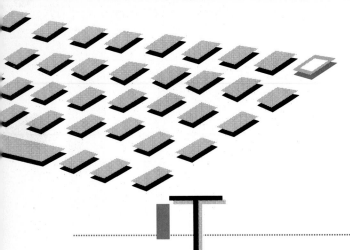

THIS chapter lays some groundwork for future topics and introduces you to some basic principles of electricity. In particular, circuits and transistors are defined and explained.

In this book, each working part of a computer will be called a *device*. The simplest and smallest device in a computer is the *transistor*. A computer uses hundreds of transistors to do even simple things.

ELECTRONS

You probably already know that everything in the universe is composed of atoms. The book you're holding, the water you drink, and you yourself are made of atoms.

Atoms are so small that you can't see them even with a very powerful microscope. But atoms contain even smaller particles, called *electrons*. You can find electrons wherever there are atoms. And in much the same way that the earth revolves around the sun, electrons are stuck revolving around the centers of atoms, as shown in this illustration.

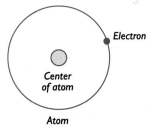

Some electrons, however, are free to move about. As you can see in the following illustration, electrons are small enough to squeeze between atoms, the way children can squeeze between adults and move through crowds. When electrons squeeze between atoms, interesting things can occur. This is how a light bulb works. Inside the glass bulb is a piece of metal called a filament. The filament is, just like everything else, made out of atoms. When the light switch is turned on, electrons move through the filament. When electrons squeeze between the atoms in the filament, they make it glow.

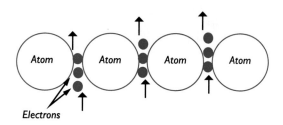

Electrons

CONDUCTORS AND INSULATORS

Electrons can move through metals very easily. There is enough space between the atoms in metals for electrons to squeeze through. Because of this, metals are called electrical *conductors*.

There are also many materials that electrons can't move through easily. These are called electrical *insulators*. Why can't electrons move through insulators? Sometimes it's because the atoms in insulators are packed too tightly for electrons to squeeze between them. Or, if electrons try to squeeze between the atoms, they just get stuck revolving around the centers of the atoms. Plastic is a good example of an insulator. It is very hard to make electrons move through plastic. Another example of an insulator is air! People can move through air easily, but electrons can't.

Have you ever wondered exactly what electrical wire is used for? Electrical wire is used to carry electrons. Typically, it consists of a long, thin piece of metal that is wrapped in plastic. Electrons can travel easily through the wire, because it is metal and therefore a conductor. Electrons cannot travel easily through the plastic, because it is an insulator. As shown in the following illustration, a wire is like a tunnel for electrons to travel through.

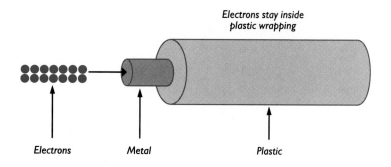

Electrons stay inside plastic wrapping

Electrons   Metal   Plastic

That's why lamps, and other electrical appliances, always have wires. The wire in the lamp is connected to the filament in the light bulb. Electrons move through the wire to the filament and make it glow.

HOW A
CIRCUIT
WORKS

W

e know that electrons travel easily through metals and other conductors. We also know that electrons can't move through plastic or other insulators. But what makes electrons move in the first place? They need something to push or pull them.

One thing that can push and pull electrons is a battery. Batteries come in many shapes and sizes, from the small, flat battery used in a digital wristwatch, to the large, boxy battery that helps start a car's engine.

Regardless of their size and shape, all batteries have two metal parts called *terminals*. One terminal is usually marked with a plus sign (+). This terminal is called the *high-voltage* terminal. A battery is always trying to pull electrons *into* the high-voltage terminal, much like someone trying to draw a thick milkshake up through a straw to their mouth.

The other terminal is marked with a minus sign (–). It is the *low-voltage* terminal. A battery is always trying to push electrons *out* of the low-voltage terminal, much like someone trying to blow air into a balloon.

Even though the battery is trying to push electrons out and pull them in, it really can't do either of these things. Remember that air is an insulator, and the air around the terminals keeps electrons from getting pushed out or pulled in. Electrons need a path made out of a conductor in order to exit the low-voltage terminal or enter the high-voltage terminal.

Suppose we touch one end of a wire to the low-voltage terminal, as shown in this illustration:

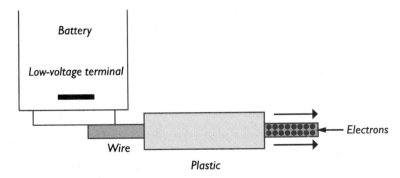

Now there is a conducting metal path for electrons to get pushed out of the battery. The wire quickly becomes filled with electrons. The battery keeps trying to push the electrons, but they have nowhere to go since the wire is surrounded by two insulators, air and plastic. Because the battery is trying to push electrons out through the wire, the wire is like a low-voltage terminal. We say that the wire is at low voltage.

Suppose we touch one end of a wire to the high-voltage terminal, as illustrated here:

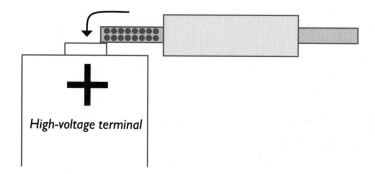

Now there is a conducting metal path for electrons to get pulled into the battery. Any electrons that may have been in the wire quickly get sucked into the battery. The battery keeps trying to pull in electrons, but no more electrons can get pulled into the wire. Again, this is because the metal of the wire is surrounded by insulators. Because the battery is trying to pull electrons in through the wire, the wire is like a high-voltage terminal. We say that the wire is at high voltage.

Now, let's touch one wire to the high-voltage terminal and one wire to the low-voltage terminal. We can then connect these wires to a light bulb, as shown in the following illustration.

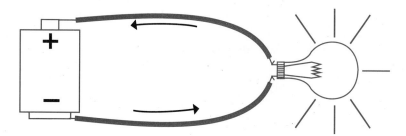

The light bulb immediately turns on. The low-voltage terminal pushes electrons through the connecting wire and into the filament of the light bulb.

They get pulled out of the filament through the wire connected to the high-voltage terminal. As electrons pass through the filament, they make it glow. The electrons travel in a circular path from the battery to the light bulb and back again. This path is called a *circuit*.

When the wire touching the low-voltage terminal is disconnected from the light bulb, the bulb goes out. Why? The battery is still trying to push electrons through the wire at the low-voltage terminal, but they can't reach the light bulb because air is an insulator. So there are no electrons moving through the filament, and the light bulb goes out.

Another thing that can push and pull electrons is an electrical *generator*. In every city there is a large electrical generator that provides electrons for the entire area. This generator pushes and pulls electrons through wires that are sometimes many miles long. These wires come to each house and are connected to the wall sockets inside. When you plug your computer into the wall, you are really providing a metal path for electrons to go into the computer and make it work. The wall sockets for the plugs have three holes. Typically, only the top two are used. Inside each hole is a piece of metal, and each piece of metal is connected to a wire that runs to the city generator. The generator is always trying to push electrons out through one wire and pull electrons in through the other. So the pieces of metal in the socket holes are like the terminals of the battery. Of course, electrons can't go in or come out unless you provide a metal path for them by plugging a wire into the wall socket.

SEMICONDUCTORS

We know that electrons move easily through conductors like metal. We know that they don't move easily through insulators like plastic and air. There are also materials that can act like conductors sometimes and like insulators at other times. These materials are called *semiconductors*.

Both sand and glass are composed of the same kind of atoms. They are made mostly out of *silicon* atoms. Pure silicon is a semiconductor, which means that sometimes electrons can pass easily through things made from silicon, and sometimes they can't. There is a way to make silicon act like a conductor or an insulator, whichever we want. You will learn about this in the next section.

TRANSISTORS

A

t the beginning of the chapter, you read that the simplest and smallest device in a computer is the transistor. The following illustration shows a *planar NPN transistor*. Planar means flat. As you can see, the transistor is made out of thin flat layers, like a sandwich. That's why this is called a *planar* NPN transistor.

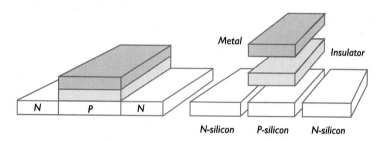

The bottom layer of the transistor is made of two kinds of silicon. One is called *n-silicon* and the other is called *p-silicon.* N-silicon and p-silicon are made by adding different chemicals to pure silicon. As I mentioned, pure silicon is a semiconductor, but after chemicals have been added, the bottom layer of the transistor acts like an insulator. Both n-silicon and p-silicon are needed to make the transistor work. A strip of p-silicon sits between two strips of n-silicon, which is why it is called a planar *NPN* transistor.

The middle layer of the transistor is a thin insulator. It doesn't really matter what kind of insulator is used, as long as electrons can't pass through it.

The top layer of the transistor is made out of a conductor. Sometimes metal is used, and sometimes other conductors are used.

Look at the following illustration. Two wires have been attached to the n-silicon strips in the transistor. These wires provide a conducting metal path for electrons to go into or come out of the bottom layer. But the bottom layer of n- and p-silicon usually acts like an insulator. So electrons can't pass through it from one wire to the other.

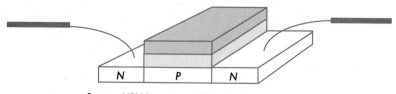

Bottom NPN layer is usually an insulator

To understand how a transistor works, you have to remember something from the discussion on batteries and voltage. Remember that if one end of a wire is touching the low-voltage terminal of a battery, the wire is said to be at low voltage. Why? Because instead of trying to push electrons out through its own low-voltage terminal, the battery now tries to push electrons out through the wire. In the same way, if one end of a wire is touching the high-voltage terminal of a battery, the wire is at high voltage. Instead of trying to pull electrons in through its own high-voltage terminal, the battery now tries to pull electrons in through the wire. In this way, we can put any conductor at high voltage or at low voltage. We just connect a wire from it to something else that is at high or low voltage.

Now let's put the top layer of the transistor at high voltage. We do this by touching one end of a wire to it and the other end to the high-voltage terminal of a battery, as shown here:

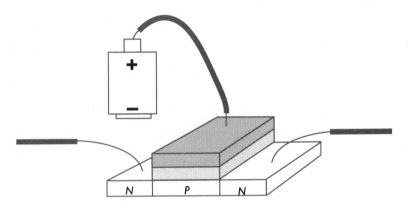

Now NPN bottom layer is a conductor

Now the battery is trying to pull in electrons through the top layer of the transistor. No electrons go into the battery, of course, because this layer is surrounded by insulators. There is air around it, and a thin insulator under it. But the battery is still trying to pull in electrons through the top layer, and so the top layer of the transistor is now at high voltage.

Because the top layer of the transistor is at high voltage, the bottom layer turns into a conductor! The reason that this happens is pretty complicated but, in general, it has to do with the two types of silicon in the bottom layer. This layer changes when the top layer is at high voltage. Now, electrons can pass from one wire, through the bottom layer, into the other wire.

The most important thing to remember about an NPN transistor is this: usually, the bottom layer of a transistor is an insulator. But if the top layer is at high voltage, then the bottom layer turns into a conductor. We say that the transistor "turns on."

Look at the next illustration. This electrical circuit is similar to the one you saw before. There is one difference, though. There used to be a wire going straight from the light bulb to the high-voltage terminal of the battery. In this illustration, the wire goes from the light bulb to the bottom layer of a transistor, and another wire leads from the bottom layer of the transistor to the battery.

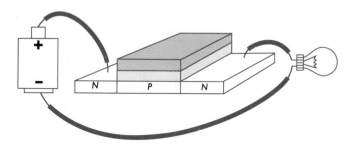

Let's see what's going on here. A wire is connected to the high-voltage terminal of the battery. The battery is trying to pull electrons in through it, but the other end of this wire is in the bottom layer of the transistor. Since this layer is usually an insulator, there are no electrons going into the battery. The battery can push a few electrons out of its low-voltage terminal. These electrons go through one wire, through the light bulb filament, and then through the other wire. But the end of this wire is also in the bottom layer of the transistor. These electrons have no place to go. They stop moving and the light bulb doesn't turn on.

Now, suppose the top layer of the transistor is put at high voltage as in the following illustration. Suddenly, the bottom layer has become a conductor, and electrons can move through it. There is now a circuit for electrons to go into and come out of the battery, and the light bulb turns on.

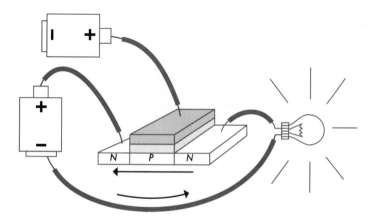

In this circuit, the transistor is like a light switch. When the high-voltage battery terminal is not connected to the top layer, the bottom layer remains an insulator, and the light bulb stays off. But if the high-voltage battery terminal is connected to the top layer, the bottom layer becomes a conductor, and the light bulb turns on.

The next illustration shows another type of planar transistor. This transistor is called a PNP transistor. This is because the bottom layer has a strip of n-silicon between two strips of p-silicon. This arrangement makes this transistor behave differently from an NPN transistor.

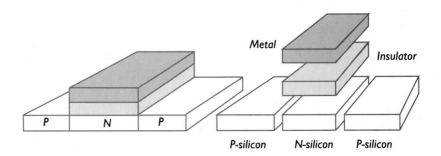

Usually, the bottom layer of the PNP transistor is an insulator. But when the top layer is put at low voltage, the bottom layer turns into a conductor.

So, when the top layer of an NPN transistor is at *high* voltage, the bottom layer becomes a conductor. When the top layer of a PNP transistor is at *low* voltage, the bottom layer becomes a conductor. Because they do the same things with opposite voltages, the two types of transistors, shown here, are called *complementary* transistors.

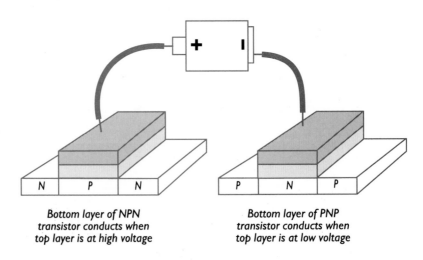

Bottom layer of NPN
transistor conducts when
top layer is at high voltage

Bottom layer of PNP
transistor conducts when
top layer is at low voltage

Review

- Electrons are invisible particles that are smaller than atoms.

- Some electrons revolve around the centers of atoms. Others are free to squeeze between atoms.

- Electrons can move through conductors easily. Most metals are conductors.

- Electrons cannot move through insulators easily. Plastic and air are insulators.

- Batteries and generators can push and pull electrons through conductors.

- Batteries always try to push electrons out of their low-voltage terminals.

- Batteries always try to pull electrons into their high-voltage terminals.

- If a conductor touches a high-voltage battery terminal, then the battery will try to pull electrons in through the conductor. The conductor is said to be at high voltage.

- If a conductor touches a low-voltage battery terminal, then the battery will try to push electrons out through the conductor. The conductor is said to be at low voltage.

- Using a battery and wires, we can put any conductor at high or low voltage.

- Semiconductors are materials that act sometimes like conductors and sometimes like insulators.

- Planar transistors have three layers. The bottom layer is made of two kinds of silicon. The middle layer is made of an insulator. The top layer is made of a conductor.

- Usually, the bottom layer of an NPN transistor acts like an insulator. But if the top layer is at high voltage, then the bottom layer becomes a conductor. Usually, the bottom silicon layer of a PNP transistor acts like an insulator. But if the top layer is at low voltage, then the bottom layer becomes a conductor. When a transistor's bottom layer becomes a conductor, the transistor "turns on."

2

How Gates Work

I N this chapter, I will show you how transistors are used to make electrical *gates*. Gates are the building blocks for more complex devices in a computer. A microcomputer chip is made up of gates that control the flow of electrons and therefore the information your computer is processing. Each type of gate is designed to yield specific results. In later chapters, you will see how gates are used to remember things, and to do math.

SCHEMATIC SYMBOLS FOR TRANSISTORS

W hen transistors are connected together they can do interesting things, as you'll see in this chapter. But first, suppose we had eight transistors connected together. If I drew a picture to represent this, like the one in Figure 2-1, it would be very confusing!

Instead, I am going to do what computer engineers do. To keep things from getting confusing, I'm going to use *schematic symbols*. Schematic symbols are simple pictures. We all use stick figures when we don't want to draw complete pictures of people. In the same way, computer engineers use schematic symbols when they don't want to draw complete pictures of transistors, batteries, and wires.

In Table 2-1, on the left are detailed pictures of some common objects used by computer engineers, and on the right are the schematic symbols used for these objects. Using these schematic symbols, the confusing picture you saw earlier would look much cleaner, like the one in Figure 2-2. A big improvement, isn't it? This kind of picture is called a *schematic diagram*. Take a moment to match the components in the confusing picture with the symbols in the schematic diagram. You'll be seeing these symbols throughout the chapter.

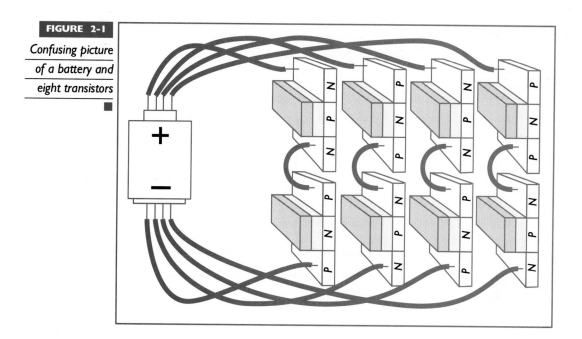

FIGURE 2-1

Confusing picture
of a battery and
eight transistors

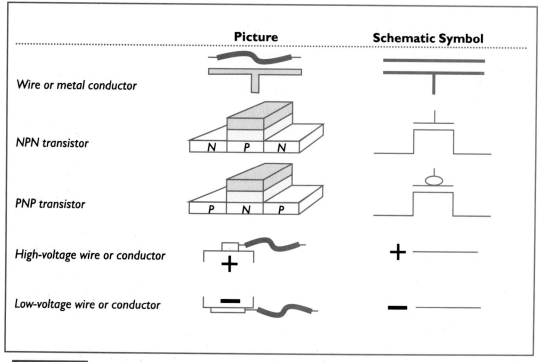

	Picture	Schematic Symbol
Wire or metal conductor		
NPN transistor		
PNP transistor		
High-voltage wire or conductor		
Low-voltage wire or conductor		

TABLE 2-1   Pictures and Schematic Symbols for Common Engineering Objects ■

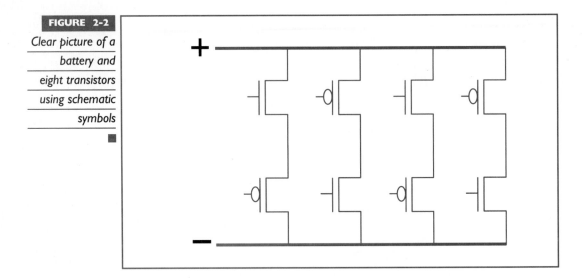

THE NOT GATE

Figure 2-3 shows one PNP transistor, one NPN transistor, and two batteries labeled A and B. The high-voltage terminal of Battery A is connected to the bottom layer of the PNP transistor, and the low-voltage terminal of Battery B is connected to the bottom layer of the NPN transistor. One metal conductor connects the top layers of both transistors, and I'll call this conductor IN. Another conductor connects the bottom layers of both transistors. I'll call this conductor OUT. Two transistors connected in this configuration form a NOT gate. The schematic diagram for the NOT gate is also shown in Figure 2-3.

Suppose IN is connected to the high-voltage terminal of a battery as shown in Figure 2-4. Now the top layers of both transistors are at high voltage. Remember from Chapter 1 that an NPN transistor turns on when its top layer is at high voltage. The lower transistor in the NOT gate is an NPN transistor, so it turns on, meaning its bottom layer becomes a conductor. The upper transistor in the NOT gate is a PNP transistor, so it stays off. Its bottom layer remains an insulator.

Now there is a conducting path from the low-voltage terminal of Battery B to OUT. This path passes through the conducting bottom layer of the NPN transistor. The path from the high-voltage terminal of Battery A is blocked because the PNP transistor is off. So the conductor called OUT is at low voltage.

FIGURE 2-3

Picture and schematic of a NOT gate

■

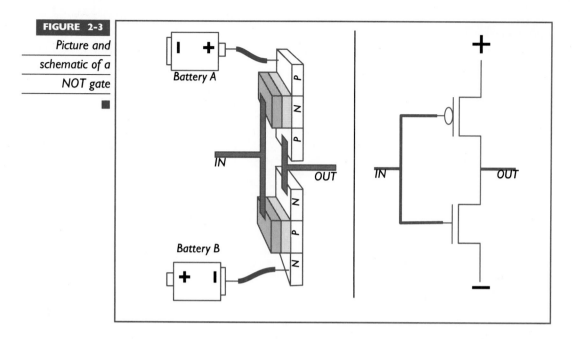

Suppose IN is connected to the low-voltage terminal of a battery as shown in Figure 2-5. Now, the top layers of both transistors are at low voltage. Remember that a PNP transistor turns on when its top layer is at low voltage.

FIGURE 2-4

A NOT gate with IN connected to the high-voltage terminal of a battery. OUT is at low voltage

■

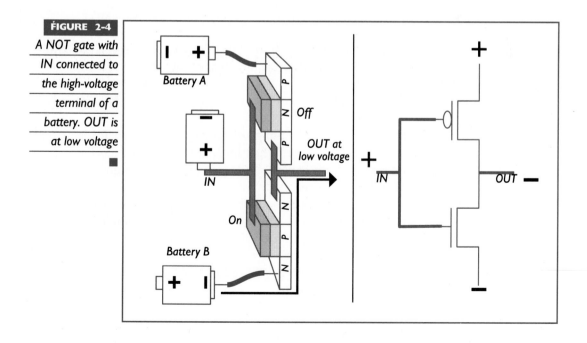

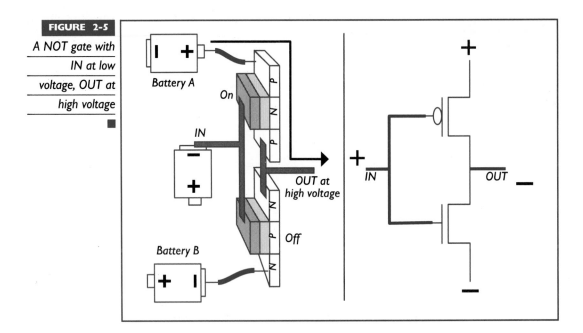

The upper transistor in the NOT gate is a PNP transistor, so it turns on, which means its bottom layer becomes a conductor. The lower transistor in the NOT gate is an NPN transistor, so it turns off. Its bottom layer switches back to being an insulator.

Now there is a conducting path from the high-voltage terminal of Battery A to OUT. This path passes through the conducting bottom layer of the PNP transistor. The path from the low-voltage terminal of Battery B is blocked, because the NPN transistor is off. So the conductor called OUT is at high voltage.

You probably noticed something interesting here. When IN is at high voltage, OUT is at low voltage. When IN is at low voltage, OUT is at high voltage. That is why this is called a NOT gate. OUT is at high voltage only if IN is *NOT* at high voltage.

We can use a *truth table* that shows the voltage of OUT for each voltage of IN to summarize how the NOT gate works. In the left column of Table 2-2, we put what voltage IN is at. In the right column, we put the corresponding OUT voltage.

If we know what voltage IN is at, we can look at this table and quickly see what voltage OUT will be at.

IN	OUT
LOW	HIGH
HIGH	LOW

TABLE 2-2   *Truth Table for a NOT Gate* ■

THE NOR GATE

n Figure 2-6, the arrangement of transistors is called a *NOR gate*. There are two PNP transistors, labeled P1 and P2. There are two NPN transistors, labeled N1 and N2. There are also two batteries, labeled A and B. The high-voltage terminal of Battery A is connected to the bottom layer of P1. The bottom layer of P1 is connected to the bottom layer of P2 with a conducting wire. The low-voltage terminal of Battery B is connected directly to the bottom layers of both N1 and N2. A conductor, labeled IN1, connects the top layers of N1 and P1. Another conductor, IN2, connects the top layers of N2 and P2. Finally, a third conductor connects the bottom layers of N1, N2, and P2. I will call this conductor OUT.

We're going to look at what happens when IN1 and IN2 are connected to the high- and low-voltage terminals of the batteries. There are four situations for us to test, so the IN columns of the truth table for the NOR gate look like this:

IN1	IN2	OUT
LOW	LOW	
LOW	HIGH	
HIGH	LOW	
HIGH	HIGH	

Situation 1 is shown in Figure 2-7. Both IN1 and IN2 are connected to the low-voltage terminals of batteries. So, the top layers of all four transistors are at low voltage. Remember that a PNP transistor turns on when its top layer is at low voltage, and an NPN transistor stays off when its top layer is at low voltage. So P1 and P2 turn on, and N1 and N2 stay off. Now there is a direct conducting path from the high-voltage terminal of Battery A to OUT. This path passes through the conducting bottom layers of P1 and P2.

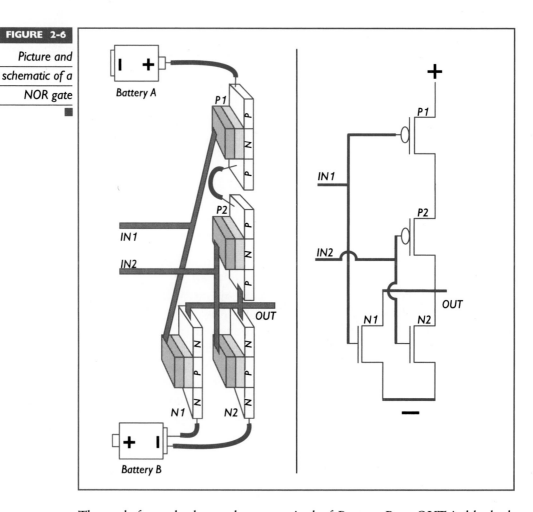

FIGURE 2-6

Picture and schematic of a NOR gate

The path from the low-voltage terminal of Battery B to OUT is blocked, because both N1 and N2 are off. So OUT is at high voltage.

We can now add one entry to the OUT column of our NOR gate truth table:

IN1	IN2	OUT
LOW	LOW	HIGH
LOW	HIGH	
HIGH	LOW	
HIGH	HIGH	

Situation 2 is shown in Figure 2-8. IN1 is connected to a low-voltage terminal, and IN2 is connected to a high-voltage terminal. Therefore, the

FIGURE 2-7

*A NOR gate with
IN1 and IN2 at
low voltage,
OUT at high
voltage*

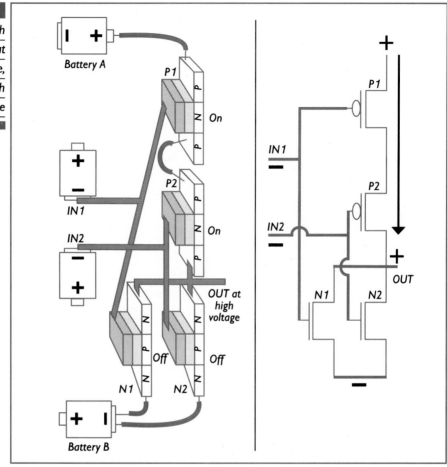

top layers of N1 and P1 are at low voltage, and the top layers of N2 and P2 are at high voltage. P1 and N2 turn on, P2 and N1 stay off. Now there is a direct conducting path from the low-voltage terminal of Battery B to OUT. This path passes through the conducting bottom layer of N2. The path from the high-voltage terminal of Battery A to OUT is blocked, because P2 is off. So OUT is at low voltage.

At this point, our truth table looks like this:

IN1	IN2	OUT
LOW	LOW	HIGH
LOW	HIGH	LOW
HIGH	LOW	
HIGH	HIGH	

FIGURE 2-8

A NOR gate with
IN1 at low
voltage, IN2 at
high voltage,
OUT at low
voltage

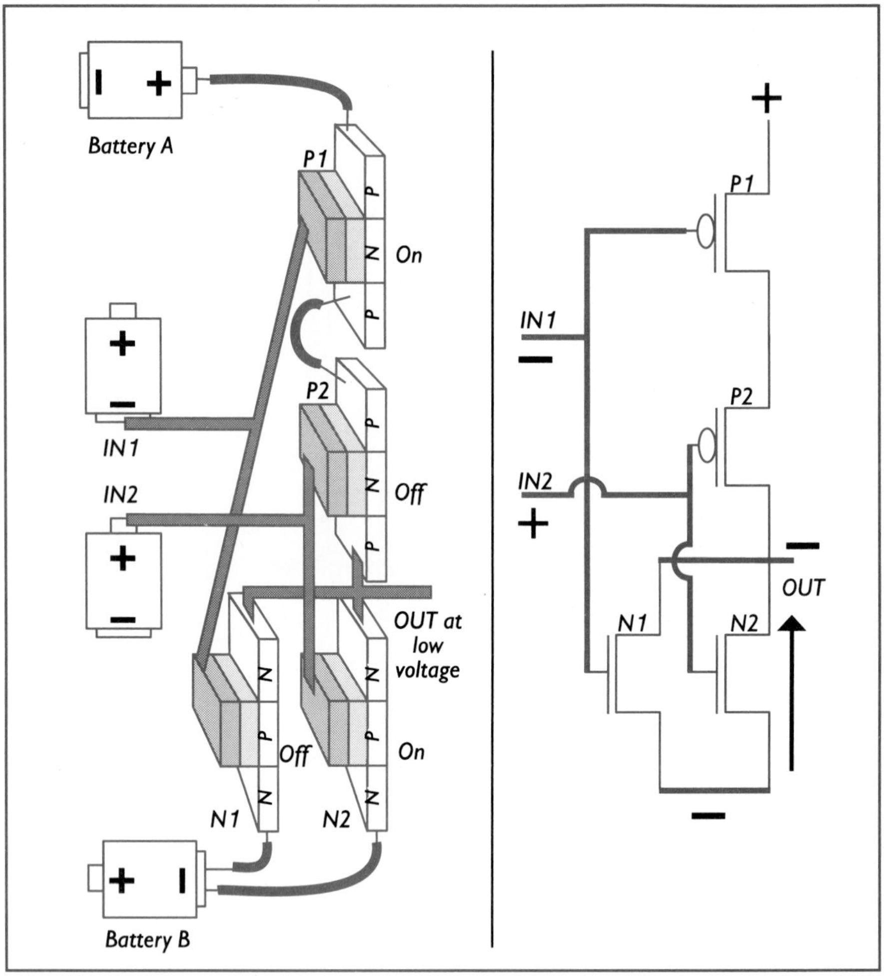

Situation 3 is shown in Figure 2-9. IN1 is connected to a high-voltage terminal, and IN2 is connected to a low-voltage terminal. Therefore, the top layers of N1 and P1 are at high voltage, and the top layers of N2 and P2 are at low voltage. P2 and N1 turn on, P1 and N2 stay off. Now there is a direct conducting path from the low-voltage terminal of Battery B to OUT. This path passes through the conducting bottom layer of N1. The path from the high-voltage terminal of Battery A to OUT is blocked again. This time it is because P1 is off. So OUT is at low voltage.

Situation 4 is shown in Figure 2-10. Both IN1 and IN2 are connected to high-voltage terminals. The top layers of all four transistors are at high voltage. N1 and N2 turn on, and P1 and P2 stay off. Now there are two conducting paths from the low-voltage terminal of Battery B to OUT. One path passes through N1. The other passes through N2. The path from the

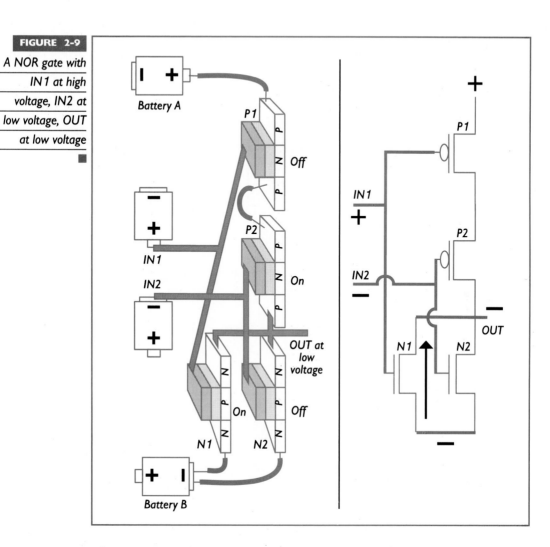

A NOR gate with IN1 at high voltage, IN2 at low voltage, OUT at low voltage ∎

high-voltage terminal of Battery A to OUT is blocked again, because both P1 and P2 are off. So OUT is at low voltage.

Our truth table, shown in Table 2-3, is now complete.

IN1	IN2	OUT
LOW	LOW	HIGH
LOW	HIGH	LOW
HIGH	LOW	LOW
HIGH	HIGH	LOW

TABLE 2-3   *Truth Table for a NOR Gate* ∎

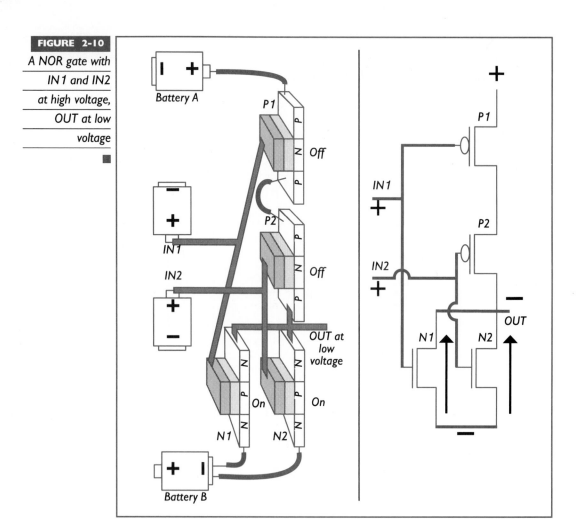

FIGURE 2-10

A NOR gate with
IN1 and IN2
at high voltage,
OUT at low
voltage

Again, if we know the voltages at IN1 and IN2, we can quickly tell what voltage OUT will be at by looking at this table. As you can see, OUT is at high voltage only if both IN1 and IN2 are at low voltage. That is why this is called a NOR gate. OUT is at high voltage only if neither IN1 *NOR* IN2 are at high voltage.

THE NAND GATE

The arrangement of transistors shown in Figure 2-11 is called a *NAND gate*. It looks almost like a NOR gate turned upside-down. We are going to

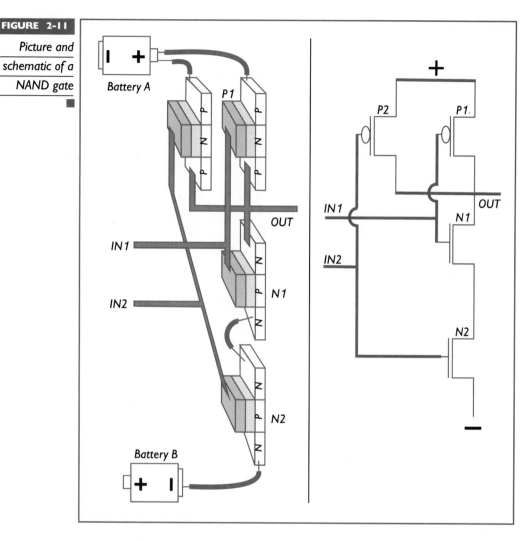

FIGURE 2-11

Picture and

schematic of a

NAND gate

examine what happens when IN1 and IN2 are connected to the high- and low-voltage terminals of the batteries, just as we did for the NOR gate. Again, there are four situations to test.

Situation 1 is shown in Figure 2-12. Both IN1 and IN2 are connected to the low-voltage terminals of batteries, so the top layers of all four transistors are at low voltage. Remember that a PNP transistor turns on when its top layer is at low voltage, and an NPN transistor stays off when its top layer is at low voltage. P1 and P2 turn on, and N1 and N2 stay off. Now there are two direct conducting paths from the high-voltage terminal of Battery A to OUT. One path passes through P1. The other passes through P2. The path from the low-voltage terminal of Battery B to OUT is blocked, because both N1 and N2 are off. So OUT is at high voltage.

A NAND gate
with IN1 and
IN2 at low
voltage, OUT at
high voltage

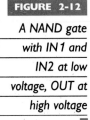

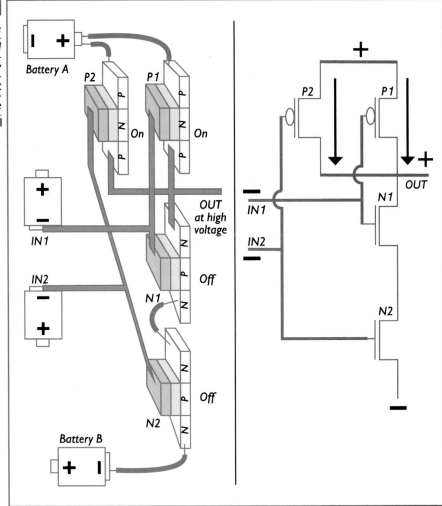

Situation 2 is shown in Figure 2-13. IN1 is connected to a low-voltage terminal and IN2 is connected to a high-voltage terminal. Therefore, the top layers of N1 and P1 are at low voltage, and the top layers of N2 and P2 are at high voltage. P1 and N2 turn on, P2 and N1 stay off. Now there is a direct conducting path from the high-voltage terminal of Battery A to OUT. This path passes through the conducting bottom layer of P1. The path from the low-voltage terminal of Battery B to OUT is blocked, because N1 is off. So OUT is at high voltage.

Situation 3 is shown in Figure 2-14. IN1 is connected to a high-voltage terminal and IN2 is connected to a low-voltage terminal. Therefore, the top layers of N1 and P1 are at high voltage, and the top layers of N2 and P2 are at low voltage. P2 and N1 turn on, P1 and N2 stay off. Now there is a direct

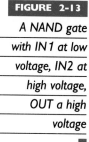

FIGURE 2-13

*A NAND gate
with IN1 at low
voltage, IN2 at
high voltage,
OUT a high
voltage*

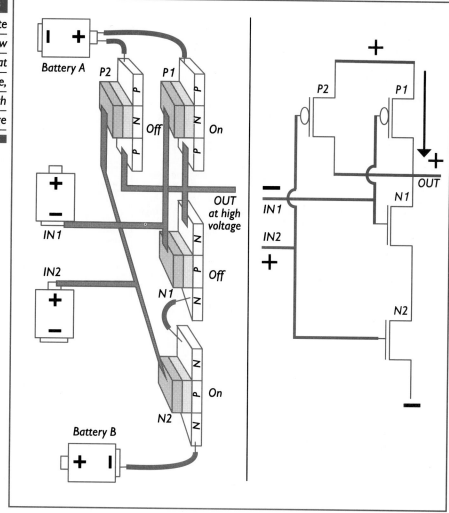

conducting path from the high-voltage terminal of Battery A to OUT. This
path passes through the conducting bottom layer of P2. The path from the
low-voltage terminal of Battery B to OUT is blocked, because N2 is off. So
OUT is at high voltage.

Situation 4 is shown in Figure 2-15. Both IN1 and IN2 are connected to
high-voltage terminals. The top layers of all four transistors are at high
voltage. N1 and N2 turn on and P1 and P2 stay off. Now there is a direct
conducting path from the low-voltage terminal of Battery B to OUT. This
path passes through N1 and N2. The path from the high-voltage terminal
of Battery A to OUT is blocked, because both P1 and P2 are off. So OUT is
at low voltage.

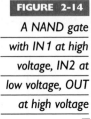

FIGURE 2-14

A NAND gate with IN1 at high voltage, IN2 at low voltage, OUT at high voltage

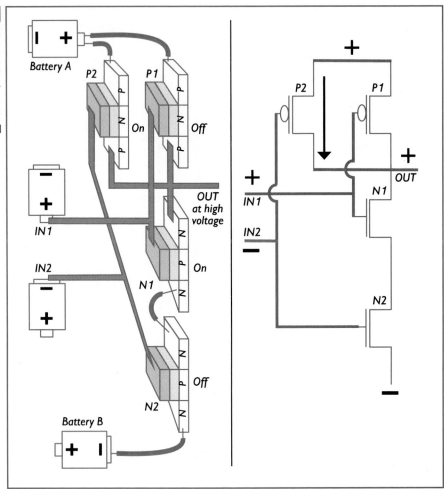

Our truth table, shown in Table 2-4, is now complete.

As you can see, OUT is at low voltage only if both IN1 and IN2 are at high voltage. That is why this is called a NAND gate. OUT is *Not* at high voltage only if IN1 *AND* IN2 are at high voltage.

IN1	IN2	OUT
LOW	LOW	HIGH
LOW	HIGH	HIGH
HIGH	LOW	HIGH
HIGH	HIGH	LOW

TABLE 2-4   *Truth Table for a NAND Gate* ■

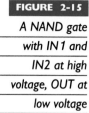

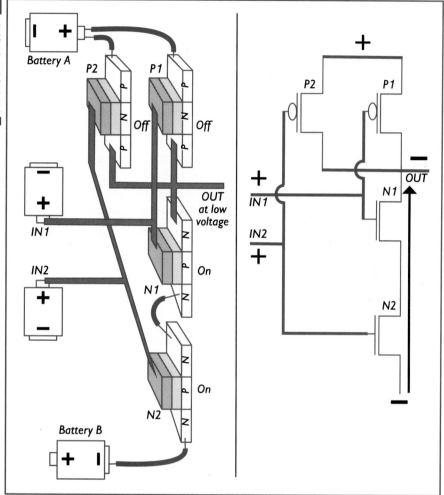

CMOS TECHNOLOGY

Y ou have seen the simplest way to build gates with transistors using one NPN transistor for every PNP transistor—in other words, using complementary transistors. Most modern computers use gates that are built this way.

This method of building gates and other devices using complementary transistors is called *CMOS technology*. CMOS stands for complementary metal-oxide semiconductor. Metal, oxide, and semiconductor are names for the three layers in a transistor.

SYMBOLS FOR GATES

In this chapter, we've looked at how transistors could be put together to make three basic gates. To keep diagrams of these configurations simple, we used schematic symbols for transistors. In the next section, we're going to look at how the three basic gates can be put together to make more complicated gates. Again, to keep our diagrams simple, we're going to use schematic symbols, but this time they'll represent the gates.

Table 2-5 shows the three basic gates and the schematic symbols used for them. It also shows the truth table for each gate.

Gate	Diagram	Schematic Symbol	Truth Table

NOT

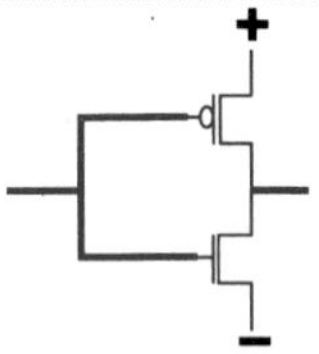

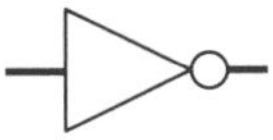

IN	OUT
LOW	HIGH
HIGH	LOW

NOR

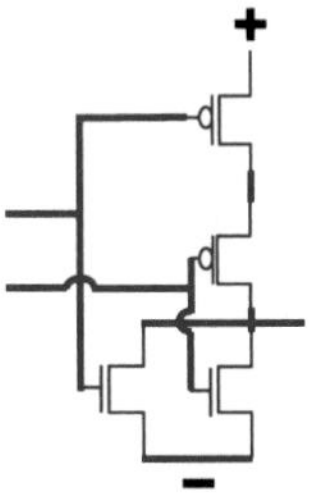

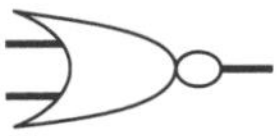

IN1	IN2	OUT
LOW	LOW	HIGH
LOW	HIGH	LOW
HIGH	LOW	LOW
HIGH	HIGH	LOW

NAND

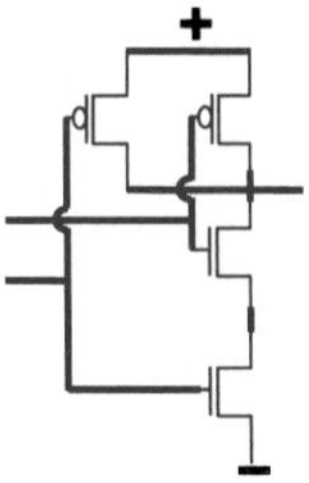

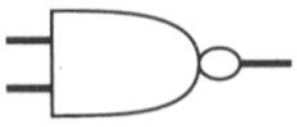

IN1	IN2	OUT
LOW	LOW	HIGH
LOW	HIGH	HIGH
HIGH	LOW	HIGH
HIGH	HIGH	LOW

TABLE 2-5 *Diagrams, Schematic Symbols, and Truth Tables for Basic Gates* ■

Schematic symbols emphasize the *inputs* and *outputs* of devices. Inputs are things you give to a device and outputs are things you get from devices. In the case of gates, the inputs and outputs are high and low voltages. You give a gate high or low voltage, and it gives you high or low voltage.

In a NOT gate, IN is the input and OUT is the output. When you put IN at high voltage or low voltage, the NOT gate puts OUT at low voltage or high voltage.

In NOR gates and NAND gates, IN1 and IN2 are inputs. OUT is the output. When you put IN1 and IN2 at high voltage or low voltage, the NOR gate and NAND gate put OUT at low voltage or high voltage.

When computer engineers draw schematic diagrams, they try to keep the inputs of a device on the left, and the outputs on the right. If this is inconvenient, they may try to keep the inputs above the device, and the outputs below it.

In later chapters, I will show you devices that have three or more inputs and two or more outputs.

MORE COMPLICATED GATES

So far, we have talked about three basic gates. Each of these gates has a different truth table, as was shown in Table 2-5.

But what if we wanted a gate with a different truth table? Luckily, we can combine the three basic gates to make more complicated ones. We can build new gates that have any truth table we want. For example, suppose we wanted to build a gate that had the following truth table:

IN1	IN2	OUT
LOW	LOW	LOW
LOW	HIGH	LOW
HIGH	LOW	LOW
HIGH	HIGH	HIGH

We can put a NOT gate after a NAND gate to create this new gate:

AND gate

The following table shows the voltages at different points in the diagram.

IN1	IN2	MIDDLE	OUT
LOW	LOW	HIGH	LOW
LOW	HIGH	HIGH	LOW
HIGH	LOW	HIGH	LOW
HIGH	HIGH	LOW	HIGH

This gate is called an *AND gate.* The OUT wire is at high voltage only if both IN1 *AND* IN2 are at high voltage.

Suppose we wanted to build a gate that had the following truth table:

IN1	IN2	OUT
LOW	LOW	LOW
LOW	HIGH	HIGH
HIGH	LOW	HIGH
HIGH	HIGH	HIGH

We can put a NOT gate after a NOR gate to create this gate:

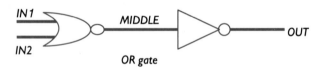

OR gate

The following table shows the voltages at different points in the diagram.

IN1	IN2	MIDDLE	OUT
LOW	LOW	HIGH	LOW
LOW	HIGH	LOW	HIGH
HIGH	LOW	LOW	HIGH
HIGH	HIGH	LOW	HIGH

This gate is called an *OR* gate. The OUT wire is at high voltage if IN1 is at high voltage *OR* if IN2 is at high voltage *OR* if both of them are at high voltage.

In the next chapter, we will look at how basic and complicated gates can be used for logic.

Review

- Gates are the building blocks for more complex devices in a computer.

- We can use transistors, wires, and batteries to build gates.

- When we connect many transistors and batteries together, we get very complicated arrangements. To draw simple pictures of complicated arrangements, we use schematic symbols.

- In a NOT gate, OUT is at high voltage when IN is *NOT* at high voltage.

- In a NOR gate, OUT is at high voltage when neither IN1 *NOR* IN2 is at high voltage.

- In a NAND gate, OUT is *Not* at high voltage when IN1 *AND* IN2 are at high voltage.

- We can combine the three basic gates to make more complicated gates, such as AND or OR gates. We can build a gate that has any truth table we want.

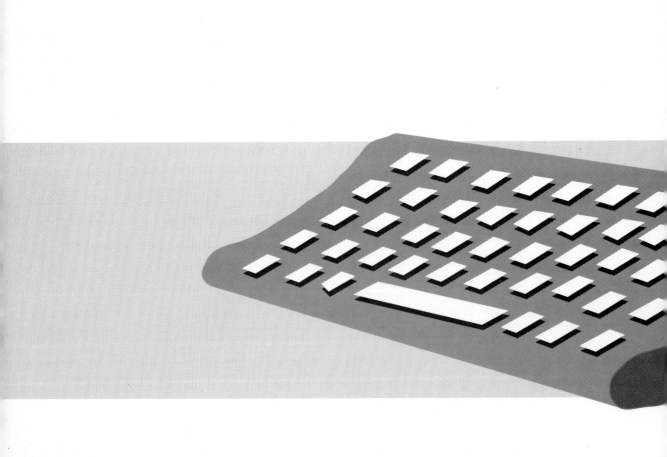

3

What Logic Is

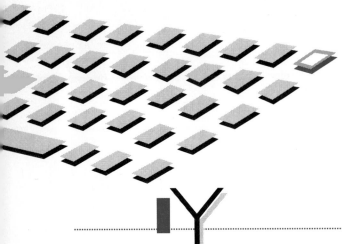

YOU have probably heard people say that computers are totally logical. But what exactly does this mean? *Logic* means taking something you know and drawing a correct conclusion from it. For example, suppose someone told you, "There is not a cloud in the sky." You know that if there are no clouds in the sky, it can't be raining. If you then say, "It is not raining," you have used logic.

Now, suppose your friend said, "A leaf just fell from that tree," and you replied, "Then I have to walk the dog." Your reply is unrelated to what your friend said. There is no real connection between a leaf falling from a tree and your having to walk the dog. You did not draw a logical conclusion from what your friend said.

In this chapter, I'm going to show you how a computer can use gates to make logical decisions. These decisions are going to seem ridiculously simple. The main thing you should learn from this chapter is that high and low voltages can represent statements or facts, such as, "There are no clouds in the sky." If you give these statements or facts to gates in the form of high or low voltages, gates can give you back logical conclusions about this information in the form of high or low voltages.

SIMPLE DECISIONS

Suppose that you've checked out a book from the library and the due date is drawing near. You know that if you return the book on or before the due date, you won't have to pay a fine. But if you return the book after the due date, then you will have to pay the fine. You could organize these instructions into a table:

I returned the library book	I have to pay the overdue fine
True	False
False	True

Does this look familiar? It should. This table is very much like the truth table for the NOT gate that you saw in Chapter 2, except here "true" replaces high voltage and "false" replaces low voltage. In fact, you can use a NOT gate, such as the one shown here, to see if you will have to pay the overdue fine.

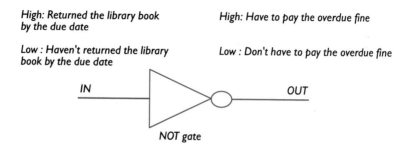

High: Returned the library book by the due date

Low : Haven't returned the library book by the due date

High: Have to pay the overdue fine

Low : Don't have to pay the overdue fine

IN OUT

NOT gate

If you haven't returned the library book by the due date, you can put IN at low voltage. If you have returned the library book by the due date, you can put IN at high voltage. Now, OUT will tell you whether or not you have to pay the overdue fine. If OUT is at high voltage, then you have to pay. If OUT is at low voltage, then you don't have to pay. The gate draws a correct conclusion from what you tell it. It does the logic for you. All you have to do is check which voltage OUT is at.

Suppose your friend invites you to go sailing and says, "If it's either clear or warm then we can go, but if it's neither clear nor warm then we'll have to cancel the trip." These instructions are a little more complicated than in the last example, so let's organize them this way:

It's clear	It's warm	You cannot go sailing
False	False	True
False	True	False
True	False	False
True	True	False

This table is very much like the truth table for the NOR gate. Here again, "true" replaces high voltage and "false" replaces low voltage. You can use a NOR gate, like the one shown in the following illustration, to decide whether or not you'll be able to go sailing.

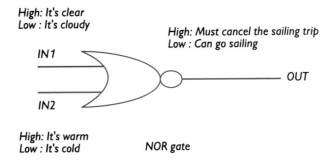

If it's clear, you can put IN1 at high voltage. If it's not clear (cloudy), you can put IN1 at low voltage. If it's warm, you can put IN2 at high voltage. If it's not warm (cold), you can put IN2 at low voltage. Now, OUT tells you whether or not you'll be able to go sailing. If OUT is at high voltage, then the trip will be canceled. If OUT is at low voltage, then you can go. The gate draws a correct conclusion from what you tell it. It does the logic for you. Again, all you have to do is check which voltage OUT is at.

Suppose you need to mail a package. You know that the post office requires that packages must be wrapped according to postal regulations and must have the correct amount of postage affixed in order to be delivered. Again, we can organize this information in a table:

Package is wrapped correctly	Package has sufficient postage	Package will not be delivered
False	False	True
False	True	True
True	False	True
True	True	False

You've probably guessed that this table is much like a NAND gate truth table and that you can use a NAND gate, such as the one shown in the following illustration, to help make the decision.

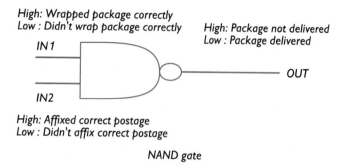

High: Wrapped package correctly
Low : Didn't wrap package correctly

High: Package not delivered
Low : Package delivered

IN1

IN2

OUT

High: Affixed correct postage
Low : Didn't affix correct postage

NAND gate

If you wrapped the package correctly, you can put IN1 at high voltage. If you didn't, you can put IN1 at low voltage. If you affixed the correct postage, you can put IN2 at high voltage. If you didn't, you can put IN2 at low voltage. If OUT is at high voltage, then you know the package won't be delivered. If OUT is at low voltage, then you know it will. Again, the gate does all the logic for you. You just have to check the voltage that OUT is at.

Right now, you probably don't have an appreciation for how useful gates can be. The decisions they have made for you in the examples provided have been very simple. A computer has many transistors and gates, but not much else. You will see that computers need to be "taught" how to do many simple functions before they can perform more difficult and useful ones. In the next section, you'll see how gates can make complicated decisions.

COMPLICATED DECISIONS

ISuppose you're a scorekeeper for a team at a track meet. The runners belong to teams from different schools. In any race, the team whose runner comes in first gets two points. The team whose runner comes in second gets one point. But, if anyone on a team is disqualified, then that team doesn't get any points no matter what. Your job is to determine how many points your team gets in a particular race. This can get confusing, so, again, let's make a table:

Status of your team's runner			Your team gets	
Disqualifies	**Comes in 1st**	**Comes in 2nd**	**2 points**	**1 point**
False	False	False	False	False
False	False	True	False	True
False	True	False	True	False
False	True	True	True	True
True	False	False	False	False
True	False	True	False	False
True	True	False	False	False
True	True	True	False	False

This table probably does not look familiar. But you can still use gates to help keep track of this information by assigning voltages to correspond with the words "true" and "false" in the table. The arrangement of gates shown here can be used to keep track of your team's score:

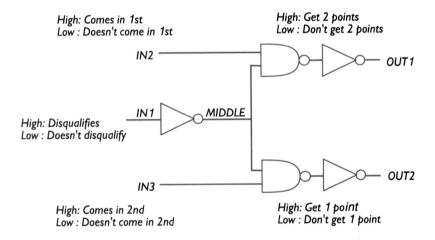

The following table shows all possible voltages at different points in the diagram:

IN1	IN2	IN3	MIDDLE	OUT1	OUT2
Low	Low	Low	High	Low	Low
Low	Low	High	High	Low	High
Low	High	Low	High	High	Low
Low	High	High	High	High	High
High	Low	Low	Low	Low	Low
High	Low	High	Low	Low	Low
High	High	Low	Low	Low	Low
High	High	High	Low	Low	Low

If a runner on your team is disqualified, or comes in first, or comes in second, you can put IN1 or IN2 or IN3 at high voltage. If OUT1 is at high voltage, your team gets at least two points. If OUT2 is also at high voltage, your team gets an additional point.

There is a name for several gates connected together. A group of gates connected together to do one thing is called a *logic block*. As you can see, we can combine gates to build logic blocks that have any truth table we want.

Review

- Logic means taking something you know and drawing a correct conclusion from it.

- We can use gates to do logic for us.

- A group of gates connected together to do one thing is called a logic block.

4

How Transistors and Chips Are Made:
VLSI

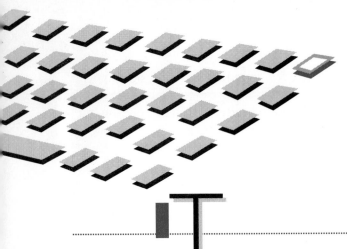

THE first computers ever built were so large they took up one or more rooms. In contrast, computers now can fit on a desktop or even in your pocket. They are also much faster and more powerful than the first computers.

If you look inside a computer today you will see, among other things, several small black boxes fastened to one or more green plastic boards. Transistors that fit inside these small boxes do the work of the computer. They can do the same work previously done by larger electrical devices that made computers take up so much space. In this chapter, you will learn how transistors can be made to fit inside these small black boxes.

Don't worry if you don't understand every bit of this chapter. In the following chapters, I am going to talk about devices that are made from hundreds of transistors. This chapter is meant to give you an idea of how these devices can be produced in such small sizes.

FROM VACUUM TUBES TO TRANSISTORS

You know that the simplest, most fundamental component of a computer is the transistor. To function properly, the most important devices in a computer need transistors. These are the devices that

- perform mathematical calculations,
- let people communicate with the computer, and
- let the computer communicate with people.

The more powerful the computer, the more transistors it uses. Today's computers use millions of transistors.

The first computers were built before the transistor was invented. Instead of transistors, they used *vacuum tubes*. Vacuum tubes look like large flashlight bulbs, and emit a great deal of heat. These computers used thousands and thousands of vacuum tubes and required a lot of special refrigeration equipment to keep them from overheating. You can see why they took up so much space.

The transistor was invented at Bell Telephone Laboratories, a branch of AT&T, in 1948 by John Bardeen, Walter H. Brattain, and William B. Shockley. Transistors do the same job that vacuum tubes did, but they produce very little heat and they are also much smaller. Scientists decided that transistors should be used in place of vacuum tubes in computers. Then they discovered that they could build very small, flat (planar) transistors. They were able to build up to 100 of them together on a small piece of silicon called a *chip*. Today, we call this *small-scale integration, or SSI*. In comparison to what can be done today, 100 is a small number of transistors to put on a chip.

Scientists continued to invent reliable ways of making transistors smaller and of putting more transistors on small silicon chips. The size and cost of computers decreased, while their speed and ability to perform complicated calculations increased. Eventually, scientists were able to put up to 5,000 transistors on a single chip. This is called *large-scale integration, or LSI*. Today, with the use of machines, up to 50,000 transistors can be placed on a silicon chip that is one-half inch long and equally wide. This is called *very-large-scale integration, or VLSI.*

1/2 inch

THE MASKING PROCESS

Try to imagine how tens of thousands of transistors might be built on a silicon chip roughly the size of your thumbnail. This is a difficult problem that has been solved reliably and cheaply using a process called *masking*. The masking process demonstrates how a solution to a very difficult problem can be obtained by solving a series of related smaller problems.

As you read in Chapter 1, planar NPN and PNP transistors are comprised of layers of a few substances that include conductors, insulators, and semiconductors. To build small transistors on a silicon layer, tiny, flat pieces of the proper substances must be placed exactly where they are needed.

The first problem is how to build thousands of transistors on a small silicon chip. Building each transistor one at a time, one layer at a time, would take too long. Remember, though, that all transistors are made from layers of the same few substances. Instead of building them one at a time, many of them can be built at once, layer by layer. The first layer of all of the transistors can be built at once, then the second layer of all of the transistors can be built, and so on.

Now the problem is how to build one layer of all of the transistors simultaneously. Thousands of microscopic pieces of a substance must be shaped and positioned on the small chip. Placing the pieces specifically where they are needed is difficult. It is easier to coat the whole chip with the substance, and then remove it from where it is not needed. In this manner, the first layer of all of the transistors can be built simultaneously. The chip then can be coated with a second substance that also can be removed from where it is not needed. Thus, all of the layers of all of the transistors can be constructed.

But how can a substance be removed from where it is not needed? Acid can be used to wear away the substance, but the acid must only touch those areas of the substance that are to be removed. To accomplish this, a substance called *photoresist,* or *PR,* is used. PR resists acid. The process works like this:

1. The areas of substance that are to remain on the chip are protected with a coat of PR.

2. The areas that are to be removed are not coated. They are left unprotected.

3. Acid is poured over the whole chip.

Those areas that are protected by PR are unaffected by the acid, and the unprotected areas are worn away.

Now the problem becomes how to protect only certain areas of the substance. This is solved by using a special property of PR. PR becomes *polymerized* when exposed to *ultraviolet* light. (Ultraviolet light is invisible to the human eye but it can be produced with special light bulbs.) When PR becomes polymerized, its atoms get rearranged in such a way that it can no longer resist acid. So if areas of a PR coating are exposed to ultraviolet light, they become polymerized and can no longer protect the substance under them. If acid is then poured over the whole layer, it will wear away the desired areas of the substance.

How can you restrict which areas of PR are exposed to ultraviolet light? Imagine if a transparent plate with dark areas drawn on it is placed between the PR layer and the ultraviolet light. The light passes through the transparent areas, but is blocked by the dark areas. In this manner, the desired areas of photoresist can be exposed to ultraviolet light. The pattern on the plate is called a *mask*.

Because the silicon chips are so small, you might think that very small, detailed patterns need to be drawn to make a mask. However, patterns on the plate don't have to be as small as the areas on the PR. A demagnifying lens can be held between the transparent plate and the PR. The pattern on the plate can be shrunk to the size of the PR layer.

To summarize, the masking process, shown in Figure 4-1, is used to remove specific areas of a substance from a layer. The first step in the process is to create a mask, which is a dark pattern on a transparent plate. The mask is clear in areas where the substance is to be removed and is dark in areas where the substance is to remain. The entire surface of the substance is coated with PR. Ultraviolet light is passed through the mask, then through a demagnifying lens, and cast onto the PR. Small areas of the PR become polymerized, as shown here:

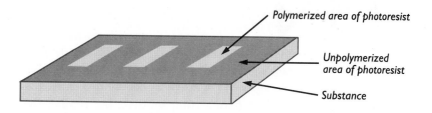

Acid is poured over the PR, and areas of the substance under the polymerized PR are worn away. Areas of the substance under the unpolymerized PR are left unaffected, as shown here:

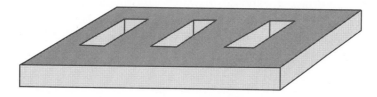

As you can see, the lines on the mask must be precisely drawn. When masks are precisely drawn, transistors can be built that are only 1.5 microns wide.

NOTE: *One million microns = one meter. One millionth of a meter = one micron.*

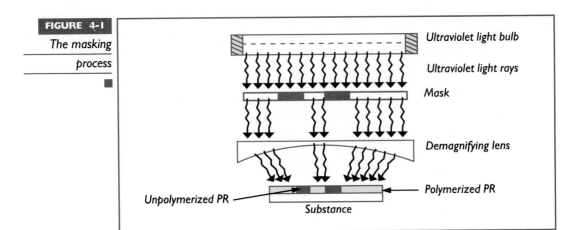

FIGURE 4-1

The masking process

Ultraviolet light bulb

Ultraviolet light rays

Mask

Demagnifying lens

Polymerized PR

Unpolymerized PR

Substance

BUILDING TRANSISTORS ON CHIPS

Now that you're familiar with the masking process, I am going to describe how it is used to build circuits and devices on silicon chips. I'll explain each step and demonstrate it by building a NOT gate.

Scientists start with a circular sheet of n-silicon called a *wafer*. This wafer is slightly wider than a compact disk, but thinner than a dime. The wafer forms the *substrate,* or base, for circuits and devices. Hundreds of separate chips are eventually cut from a wafer. Sometimes, different circuits and devices are built on each of the chips. Sometimes, the same circuits and devices are built on each of the chips. When all the circuits and devices are the same, there are many spares to choose from if one of the chips is defective.

The wafer is heated to between 900 and 1000 degrees Celsius and its surface is exposed to water vapor. The surface absorbs oxygen from the water. This forms a layer of *silicon dioxide* on the substrate, as shown here. The chemical formula for silicon dioxide is SiO_2.

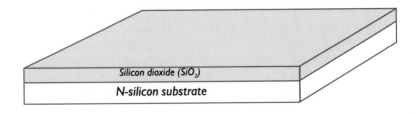

Silicon dioxide (SiO_2)

N-silicon substrate

PNP transistors can be built on an n-silicon substrate. However, NPN transistors must be built on p-silicon. The substrate must be treated with p-chemical to form p-silicon where the NPN transistors will be built. Using the masking process, the SiO2 is removed from these areas. The substrate is then exposed to p-chemical. The p-chemical sinks into the exposed areas of the substrate the way water sinks into a brick or a sponge. In these exposed areas, the n-silicon substrate is changed into p-silicon. The p-silicon areas are called p-wells. The SiO2 shields other areas of the wafer from the p-chemical. The result is that the substrate remains n-silicon in some places, and becomes p-silicon in other places as shown in this illustration.

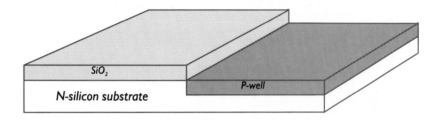

Now that the p-wells have been formed, the SiO2 can be removed using the masking process.

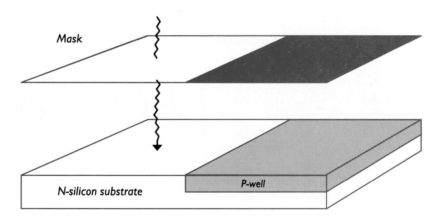

The substrate will form the bottom layer for both PNP and NPN transistors. The next step is to form the middle layer of the transistors, which is an insulator. A special form of silicon called *thin oxide* is used for this layer. Thin oxide is always an insulator. The entire wafer is covered with a thin layer of thin oxide. Then, the masking process is used to remove it from places it is not needed. The result is shown in the following illustration.

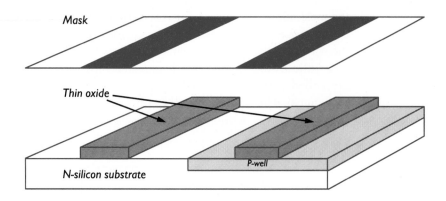

The next step is to form the top layer of the PNP and NPN transistors. A special form of silicon called *polysilicon* is used for this layer. Polysilicon is always a conductor. The entire wafer is covered with a layer of polysilicon. Then, the masking process shown here is used to remove it from places it is not needed.

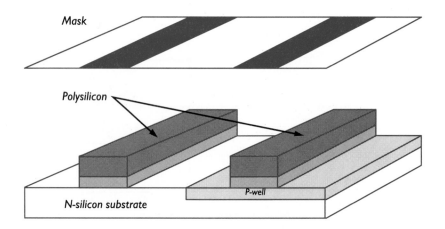

The next step, shown in Figure 4-2, is to finish the bottom layers of the PNP and NPN transistors. Using a process similar to masking, the PNP transistors are exposed to p-chemical. The p-chemical sinks into the wafer, but cannot pass through the polysilicon. Because of this, two strips of p-silicon form on either side of the n-silicon that is under the polysilicon. The PNP transistors are now complete.

The process is repeated for NPN transistors, as shown in Figure 4-3. They are exposed to n-chemical. The n-chemical sinks into the substrate, but cannot pass through the polysilicon. Because of this, two strips of n-silicon

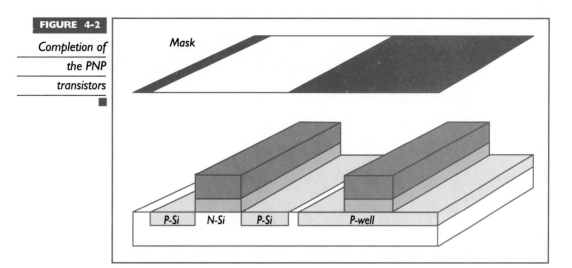

FIGURE 4-2

Completion of the PNP transistors

Mask

P-Si | N-Si | P-Si | P-well

form on either side of the p-silicon that is under the polysilicon in the p-well. The NPN transistors are now complete.

For protection, a layer of SiO$_2$ is added over the transistors. Then, using the masking process, holes are made in the SiO$_2$. These holes, called *contact cuts*, expose the bottom and top layers of the transistors. This allows the transistors to be connected together, as shown in Figure 4-4.

The masking process is used again to form metal connections between the bottom and top layers of the transistors. Figure 4-5 shows what the metal connections would look like for a NOT gate. The diagram for the NOT gate you saw in Chapter 2 is also shown.

Once all the proper metal connections have been made, the wafer is cut into separate chips. Each chip is encased in a small rectangular box of plastic

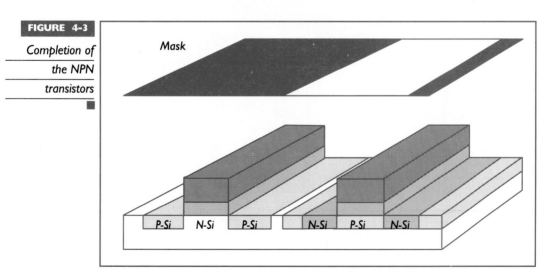

FIGURE 4-3

Completion of the NPN transistors

Mask

P-Si | N-Si | P-Si | N-Si | P-Si | N-Si

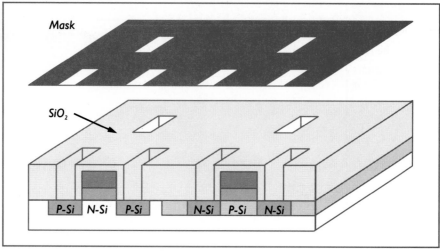

FIGURE 4-4

Using the masking process to make contact cuts

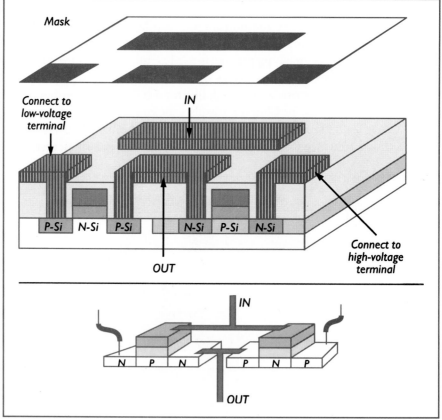

FIGURE 4-5

Completed transistors with metal connections for a NOT gate

or ceramic, called a *package*. The package helps to protect the delicate transistors. Transistors can become hot when electrons pass through their bottom layers and can be damaged if exposed to too much heat. The package helps to move the heat away from the transistors.

Small metal pins on the package are connected to the conductors inside. These pins are shown in Figure 4-6.

At least one of the pins is always meant to be connected to a high-voltage terminal. At least one more is always meant to be connected to a low-voltage terminal. That way, electrons can move in and out of the chip to make the transistors work. The other pins are connected to the inputs and outputs of the circuits and devices on the chip.

If the pins are arranged in two parallel lines on the package, it is called *dual in-line package*, or *DIP*, shown here. (A long, thin package is called a skinny-DIP. Really!) If the pins are arranged in just one long line, the package is called a *single in-line package*, or *SIP*. And, if there are too many pins to fit on the sides of the package, they can be arranged on the bottom. This kind of package is called a *pin grid array*, or *PGA*.

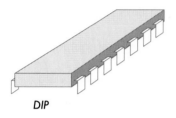

DIP

SIP

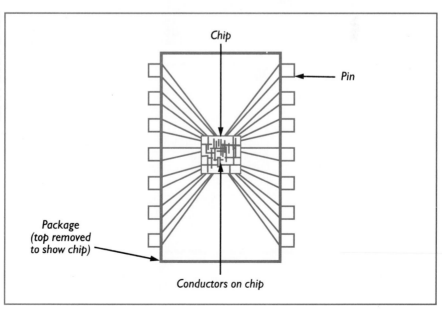

PGA

FIGURE 4-6

Pins are connected to the conductors on a chip

■

Chip

Pin

Package (top removed to show chip)

Conductors on chip

COMPUTER-AIDED VLSI DESIGN

The most important step in building circuits and devices on chips is making accurate masks. This is because the masks determine where different substances will be placed on the chip. If there is a mistake in the mask, the transistors that are built may be unreliable. Worse, they may not work at all. And if just one transistor fails to work, the whole circuit may be ruined.

Engineers use computers to make accurate masks. First, they use computers to draw pictures of the transistors. This is one example of *computer-aided design*, or *CAD*. Computers allow engineers to use pictures to describe precisely how circuits and devices should be built. The pictures show an overhead view of where layers of different substances should be placed. For example, if a computer engineer were designing a NOT gate, the picture on the monitor would look something like Figure 4-7.

Using a computer, the engineer can rearrange, make copies of, stretch, shrink, and zoom in on or zoom out from parts of the picture. The computer

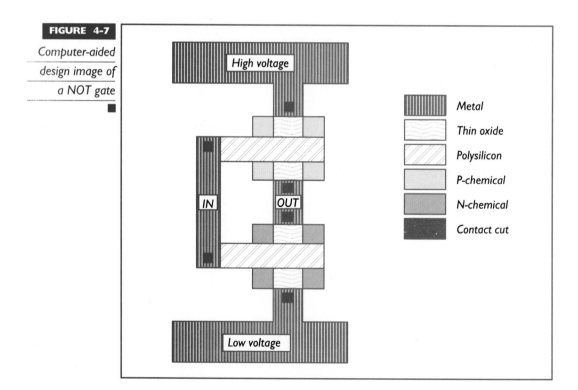

FIGURE 4-7

Computer-aided design image of a NOT gate

Metal

Thin oxide

Polysilicon

P-chemical

N-chemical

Contact cut

can display the picture one substance at a time, or with all of the layers together. The computer can even warn the engineer if errors have been made in the design. Using such computers, an engineer can easily design a whole chip with thousands of transistors.

Once a drawing has been completed, the computer tells other machines to create precise masks on glass. These masks are then used to build the circuits and devices on chips.

Engineers have to be very careful when designing chips. If two conductors are drawn too close together, they might accidentally touch when the chip is actually built. This would result in "crossed wires," and the chip would not work. If a high-voltage terminal is accidentally connected to a low-voltage terminal, a huge burst of electrons might travel through the chip and damage it.

Another factor engineers have to consider is *switching times*. The switching time of a transistor is the time it takes for a change in voltage to travel across its bottom layer. For example, suppose two conductors, A and B, are connected to the bottom layer of a transistor that is on. Suppose that conductor A is at high voltage. Since the transistor is on, conductor B is also at high voltage. Now suppose that A suddenly goes to low voltage. Approximately one nanosecond of time passes before conductor B goes to low voltage. Therefore, the switching time of this transistor is one nanosecond.

NOTE: *One billion nanoseconds = one second. One nanosecond = one billionth of one second.*

Now, suppose that A goes from low voltage to high voltage and back to low voltage in less than one nanosecond. Since the switching time for this transistor is one nanosecond, B never changes voltages. It doesn't have time to "notice" the voltage changes in A.

A circuit containing transistors with small switching times is faster than one containing transistors with large switching times. When engineers want fast circuits, they use wider transistors. The disadvantage is that wider transistors take up more space. When conserving space is more important than fast circuits, engineers use narrow transistors.

Review

- Vacuum tubes look like large flashlight bulbs and emit a great deal of heat.

- The first computers took up many rooms because they used vacuum tubes instead of transistors.

- The transistor was invented at Bell Telephone Laboratories in 1948 by John Bardeen, Walter H. Brattain, and William B. Shockley.

- Transistors do the same job that vacuum tubes did. However, transistors produce very little heat and are much smaller than vacuum tubes.

- A mask is a dark pattern on a transparent plate.

- The masking process can be used to remove microscopic areas of a substance from a layer. Using the masking process, microscopic transistors can be built on small silicon chips.

- For protection and to dissipate heat, chips are enclosed in ceramic or plastic packages.

- Engineers use computers to draw complicated masks precisely. This is one example of computer-aided design.

- The switching time of a transistor is the time it takes for a change in voltage to travel across its bottom layer.

- Wide transistors have quick switching times.

- Narrow transistors have slower switching times.

5

How Computers Represent Numbers

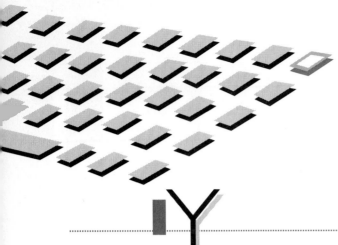

O U ' V E read how transistors can be used to make basic gates. You've read how basic gates can be used to make logic blocks. Computers use logic blocks to perform mathematical calculations. Even complicated logic blocks are simple in a way because they use just two voltages: high and low. How can computers do complicated math with such simple logic blocks? In this chapter, I will start to answer this question. You will learn how just two voltages can represent any number.

DECIMAL NUMBER REPRESENTATION

We use symbols to represent quantities, or numbers. For example, when we see this many objects,

we write the symbol 3. This symbol indicates there are three objects. We use a total of ten symbols when we count a number of objects. They are 0, 1, 2, 3, 4, 5, 6, 7, 8, and 9. These symbols are called *numerals*. They are also called *digits*.

How can we use just ten symbols to count any number of objects? When we count from zero to nine objects, we use just one symbol at a time. This symbol is written in the ones place, as shown in the following illustration:

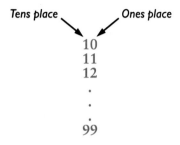

Ones place

0
1
2
.
.
.
9

When we count from ten to ninety-nine objects, we have to use two symbols at a time to represent the quantity. One symbol goes in the ones place to show how many single items there are in the quantity and the second symbol goes in the tens place to show how many multiples of ten there are in the quantity, like this:

Tens place   _Ones place_

10
11
12
.
.
.
99

When we count from one hundred to nine hundred ninety-nine objects, we must use three symbols at a time to represent the number we have. As before, the first symbol is put in the ones place and the second symbol is put in the tens place. The third symbol shows how many multiples of one hundred there are in the quantity. We put that symbol in the hundreds place, as shown here:

Tens place

Hundreds place   _Ones place_

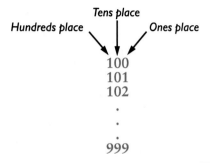

100
101
102
.
.
.
999

Continuing like this, we put numerals in the thousands place, the ten-thousands place, the hundred-thousands place, and so on. With this method, we can represent any number by using just ten different symbols. This is called *decimal number representation*. The prefix "deci" means "ten."

When one or more of these symbols are written together, then the symbol farthest to the right counts ones, or 10^0s. The symbol to its left counts tens, or 10^1s. The next symbol to the left counts hundreds, or 10^2s. And the next symbol to the left counts thousands, or 10^3s, and so on. For example, when we see 1403, we know that these symbols represent three ones, no tens, four hundreds, and one thousand. Adding these up, we get one thousand four hundred three.

BINARY NUMBER REPRESENTATION

Computers also use symbols to represent quantities and the symbols they use are voltages. We have ten numerals to represent quantities with. But computers only have two voltages to represent quantities with: high voltage and low voltage.

Even with only two symbols to use, computers can still represent any number. Instead of using decimal number representation, however, they must use *binary number representation*. The prefix "bi" means "two." Symbols in binary number representation are called *bits*. Bits is an abbreviation for binary digits.

In binary number representation, low voltage means "zero" or "none" and high voltage means "one." If we see one or more voltages, then the voltage farthest to the right counts ones, or 2^0s. The voltage to its left counts twos, or 2^1s. The voltage to its left counts fours, or 2^2s. The voltage to its left counts eights, or 2^3s. The voltage to its left counts sixteens, or 2^4s, and so on.

Look at the five batteries shown here. The voltages are high, low, low, high, high. The rightmost voltage counts 2^0s or ones. The next voltage counts 2^1s or twos. The next voltage counts 2^2s or fours. The next voltage counts 2^3s or eights. The next voltage counts 2^4s or sixteens.

The number represented by these voltages is 1 one, 1 two, 0 fours, 0 eights, and 1 sixteen. Adding these up, we get nineteen. So these five voltages represent the number nineteen in binary number representation.

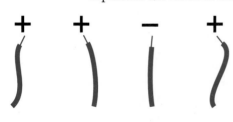

Suppose we have four wires at the voltages shown here: high, high, low, high. The number represented by these voltages is 1 one, 0 twos, 1 four, and 1 eight. Adding these up, we get thirteen. So these four voltages represent the number thirteen in binary number representation.

Suppose we have five conductors that are at the following voltages: low, high, low, high, low. The number represented by these voltages is 0 ones, 1 two, 0 fours, 1 eight, 0 sixteens. Adding these up, we get ten. So these five voltages represent the number ten in binary number representation.

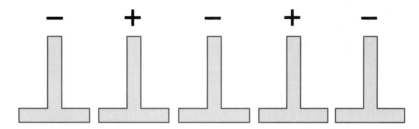

Drawing pictures of various conductors can get complicated. From now on, when I use binary number representation, I will use the symbol 1 for high voltage, and the symbol 0 for low voltage. Therefore, the battery voltages we saw would be represented with 10011. The wire voltages would be replaced with 1101 and the conductor voltages with 01010.

BITS, BYTES, AND NYBBLES

Suppose I write a number using decimal number representation. If I count how many symbols I used, I can say that the number is that many digits long. For example, 34 is two digits long, 3459 is four digits long, and 9 is one digit long.

Now suppose I write a number using binary number representation. If I count how many symbols I used, I say that the number is that many bits long. For example, 10110 (twenty-two) is five bits long, 101 (five) is three bits long, and 1 is one bit long.

Computer engineers have special names for numbers that are four bits long and numbers that are eight bits long. You know that a nibble contains a few bits of food. Computer engineers call four computer bits a *nybble*. You know that a bite contains several bits of food. Computer engineers call eight computer bits a *byte*. For example, 1001, 1101, and 0111 are all nybbles. 10101010, 01010101, and 01101001 are all bytes.

In a number written using binary number representation, the bits at the far left are called the *most significant bits* (MSB). This is because they count the highest powers of two. The bits at the far right are called the *least significant bits* (LSB). This is because they count the lowest powers of two.

For example, in the number 01101001, the most significant bit is 0. The least significant bit is 1. The three most significant bits are 011. The three least significant bits are 001. In the number 10110101, the most significant bit is 1. The least significant bit is also 1. The three most significant bits are 101. The three least significant bits are also 101.

ADDITION

Adding two numbers (called *addends*) in decimal number representation is easy. All we have to do is add up the ones, then add up the tens, then the hundreds, and so on. The only thing we have to be careful about is "carrying." If we are adding up ones and we get multiples of ten, then we have to count them with the other tens. If we are adding up tens and we get multiples of one hundred, then we have to count them with the other hundreds.

Adding two numbers in binary number representation is even easier. All we have to do is add up the ones, then add up the twos, then the fours, then the eights, and so on. Again, however, we have to be careful about carrying. If we are adding up ones and we get multiples of two, then we have to count them with the other twos. If we are adding twos and we get multiples of four, then we have to count them with the other fours.

Let's look at some examples:

```
   1            0            0
  +0           +1           +0
  ---          ---          ---
   1            0            0
```

These should be pretty simple. Let's look at a few more binary additions:

```
   10                01
  +01               +01
  ----              ----
   11                10
```

The first addition is two (represented by 10) plus one (01). When I add the ones, I get one. So I write a 1 in the ones column. When I add the twos, I get one, so I write a 1 in the twos column. The result is 1 two and 1 one. Adding these up, I get my answer, three.

The second addition is one plus one. When I add the ones, I get two, but I can't write a "2" because the only symbols that can be used in binary number representation are 0 and 1. What I do instead is carry a 1 into the twos column, and write a 0 in the ones column. Now, when I add the twos, I get one, so I write a 1 in the twos column. The result is 1 two and 0 ones. Adding these up, I get my answer, two.

Let's try one more addition:

```
   1001
  +0101
  --------
   1110
```

You can see that this addition is correct. The first addend is 1 one, 0 twos, 0 fours, and 1 eight, or nine. The second addend is 1 one, 0 twos, 1 four, and 0 eights, or five. The answer is 0 ones, 1 two, 1 four, and 1 eight, or fourteen. I'll go through this addition step by step.

1. First, add the ones to get two. Carry a 1 into the twos column, and write a 0 in the ones column.

```
      1
   1001
  +0101
  --------
      0
```

2. Next, add the twos to get one. Write a 1 in the twos column.

```
      1
   1001
  +0101
  --------
     10
```

3. Next, add the fours to get one. Write a 1 in the fours column.

```
   1
 1001
+0101
--------
  110
```

4. Finally, add the eights to get one. Write a 1 in the eights column.

```
   1
 1001
+0101
--------
 1110
```

Now let's try adding two very long binary numbers:

```
+   11111111111  111
  100101010110110111
 +010010101001010011
--------------------------------
  111000000000001010
```

As you can see, you have to do a lot of carrying in this addition. Look at the twos column. I added up how many multiples of two there were and got three. Three groups of twos equals six (2+2+2, or 4+2). So I wrote a 1 in the twos column and carried a 1 into the fours column.

Addition is very simple in binary number representation. You just work one column at a time from right to left. Each column will have two numbers to add. You might also have to add in a number carried in from the previous column. For each column, use the rules listed in Table 5-1.

SUBTRACTION IS

ubtracting one number (called the *subtrahend*) from another (called the *minuend*) in decimal number representation is also easy. All we have to do is subtract in the ones column, subtract in the tens column, then the hundreds, and so on. The only thing we have to be careful about is "borrowing." For example, if we are subtracting ones and we run out of ones, we can borrow ten ones from the tens column. Now we have ten more

keep in mind that will be useful when we look at how a computer can do multiplication.

In binary number representation, when you multiply one number by a second number:

- You multiply the multiplicand by each bit in the multiplier.

- The results of these multiplications are either the multiplicand or zero. This is because each bit in the multiplier is either 1 or 0.

- You shift each successive partial product one place to the left (except the first one) and then add them to get the product.

- The number of bits in the product is at most the number of bits in the multiplicand plus the number of bits in the multiplier.

Review

- In decimal number representation, we use ten symbols. If we see one or more of these symbols, then the rightmost symbol counts ones, or 10^0s. The next symbol counts tens, or 10^1s. The next symbol counts hundreds, or 10^2s. The next symbol counts thousands, or 10^3s, and so on.

- In binary number representation, computers use two symbols. Low voltage means "zero" or "none." High voltage means "one." If we see one or more voltages, then the rightmost voltage counts ones, or 2^0s. The next voltage counts twos, or 2^1s. The next voltage counts fours, or 2^2s. The next voltage counts eights, or 2^3s. The next voltage counts sixteens, or 2^4s, and so on.

- When adding two numbers in binary number representation, use the rules listed in Table 5-1.

- When subtracting two numbers in binary number representation, use the rules listed in Table 5-2.

- When multiplying two numbers in binary number representation, keep the following in mind:

  You multiply the multiplicand by each bit in the multiplier.

  The results of these multiplications are either the multiplicand or zero. This is because each bit in the multiplier is either 1 or 0.

  You shift each successive partial product one place to the left (except the first one) and then add them to get the product.

  The number of bits in the product is at most the number of bits in the multiplicand plus the number of bits in the multiplier.

6

How Computers Do Math

I N the last chapter, you learned how high and low voltages could be used to represent numbers. In the chapter before that, you learned how basic gates could be combined to make logic blocks with whatever truth table we wanted. In this chapter, we are going to combine these two ideas to show how we can do addition and subtraction using gates.

DOING ADDITION WITH GATES

We'll start by working through some examples of four-bit addition. Remember the table of rules (from the previous chapter) for addition of two numbers in binary number representation:

If One Digit Is	and the Other Digit is	and the Carry is	Write	and Carry
0	0	0	0	0
0	0	1	1	0
0	1	0	1	0
0	1	1	0	1
1	0	0	1	0
1	0	1	0	1
1	1	0	0	1
1	1	1	1	1

You apply these rules to each column of numbers. First you add the ones column, then the twos, then the fours, then the eights, and so on.

By replacing the 1's and 0's with high and low voltages, I can turn this table of rules into a truth table. Then, I can combine gates to create a logic block that has this truth table. This arrangement of gates is shown in Figure 6-1.

This logic block uses gates that have three inputs. Such gates are called *multiple-input* gates. They are a little more complicated than two-input gates we've seen, but they behave similarly. If all inputs to a multiple-input NAND gate are high, then its output is low. Otherwise, its output is high. If all inputs to a multiple-input NOR gate are low, then its output is high. Otherwise, its output is low.

The following table shows the voltages at different points in Figure 6-1.

NUM1	NUM2	CARRYIN	A	B	C	D	E	F	WRITE	CARRY-OUT
Low	Low	Low	High	Low	High	High	High	High	Low	Low
Low	Low	High	High	Low	High	Low	Low	High	High	Low
Low	High	Low	High	High	High	Low	Low	High	High	Low
Low	High	High	High	High	Low	Low	High	High	Low	High
High	Low	Low	High	High	High	Low	Low	High	High	Low
High	Low	High	High	High	Low	Low	High	High	Low	High
High	High	Low	Low	High	High	Low	High	High	Low	High
High	High	High	Low	High	Low	Low	High	Low	High	High

This logic block follows the rules for addition of one column of binary numbers. I put NUM1, NUM2, and CARRYIN at high or low voltage,

FIGURE 6-1

Logic block for binary addition truth table

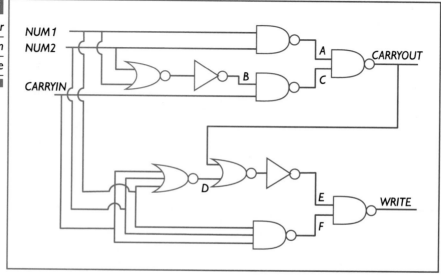

depending on whether its value is one or zero. The voltages at WRITE and CARRYOUT then tell me what numbers to write and carry. Because the logic block that does addition contains several gates, I am going to use the following schematic symbol to represent it from now on.

We now have a logic block that adds one column of numbers. This means we can add two addends that are each one bit long (which correspond to NUM1 and NUM2). If we want to add two addends that are longer than one bit each, we just connect logic blocks together. For example, suppose we wanted to add two addends in binary number representation that are four bits long. We would connect addition logic blocks together as shown in Figure 6-2. This arrangement of logic blocks is called a four-bit *adder*. (It also can be called a nybble adder.)

We can use this four-bit adder to add any two four-bit addends that are in binary number representation. For example, suppose we wanted to find the answer to the following addition:

```
  1001
+ 0101
---------
```

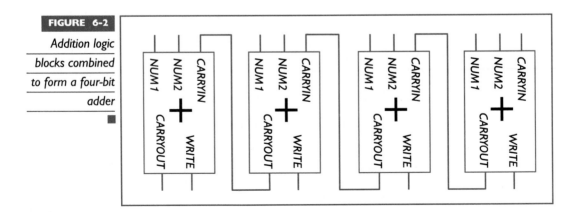

FIGURE 6-2

Addition logic blocks combined to form a four-bit adder

■

Remember that each logic block handles one column of numbers. The logic block on the right handles the ones column. The one to its left handles the twos column. The one to its left handles the fours column. And the logic block on the left handles the eights column. In the ones column, you are adding one to one. Because this is the first column, there is no carry in from a previous column to consider. So we put NUM1 at high voltage, NUM2 at high voltage, and CARRYIN at low voltage. From the table you can see that now WRITE is at low voltage and CARRYOUT is at high voltage. This is shown here:

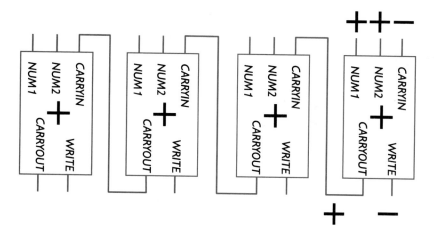

In the twos column, we are adding zero to zero. So we put NUM1 at low voltage and NUM2 at low voltage. CARRYIN is already set at high voltage for us (because CARRYOUT was at high voltage in the previous step). Now WRITE is at high voltage and CARRYOUT is at low voltage, as shown here:

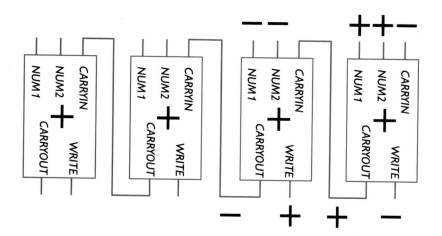

Continuing like this for the next two columns, we get the results shown in Figure 6-3.

You can read the voltages at WRITE for each column of the addition. They are high, high, high, low. (For now, we'll ignore the voltage that CARRYOUT is at in the eights column.) The answer is fourteen.

Actually, we don't need to put the NUM1s and NUM2s at high or low voltage one column at a time. We can set all the NUM1s and NUM2s at once, and still get the right answer. All the WRITEs will be at the correct voltage.

Overflow

Suppose we wanted to add eleven to thirteen. In binary number representation, this is

```
+ 1011
+ 1101
---------
```

If we try these addends on our four-bit adder, we get the results shown Figure 6-4.

The answer seems to be high, low, low, low, or eight. This is wrong. The answer should be twenty-four. But notice that CARRYOUT is at high voltage in the eights column. This is the logic block's way of representing a sum that is more than four bits long.

We are adding two four-bit addends. If the answer turns out to be more than four bits long, we say that *overflow* has occurred. If the answer to the addition has more than four bits, then CARRYOUT is at high voltage in the eights column. The logic block is saying, "I carried a sixteen out to get this

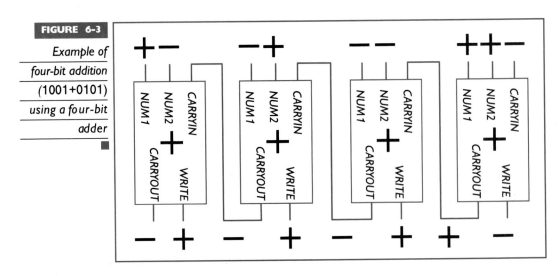

FIGURE 6-3

Example of

four-bit addition

(1001+0101)

using a four-bit

adder

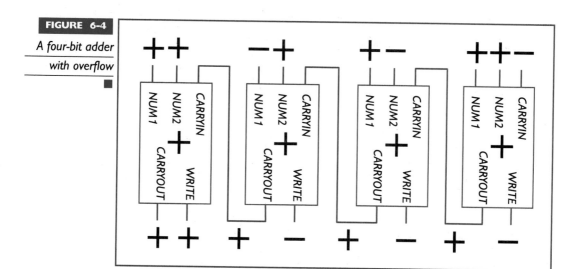

FIGURE 6-4

A four-bit adder with overflow

answer." This tells us that the real answer is sixteen more than the number that appears on the WRITE lines. In this example, the real answer is sixteen more than eight, or twenty-four.

So, if we have to do some extra addition to correctly interpret the adder's answer, what use is it? Remember that this extra addition is necessary only when the answer is more than four bits long. For all other additions, the adder gives the correct answer directly. Also, remember that CARRYOUT in the eights column warns us if overflow has occurred. In this case, the CARRYOUT in the eights column can also be used as a fifth bit in the answer.

DOING SUBTRACTION WITH GATES

Now let's try some four-bit subtraction. Remember the table of rules for subtraction of one number from another in binary number representation:

If One Digit is	and the Other Digit is	and you Borrowed	Write	Borrow
0	0	0	0	0
0	0	1	1	1
0	1	0	1	1
0	1	1	0	1

If One Digit is	and the Other Digit is	and you Borrowed	Write	Borrow
1	0	0	1	0
1	0	1	0	0
1	1	0	0	0
1	1	1	1	1

You apply these rules to each column of numbers. First you subtract the ones column, then the twos, then the fours, then the eights, and so on.

By replacing 1's and 0's with high and low voltages, I can turn these rules into a truth table. Then, I can combine gates to create a logic block that has this truth table. This arrangement of gates is shown in Figure 6-5. It uses just one more gate than the addition logic block. The following table shows the voltages at each point in Figure 6-5.

NUM1	NUM2	BOR-ROW	A	B	C	D	E	F	WRITE	BOR-ROW
Low	Low	Low	High	High	High	High	High	High	Low	Low
Low	Low	High	High	High	Low	High	Low	High	High	High
Low	High	Low	Low	High	High	High	Low	High	High	High
Low	High	High	Low	High	Low	Low	High	High	Low	High
High	Low	Low	High	Low	High	High	High	Low	High	Low
High	Low	High	High	Low	High	High	High	High	Low	Low
High	High	Low	High	High	High	High	High	High	Low	Low
High	High	High	High	High	Low	High	Low	High	High	High

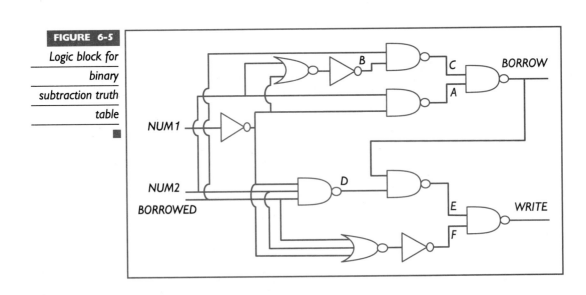

FIGURE 6-5

Logic block for binary subtraction truth table

This logic block follows the rules for subtraction of one column of binary numbers. You put NUM1, NUM2, and BORROWED at high or low voltage, depending on whether its value is one or zero. The voltages at WRITE and BORROW then tell you what numbers to write and borrow. I am going to use the following schematic symbol for the logic block that does subtraction:

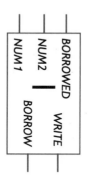

We now have a logic block that subtracts one column of numbers. If the minuend and the subtrahend are more than one bit long, we just connect logic blocks together. For example, suppose we wanted to subtract one four-bit number from another in binary number representation. We would connect subtraction logic blocks together as shown in Figure 6-6. This arrangement of logic blocks is called a four-bit *subtracter*. (It also can be called a nybble subtracter.)

We can use a four-bit subtracter to find the difference of any two numbers that are in binary number representation. For example, suppose we wanted to find the answer to the following subtraction:

```
 – 1101
 – 0101
---------
```

FIGURE 6-6

Subtraction logic blocks combined to form a four-bit subtracter

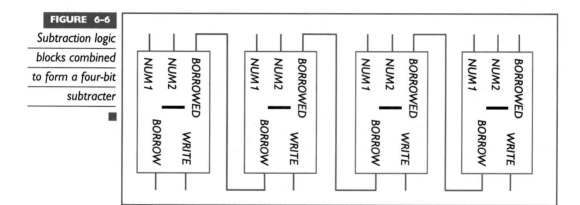

Remember that each logic block handles one column of numbers. In the ones column, we are subtracting one from one. We haven't borrowed from this column nor do we have to borrow in order to do this subtraction. So we put NUM1 at high voltage, NUM2 at high voltage, and BORROWED at low voltage. Now WRITE is at low voltage, and BORROW is at low voltage, as is shown here:

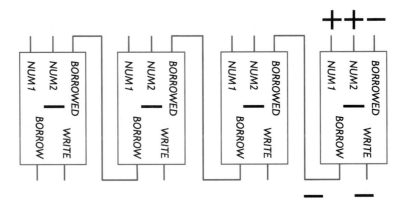

In the twos column, we are subtracting zero from zero. So we put NUM1 at low voltage and NUM2 at low voltage. BORROWED is already at low voltage, because we didn't need to borrow from this column to subtract the ones. Now WRITE is at low voltage, as shown here. BORROW is at low voltage, because we didn't have to borrow from the fours column to do this subtraction.

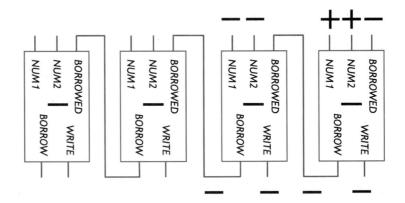

Continuing like this for the remaining columns, we get the results shown in Figure 6-7.

You can read the voltages at WRITE for each column of the subtraction. They are high, low, low, low. (For now, we'll ignore the voltage that BORROW is at in the eights column.) The answer is eight.

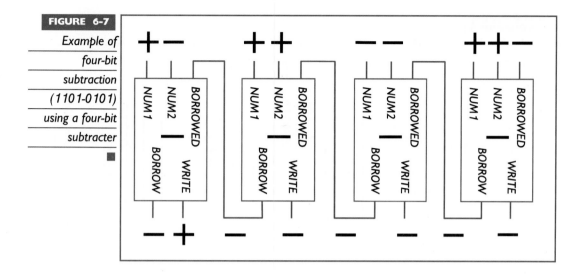

Underflow

Suppose we wanted to subtract thirteen from eleven. In binary number representation, this is

```
 -1011
 - 1101
 ---------
```

If we try these numbers on the four-bit subtracter, we get the results shown in Figure 6-8.

The answer would appear to be high, high, high, low, or fourteen. This is wrong. The answer should be negative two. But notice that BORROW is at high voltage in the eights column. This is the logic block's way of representing a negative difference. The logic block is saying, "I borrowed a sixteen to get this answer."

We are subtracting one four-bit number from another. If the answer turns out to be less than zero, we say that *underflow* has occurred. If the answer to the subtraction is less than zero, then BORROW is at high voltage in the eights column. This tells us that the real answer is sixteen less than it appears to be. In this example, the real answer is sixteen less than fourteen, or negative two.

Again, remember that this extra subtraction is necessary only when our answer is less than zero. For all other subtractions, the subtracter gives us the correct answer directly. Also, remember that BORROW in the eights column warns us that underflow has occurred.

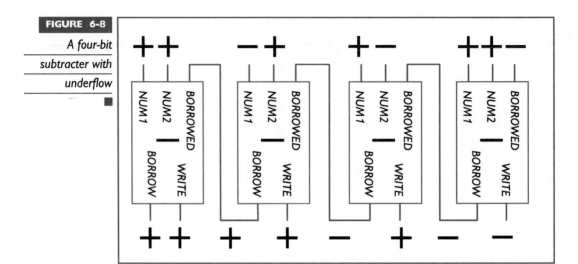

It would seem natural to cover multiplication now. Unfortunately, you saw in the last chapter that there is no table of rules for multiplication of two numbers in binary number representation. Since there is no table of rules, we can't make a truth table. And since we can't make a truth table, we can't do multiplication using just gates. The question of how a computer performs multiplication will have to wait a few chapters.

Review

- We can turn the table of rules for binary addition into a truth table. Then, we can build a logic block that has this truth table.

- We can turn the table of rules for binary subtraction into a truth table. Then, we can build a logic block that has this truth table.

- If we want to add or subtract numbers that are four (or more) bits long, we just connect four (or more) logic blocks together.

- If we are adding two numbers with a four-bit adder, and the answer is five bits long, then CARRYOUT will be at high voltage in the eights column. We say that overflow has occurred, and the real answer is sixteen more than it appears to be.

- If we are subtracting with a four-bit subtracter, and the answer is less than zero, then BORROW will be at high voltage in the eights column. We say that underflow has occurred, and the real answer is sixteen less than it appears to be.

7

How Flip-Flops Work

s you have seen, we can use gates to build logic blocks that have any truth table we want. We've built logic blocks that can do addition and subtraction. One property of the gates and logic blocks we have seen is that they produce output only when they have input. When we take away the input, the output goes away too. However, computers often need to store the output of a logic block while the inputs change. In this chapter, I will discuss circuits that store voltages.

THE RS FLIP-FLOP

igure 7-1 shows two NOR gates connected together in an unusual manner. The output of each NOR gate is connected to an input of the other NOR gate. This arrangement of gates is called an *RS flip-flop*.

Let's look at how the RS flip-flop works. Suppose that initially, Q is at high voltage and $\overline{Q}$ is at low voltage. (You will soon see that $\overline{Q}$ is always at the voltage opposite of Q.) Also, suppose that both R and S are at low

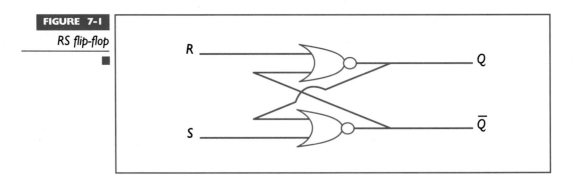

R

S

Q

$\overline{Q}$

voltage. If you remember the truth table for NOR gates (see Table 2-5 in Chapter 2), you'll see that the RS flip-flop retains this voltage configuration, as shown in the illustration. I'll call this the *initial state*.

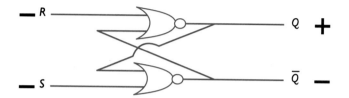

Now suppose that R suddenly goes to high voltage. Since $\overline{Q}$ is still at low voltage, Q goes to low voltage. Now both Q and S are at low voltage, so $\overline{Q}$ goes to high voltage. The RS flip-flop now looks like this:

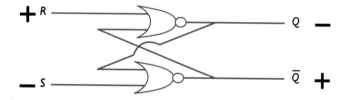

Now suppose that R goes back to low voltage. $\overline{Q}$ was at high voltage, so Q stays at low voltage. In fact, neither Q nor $\overline{Q}$ change when R goes back to low voltage. The RS flip-flop is now as shown here:

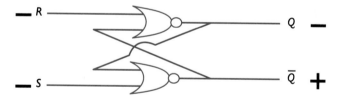

Now suppose that S suddenly goes to high voltage. Since Q is still at low voltage, $\overline{Q}$ goes to low voltage. Now both $\overline{Q}$ and R are at low voltage, so Q goes to high voltage. The RS flip-flop stays as shown here:

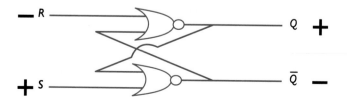

Now suppose that S goes back to low voltage. Q was at high voltage, so $\overline{Q}$ stays at high voltage. In fact, neither Q nor $\overline{Q}$ change when S goes back to low voltage. The RS flip-flop goes back to the way it was initially.

Can you see what is happening here? Whenever R goes to high voltage, Q goes to low voltage and $\overline{Q}$ goes to high voltage. When R goes back to low voltage, Q and $\overline{Q}$ stay the way they were. Whenever S goes to high voltage, Q goes to high voltage and $\overline{Q}$ goes to low voltage. When S goes back to low voltage, Q and $\overline{Q}$ stay the way they were.

You see, the R in "RS flip-flop" stands for *reset*. Whenever R goes to high voltage, Q gets reset to low. The S in "RS flip-flop" stands for *set*. Whenever S goes to high voltage, Q gets set to high. If Q is at high voltage, then $\overline{Q}$ is at low. If Q is at low voltage, then $\overline{Q}$ is at high.

Unlike most combinations of gates, we cannot use a truth table to describe how this flip-flop works. Why? Because we can't relate the output of a flop-flop to its inputs. Suppose R and S are both at low voltage. We can't be sure whether Q and $\overline{Q}$ are at high or low voltage. It depends on what R and S were before they both went to low. Also, if you try to put both R and S at high voltage at the same time, it's hard to tell what voltage Q and $\overline{Q}$ are at. They keep changing. This can be summarized by the following table:

R	S	Q	$\overline{Q}$
0	0	?	?
0	1	1	0
1	0	0	1
1	1	?	?

Since we can't use a truth table, we use something else to describe how an RS flip-flop works. Figure 7-2 is a *timing diagram*. A timing diagram shows how the voltages that conductors are at change over a period of time.

This particular timing diagram counts time in seconds. That's why the voltage changes are drawn as vertical lines. They occur almost instantly. If the diagram were counting time in nanoseconds, on the other hand, I would have to draw the voltage changes as slanted lines. This would show the amount of time a conductor took to change voltage, which depends on the switching time of the transistors. This diagram depicts the sequence of voltages we looked at before.

1. Initially (at time = 0), R, S, and $\overline{Q}$ are at low voltage and Q is at high.

FIGURE 7-2

Timing diagram

for an RS

flip-flop

■

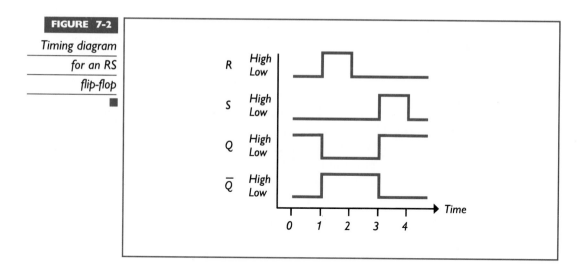

2. At time = 1, R goes to high voltage. Q immediately goes to low voltage and $\overline{Q}$ goes to high. S stays at low voltage.

3. At time = 2, R goes to low voltage. Q stays at low voltage and $\overline{Q}$ stays at high. S stays at low voltage.

4. At time = 3, S goes to high voltage. $\overline{Q}$ immediately goes to low voltage and Q goes to high. R stays at low voltage.

5. At time = 4, S goes to low voltage. $\overline{Q}$ stays at low voltage and Q stays at high. R stays at low voltage. After this, the RS flip-flop stays the way it was initially.

Figure 7-3 shows the diagram and corresponding schematic symbol for the RS flip-flop.

FIGURE 7-3

Diagram and

schematic

symbol for an

RS flip-flop

■

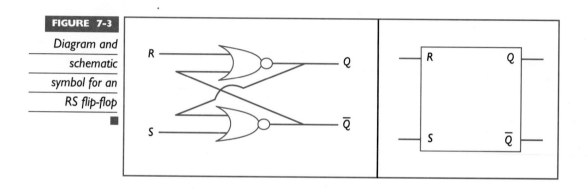

THE T FLIP-FLOP

igure 7-4 shows two NAND gates and two NOT gates connected to an RS flip-flop. These extra connections make this arrangement of gates into another kind of flip-flop called a *T flip-flop*.

Let's look at how the T flip-flop works. Suppose that initially, Q is at high voltage and $\overline{Q}$ is at low voltage. Also suppose that T is at low voltage. The T flip-flop in its initial state is shown here:

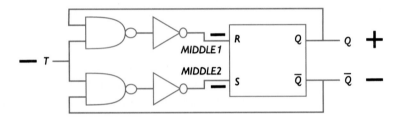

Now suppose that T goes briefly to high voltage as shown in the following illustration. MIDDLE1 (the R input to the RS flip-flop) goes to high voltage. MIDDLE2 (the S input to the RS flip-flop) is at low voltage. From the timing diagram for the RS flip-flop (Figure 7-2), you can see that Q goes to low voltage, and $\overline{Q}$ goes to high voltage.

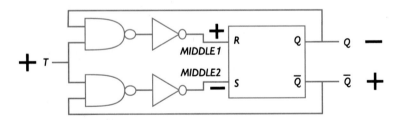

FIGURE 7-4

T flip-flop

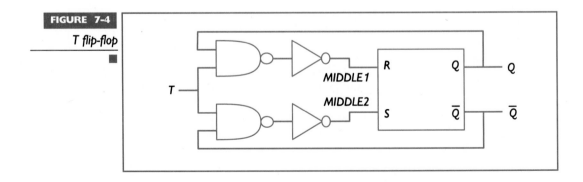

Suppose that T goes immediately to low voltage again, as shown in the next illustration. MIDDLE1 and MIDDLE2 are at low voltage. So Q stays at low voltage and $\overline{Q}$ stays at high voltage.

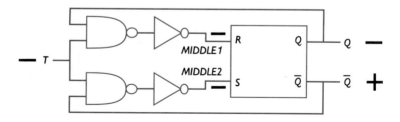

Now suppose that T goes briefly to high voltage again. MIDDLE1 stays at low voltage and MIDDLE2 goes to high voltage. From the timing diagram for the RS flip-flop, you can see that Q goes to high voltage, and $\overline{Q}$ goes to low voltage, as shown here:

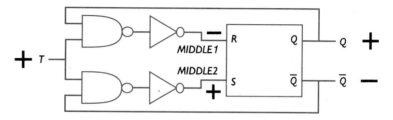

If T goes immediately to low voltage again, Q stays at high voltage and $\overline{Q}$ stays at low voltage. The T flip-flop is back to the way it was initially.

Can you see what is happening here? Whenever T goes briefly from low voltage to high voltage, Q and $\overline{Q}$ trade voltages. If T goes from high voltage to low voltage, Q and $\overline{Q}$ don't change. The T in "T flip-flop" stands for *toggle*, which means to switch back and forth between two states. When T goes to high voltage, it toggles Q and $\overline{Q}$ from low voltage to high voltage or high voltage to low voltage.

Figure 7-5 shows the timing diagram for a T flip-flop. This diagram shows the sequence of voltages that we just looked at.

1. Initially (at time = 0), T and $\overline{Q}$ are at low voltage and Q is at high voltage.

2. At time = 1, T goes to high voltage. Q immediately switches to low voltage, while $\overline{Q}$ goes to high.

3. At time = 2, T returns to low voltage. Q stays at low voltage and $\overline{Q}$ stays at high.

FIGURE 7-5

*Timing diagram
for a T flip-flop*

■

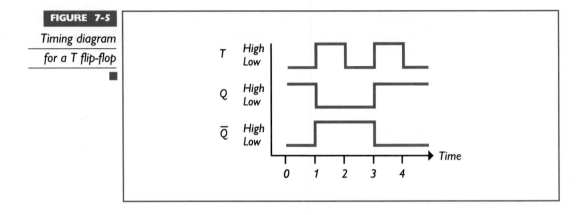

4. At time = 3, T goes to high voltage. Q immediately switches to high voltage, while $\overline{Q}$ goes to low.

5. At time = 4, T returns to low voltage. Q stays at high voltage and $\overline{Q}$ stays at low. The T flip-flop is the way it was initially.

Figure 7-6 shows the diagram and corresponding schematic symbol for the T flip-flop.

THE JK FLIP-FLOP

igure 7-7 is a picture of a *JK flip-flop*. It looks very similar to a T flip-flop. However, it behaves like a cross between an RS flip-flop and a T flip-flop. When J goes to high voltage, Q gets reset to low. When K goes to high voltage, Q gets set to high. Now, in an RS flip-flop, if both R and S went from low to high voltage at the same time, you couldn't tell what voltage Q

FIGURE 7-6

*Diagram and
schematic
symbol for a T
flip-flop*

■

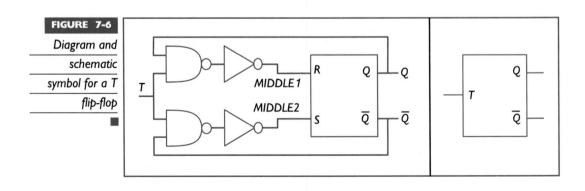

FIGURE 7-7

JK flip-flop

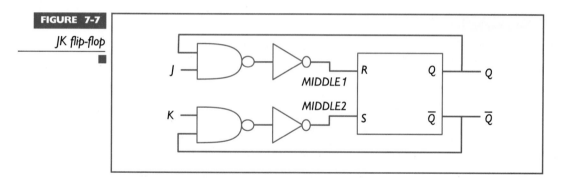

and $\overline{Q}$ were at. But in the JK flip-flop, if both J and K go just briefly from low to high voltage, then Q and $\overline{Q}$ switch voltages, like in a T flip-flop. So the JK flip-flop is a "safe" version of an RS flip-flop. You can always tell what voltage the output is at.

The timing diagram for the JK flip-flop is shown in Figure 7-8. As you can see, from time = 0 to 4 it behaves very much like an RS flip-flop. But when both J and K go from low to high voltage at time = 5 and time = 7, it behaves like a T flip-flop.

Figure 7-9 shows the diagram and corresponding schematic symbol for the JK flip-flop.

AN APPLICATION

Y ou're probably wondering what flip-flops can be used for. Flip-flops are important because they have memory. What exactly *is* memory? This is

FIGURE 7-8

Timing diagram for a JK flip-flop

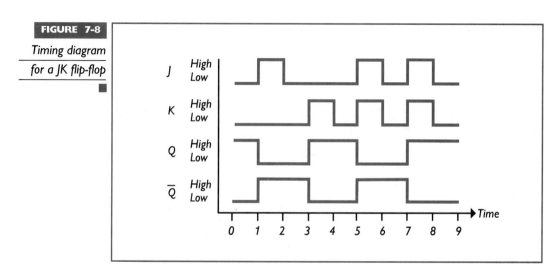

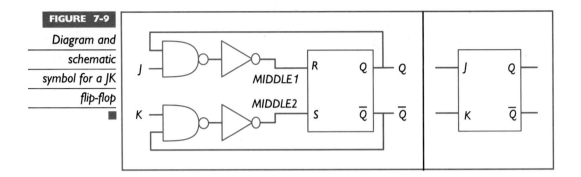

FIGURE 7-9

Diagram and schematic symbol for a JK flip-flop ∎

a very difficult question, but a simple answer for now is that memory is knowing something even after you're no longer being told it.

A flip-flop has a very simple memory. For example, suppose you have an RS flip-flop and you put S at high voltage. This tells the RS flip-flop, "Put Q at high voltage." Now Q goes to high voltage. The flip-flop will "remember" what you told it by keeping Q at high voltage. Even after S goes to low voltage, Q will stay at high voltage. Gates don't have memory. A gate will "forget" what you "told it" as soon as you stop "telling it." For example, suppose you have a NOT gate and you put IN at high voltage. This tells the NOT gate, "Put OUT at low voltage." Now OUT goes to low voltage. But if IN ever goes to low voltage, OUT will go to high voltage.

We can use the simple memory of a flip-flop to build more complicated memories. Look at Figure 7-10. It shows four T flip-flops connected together. They are labeled T0, T1, T2, and T3. Remember that in a T flip-flop, Q changes its voltage level whenever T goes briefly from low to high voltage. Suppose we quickly and continuously alternate the voltage that IN is at. Every time IN goes from low to high voltage, Q0 will change its voltage level. Every time IN goes from high to low voltage, Q0 will stay the same. Every time Q0 goes from low to high voltage, Q1 will change its voltage level. Every

FIGURE 7-10

Example of a four-bit counter ∎

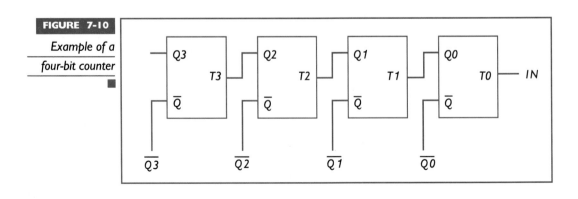

time Q0 goes from high to low voltage, Q1 will stay the same, and so on. This following table shows the voltages that the Qs are at when IN alternates like this.

IN	Q0	Q1	Q2	Q3
Low	Low	Low	Low	Low
High	High	Low	Low	Low
Low	High	Low	Low	Low
High	Low	High	Low	Low
Low	Low	High	Low	Low
High	High	High	Low	Low
Low	High	High	Low	Low
High	Low	Low	High	Low
Low	Low	Low	High	Low
High	High	Low	High	Low
Low	High	Low	High	Low
High	Low	High	High	Low
Low	Low	High	High	Low
High	High	High	High	Low
Low	High	High	High	Low
High	Low	Low	Low	High
Low	Low	Low	Low	High
High	High	Low	Low	High
Low	High	Low	Low	High
High	Low	High	Low	High
Low	Low	High	Low	High
High	High	High	Low	High
Low	High	High	Low	High
High	Low	Low	High	High
Low	Low	Low	High	High
High	High	Low	High	High
Low	High	Low	High	High
High	Low	High	High	High
Low	Low	High	High	High
High	High	High	High	High

This may look familiar. If you change all the Highs to 1's and Lows to 0's in the Q columns of the table, you'll get the numbers from zero to fifteen in binary number representation (reversed). This arrangement of flip-flops counts the number of times that IN goes from low to high voltage. It is called a four-bit *counter*.

THE CLOCKED D FLIP-FLOP

igure 7-11 shows two NAND gates and three NOT gates connected to an RS flip-flop. These extra connections turn this arrangement of gates into a *clocked D flip-flop*.

Let's look at how the clocked D flip-flop works. Assume that CLK is at high voltage. It doesn't really matter what voltage Q and $\overline{Q}$ are at. If D is at high voltage, then S gets put at high voltage, and R gets put at low. The result is that Q gets *set* to high voltage. $\overline{Q}$ is at low voltage. Now, if D goes to low voltage, then S gets put at low voltage, and R gets put at high. The result is that Q gets *reset* to low voltage. $\overline{Q}$ is at high voltage.

If CLK is at low voltage, then it doesn't matter what voltage D is at. Both R and S are at low voltage, so Q and $\overline{Q}$ don't change. The timing diagram for a clocked D flip-flop is shown in Figure 7-12.

If CLK is at high voltage, then Q matches D. However, if CLK goes to low voltage, then Q doesn't change, no matter what happens to D. If Q was at low voltage, it stays at low. If it was at high voltage, it stays at high. ($\overline{Q}$ always stays the opposite of Q.) The D in "clocked D flip-flop" stands for *data*. When CLK is at high voltage, Q stores the data, or information, given by D, which is either a high or a low voltage. When CLK goes to low voltage, Q keeps the previous information, even if the voltage at D now changes.

FIGURE 7-11
Clocked D
flip-flop
∎

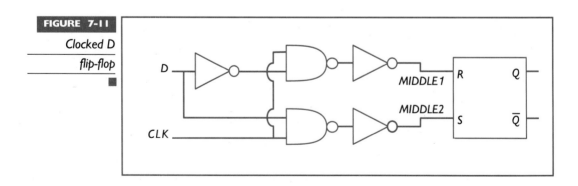

FIGURE 7-12

Timing diagram
for a clocked D
flip-flop
■

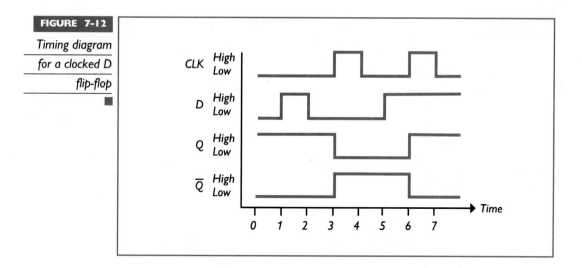

The reason this is called a *clocked* D flip-flop is that Q can only change when CLK is at high voltage. (When CLK is at low voltage, R and S are both at low voltage, and Q stays the same.) The flip-flop is made this way for a very good reason. Devices inside computers often do things just one step at a time. They may need some information at one step, and different information at the next step. While they are working on one step, they don't want to be bothered with information for the next step. The CLK input to the clocked D flip-flop allows information to be held at Q and $\overline{Q}$ while a device uses it. Even if new information becomes available at D, it doesn't appear at Q or $\overline{Q}$. But when the device is finished using the old information, it can make CLK go to high voltage, and the new information then appears at Q. The diagram and corresponding schematic symbol for a clocked D flip-flop are shown in Figure 7-13. The small triangle at the bottom left corner of the symbol represents the CLK input.

FIGURE 7-13

Diagram and
schematic
symbol for a
clocked D
flip-flop
■

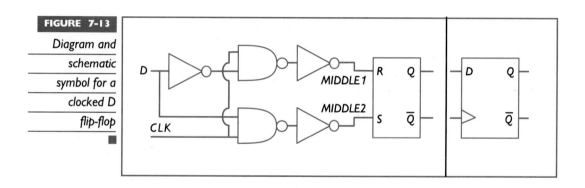

Review

- Truth tables cannot be used to describe flip-flops. Instead, we use timing diagrams to describe them. Timing diagrams tell us whether various conductors are at high voltage or low voltage at specific times.

- In an RS flip-flop, whenever R goes to high voltage, Q gets *reset* to low voltage. Whenever S goes to high voltage, Q gets *set* to high voltage. If both R and S are at low voltage, Q doesn't change. $\overline{Q}$ is always at the opposite voltage as Q. If you put both R and S at high voltage in an RS flip-flop, you can't tell what voltage Q is at.

- In a T flip-flop, whenever T goes briefly from low to high voltage, Q and $\overline{Q}$ trade voltages. If Q was at high voltage, it goes to low and $\overline{Q}$ goes to high. If Q was at low voltage, it goes to high, and $\overline{Q}$ goes to low.

- Depending on its input, a JK flip-flop can behave like an RS flip-flop or a T flip-flop.

- In a JK flip-flop, whenever J goes to high voltage, Q gets *reset* to low. Whenever K goes to high voltage, Q gets *set* to high. If both J and K are at low voltage, Q doesn't change. If both J and K are briefly at high voltage, then Q and $\overline{Q}$ trade voltages.

- Flip-flops can be connected together to make counters.

- A counter keeps track of the number of times its input goes from low voltage to high voltage.

- In a clocked D flip-flop, if CLK is at high voltage, then Q matches D. If CLK is at low voltage, then Q doesn't change, even if D does.

8

How Memory Works

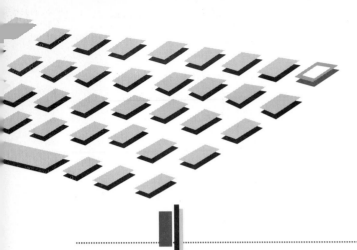

I N the last chapter, we looked at flip-flops. Flip-flops have simple memories that can store one voltage—high or low. In this chapter, we are going to build complex memories that can store much more information.

STORAGE USING TRANSISTORS

Y ou know that flip-flops can store one voltage that is either high or low. In binary number representation, a flip-flop stores a single one-bit number. We can't do much with a one-bit number. How do we store numbers that are longer than one bit? In the last chapter, you saw one way to do this. We used four flip-flops together in a counter. The counter could store numbers that were up to four bits long.

We can't do much with a single number, even if it is very long. How do we store more than one number? And once we've stored them, how do we keep track of them? To answer this question, think about how you store some of your possessions. Maybe you keep your reference books on the bottom shelf of your bookcase. Whenever you want those books, you always look there, and if you want different books, you look someplace else. Or, maybe you keep your most important papers on your desk. When you want these papers, you always know you can find them there. If you want other papers, you look elsewhere.

The important thing to remember is that you store things at certain *locations*. Whenever you want to retrieve them, you check back in those locations. This is the same principle as how a computer stores things.

There is one problem, though. A computer doesn't have tangible objects like books and papers to store. It doesn't have shelves and desks to store them in, and it doesn't have arms and legs to retrieve them. All a computer can store is high or low voltages and all it has to store them in is transistors. (Flip-flops are made from gates, which are made from transistors.) And the only way a computer can retrieve these voltages is by using conductors.

Luckily, high and low voltages can represent numbers in binary number representation. So computers can actually store numbers in transistors. Let's see how this is done.

Look at Figure 8-1. It shows a memory with PNP and NPN transistors connected to high- and low-voltage terminals. This memory stores, in four locations, four numbers that are each four bits long (therefore, it is a four-nybble memory). To retrieve a number, just put its LOCATION line at

FIGURE 8-1

A memory that stores four nybbles

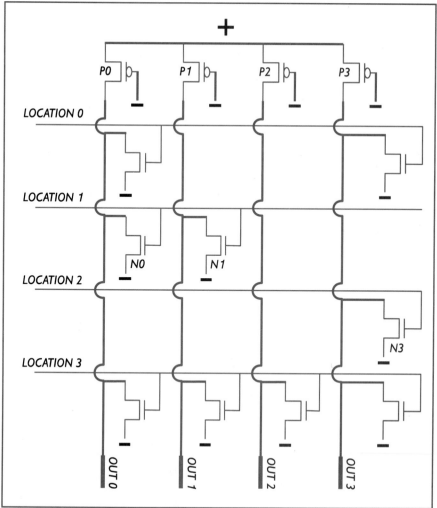

high voltage (and keep the other LOCATION lines at low voltage). The OUT lines will then be at the voltages that represent the number.

For example, suppose I want to retrieve the number that is in Location 1. First, I put the line labeled LOCATION1 at high voltage, and the other LOCATION lines at low voltage, as shown in Figure 8-2. This puts the top layers of the N0 and N1 transistors at high voltage and they turn on. All of the other NPN transistors stay off. OUT2 and OUT3 are at high voltage, because there is a direct conducting path to them from the high-voltage terminal at the top of the figure.

There is also a direct conducting path from the high-voltage terminal to OUT1, because P1 is on. P0 to P3 are special PNP transistors that are always

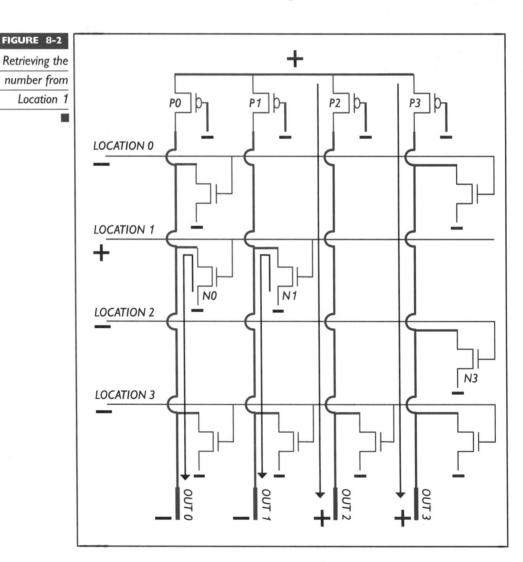

FIGURE 8-2

Retrieving the
number from
Location 1

on. (There is a direct conducting path from the low-voltage terminal at Location 1 to OUT1, because N1 is on.)

Because there are conducting paths to it from both the high-voltage terminal and a low-voltage terminal, you might think that OUT1 is at a "middle" voltage—neither high nor low. This is somewhat true. However, when this happens, the special PNP transistor, P1, helps keep OUT1 "on the low side." For all practical purposes, OUT1 is at low voltage. OUT0 is at low voltage for the same reasons. The voltages at the OUT lines then are low, low, high, high, or three. We say that a three is stored at Location 1.

Suppose I wanted to retrieve the number that is in Location 2. As shown in Figure 8-3, I put the line labeled LOCATION2 at high voltage and all of

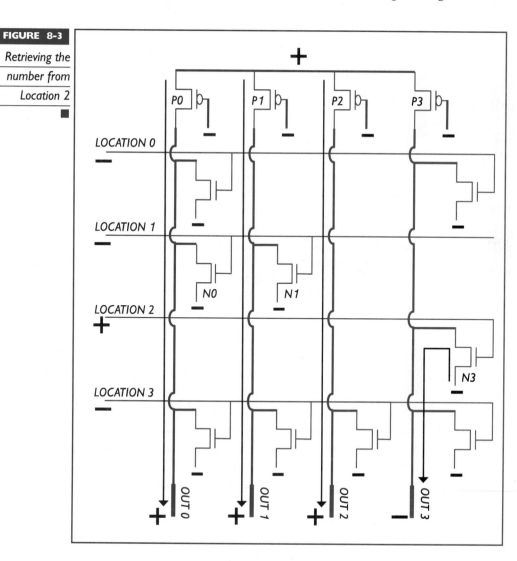

FIGURE 8-3

Retrieving the number from Location 2

the other LOCATION lines at low voltage. This puts the top layer of N3 at high voltage and this transistor turns on (all of the other NPN transistors stay off). OUT0, OUT1, and OUT2 are all at high voltage, because there are direct conducting paths to them from the high-voltage terminal. OUT3 is at low voltage, because there is a direct conducting path to it from the low-voltage terminal at N3. The voltages at the OUT lines are high, high, high, low, or fourteen. We say that a fourteen is stored at Location 2.

If you further study the figure, you'll find that there is a six stored at Location 0 and a zero stored at Location 3. An easy way to determine this is to look at places where a LOCATION line crosses an OUT line. If there is a transistor at a crossing, then that OUT line will be at low voltage. If there is not a transistor at the crossing, then that OUT line will be at high voltage. From the highs and lows, you can easily figure out what number is stored at that location.

PSEUDO-NMOS TECHNOLOGY

In Chapter 2, I talked about building gates using complementary transistors. This called CMOS technology. The gates we looked at contained one PNP transistor for every NPN transistor.

In the four-nybble memory we just looked at, there was not one PNP transistor for every NPN transistor. If there had been only NPN transistors, this memory would have been built using *NMOS technology*. NMOS technology means building devices using only NPN transistors. However, since there were a few PNP transistors, this method of building devices is called *pseudo-NMOS technology*. Pseudo-NMOS technology means building devices in a way that resembles NMOS technology.

DECODERS

In the four-nybble memory, there were four locations where four-bit numbers were stored. However, most computers have millions of memory locations. What if we wanted to retrieve a number from a huge memory? We don't want to have to keep track of millions of LOCATION lines. We also don't want to put two LOCATION lines at high voltage by accident.

That would be like trying to retrieve two numbers at the same time. It would be easier to just give the number of the location and have the correct LOCATION line put at high voltage for us. A logic block that allows us to do this is called a *decoder*.

Figure 8-4 shows a simple decoder. On the left side are two input lines, NUM0 and NUM1. On the right side are four LOCATION lines. We can put NUM0 and NUM1 at voltages that represent a number from zero to three (00, 01, 10, 11) and the LOCATION line for that number will then be at high voltage. All other lines will be at low voltage. The figure shows the outputs of the decoder when the numbers zero through three are put on the NUM lines.

We can attach this decoder to the memory we looked at before. Now, we don't have to put the LOCATION line at high voltage for the memory location we want to retrieve. We just put the number of that location on the NUM lines and the number stored at that location automatically appears at

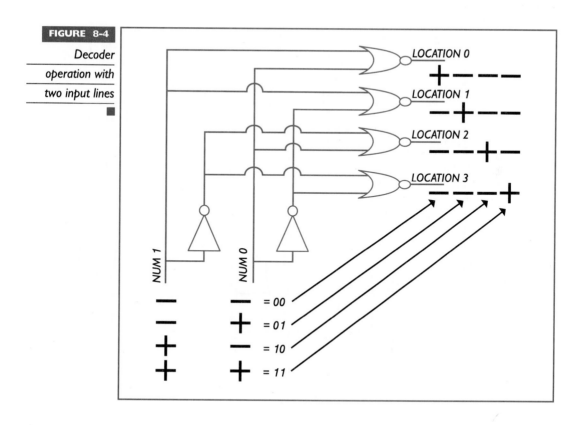

FIGURE 8-4

Decoder operation with two input lines ∎

the LOCATION lines. The operation of the decoder together with the memory is shown in Figure 8-5.

FIGURE 8-5

Decoder
operation with
memory

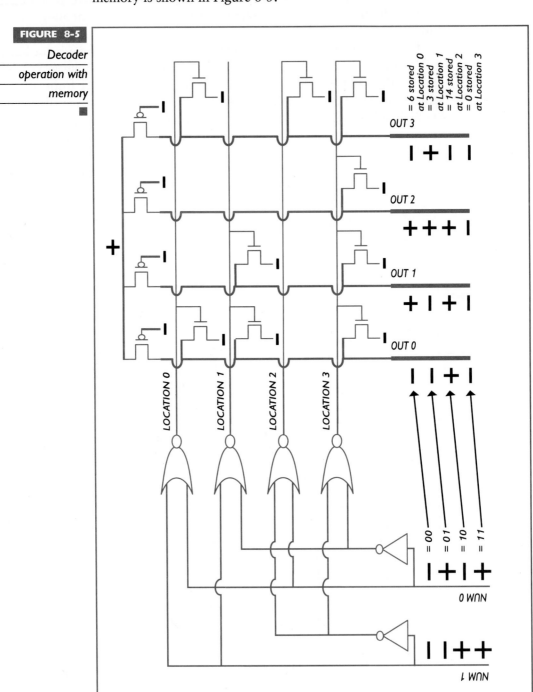

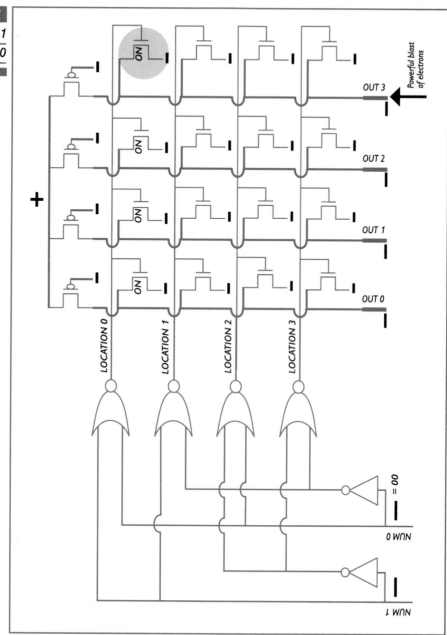

FIGURE 8-7

Storing a 0001
in Location 0

withstand the electron blast. Now the NPN transistor on the upper right is
gone and a one is stored in Location 0.

Now, suppose I wanted to store a five in Location 1. To do this, I must
remove the transistor on the far right (the ones column), as well as the
transistor second from the left (the fours column). I use the decoder to put

the LOCATION1 line at high voltage. This turns on all the transistors in the second row. Now, as shown in Figure 8-8, I send powerful blasts of electrons in through OUT1 and OUT3. The transistors are destroyed and a five is now stored in Location 1.

FIGURE 8-8

Storing a 0101

in Location 1

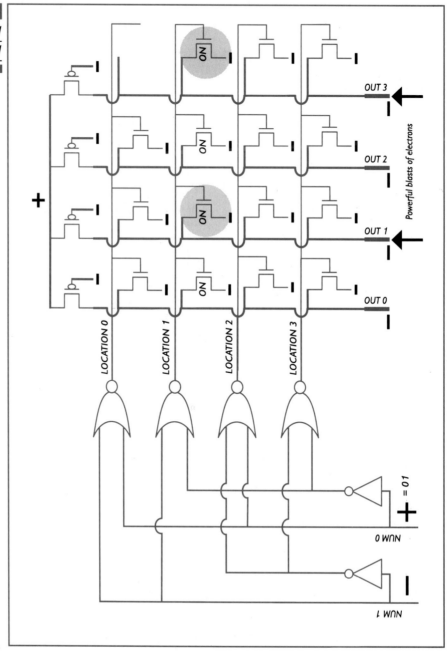

**RANDOM
ACCESS
MEMORY**

A computer usually needs to be able to change the information it stores, which means it needs *read-write memory*. Read-write memory allows you to store, or write, new numbers as well as retrieve, or read, them. And you don't have to destroy transistors or put new ones in to do it. However, read-write memory chips are larger and more expensive. They require an entire flip-flop for every bit of storage.

Read-write memory is usually called *RAM*, which stands for *random-access memory*. Read-write memory is probably called random access memory because you can get at any memory location easily and change it.

Figure 8-9 shows one way to build a read-write memory. This example stores four numbers that are each four bits long.

Let's look at the differences between this read-write memory and the read-only memory we looked at in the last section (Figure 8-6).

- Notice that along with the LOCATION inputs, there is an input line labeled W/R. Using the LOCATION lines, we tell the memory which location we are interested in. We tell the memory whether we want to read from or write to that location using the W/R line.

- Notice that the OUT lines are called DATA lines. These conductors are used to put numbers into, as well as retrieve them from, the memory. When we are reading from locations in the memory, the stored numbers appear here. When we are writing to locations in the memory, we have to put the numbers to be stored here. In either case, the numbers are in binary number representation, of course.

- In the read-only memory, there were transistors wherever a zero bit was stored. In this read-write memory, there are flip-flops—one for every bit that can be stored. This is because we need to be able to write bits as well as read them. And we don't know whether we will be writing high or low voltages. The flip-flops are prepared for either case.

- Notice that four individual transistors are connected to each flip-flop. These transistors are called *pass transistors*. They control whether a bit stored in the flip-flop is put on the DATA lines, or whether a bit put on the DATA lines is stored in the flip-flop.

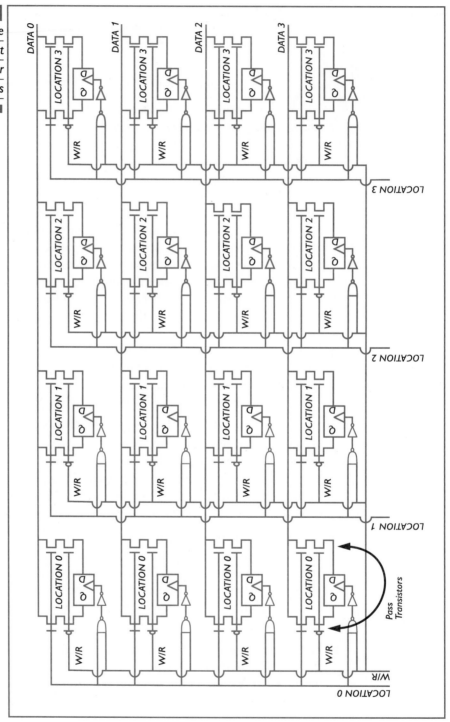

FIGURE 8-9

A read-write
memory that
stores four
nybbles

9

What Programmable Logic Arrays Are

N the last chapter, you learned about ROM, or read-only memory. In this chapter, I'm going to talk about a similar device called a *programmable logic array,* or *PLA.* PLAs are important for two reasons. First, you can easily make a wide variety of complicated logic blocks out of just one kind of PLA. Second, you can turn PLAs into *finite state machines.* Unlike gates and logic blocks, which can perform a single operation such as addition, subtraction, or simple decision-making, finite state machines can perform multiple operations, one at a time. I'll talk more about finite state machines in Chapter 11.

NOR GATES AS BUILDING BLOCKS

n Chapter 2, we built complicated logic blocks using three basic gates: the NOT gate, the NOR gate, and the NAND gate. An important feature of the NOR gate is this: *you can make the other two basic gates by using just NOR gates.* For example, if I connect the inputs of a NOR gate together, I am left with just one input and one output, as shown in this illustration:

NOR gate

This NOR gate behaves just like a NOT gate. If the input is at high voltage, then the output is at low voltage. If the input is at low voltage, then the output is at high voltage. You can check this by looking at the truth table in Chapter 2 for the NOR gate. If both inputs are at the same voltage, then the output is at the opposite voltage.

If I put these types of NOR gates at the inputs and output of a basic NOR gate, I get a NAND gate, as shown in the illustration. Just like a NAND gate, the output is at low voltage only if both inputs are at high voltage.

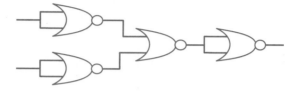

So, there is one important thing to remember about NOR gates: if we have many NOR gates available, we can use them to make any logic block that we want.

THE LOGIC ARRAY

The following illustration shows a pseudo-NMOS NOR gate with four inputs and one output. Just like a regular NOR gate, the output of this gate is at high voltage only if all of the inputs are at low voltage. If any of the inputs are at high voltage, then the output is at low voltage.

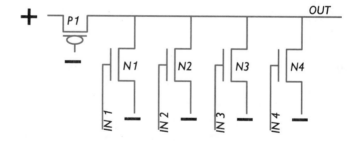

Each input is connected to an NPN transistor. As you can see, if all of the inputs are at low voltage, then all of the NPN transistors are off. There is a direct conducting path from the high-voltage terminal, through P1, to OUT. So OUT is at high voltage.

Suppose IN2 is at high voltage, as shown in the following illustration. N2 turns on, providing a direct conducting path from the low-voltage terminal through N2 to OUT. There is also still a direct conducting path from the high-voltage terminal through P1 to OUT. When this happens, the special PNP transistor, P1, helps keep OUT "on the low side." So, you can see that if any of the inputs are at high voltage, OUT is at low voltage.

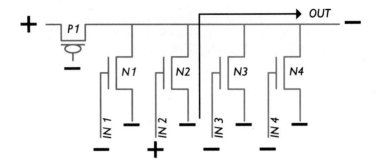

Figure 9-1 shows four of the NOR gates we looked at before. However, not all of the NOR gates have four inputs. The bottom two are missing a few transistors. The bottom NOR gate has two inputs, IN1 and IN3. The gate above it has two different inputs, IN2 and IN4. In ROMs, the presence or absence of transistors determines whether zeros or ones are stored in the memory. In these NOR gates, the presence or absence of transistors determines whether or not IN lines are inputs to the NOR gates.

As you can see, if you have a certain number of inputs, you can pick which ones are inputs to any of the NOR gates.

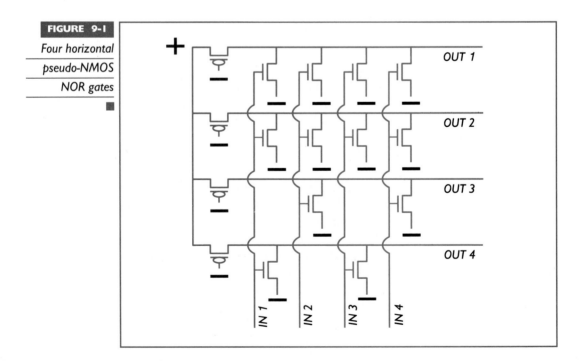

FIGURE 9-1

Four horizontal pseudo-NMOS NOR gates

We can also place NOR gates vertically. This lets us use the outputs of the horizontal NOR gates as inputs to the vertical NOR gates as shown in Figure 9-2.

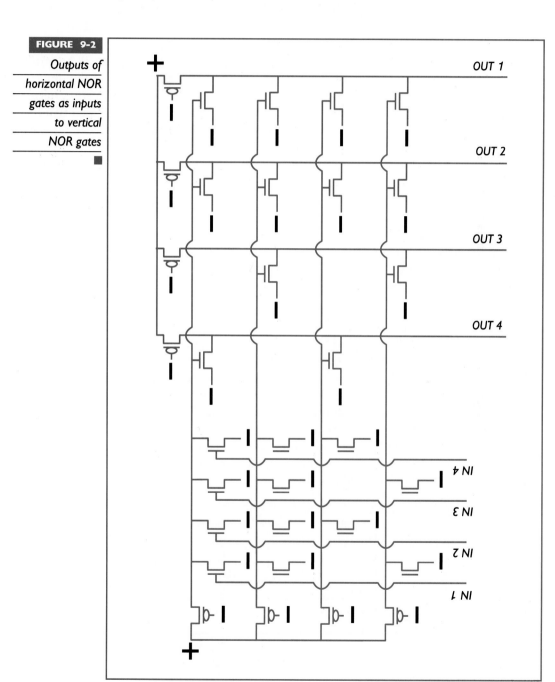

Again, the presence or absence of transistors determines whether or not the outputs of the horizontal NOR gates are inputs to the vertical NOR gates. Any or all of the IN lines can be inputs to the horizontal NOR gates. And any or all of the outputs of the horizontal NOR gates can be inputs to the vertical NOR gates. This arrangement of IN lines, horizontal NOR gates, vertical NOR gates, and OUT lines is called a *logic array*. Logic arrays are available in packages. Usually, they have anywhere from 8 to 24 horizontal NOR gates, and about as many vertical NOR gates. Half of the inputs to the horizontal NOR gates are connected to NOT gates, which are connected to the inputs of the other half. This is because it is useful to have available the opposite of each voltage that is input to the logic array. Figure 9-3 shows an example of such a logic array.

LOGIC BLOCKS FROM LOGIC ARRAYS

As sold by the manufacturer, logic arrays are not very useful. They must be programmed—turned into useful logic blocks—by removing some of their transistors. It is very easy to make logic blocks from logic arrays. This can be done because logic arrays contain many NOR gates. And as you've read, NOR gates are all we need to make logic blocks.

Let's look at how logic blocks can be made from logic arrays. We'll start with the logic array containing four horizontal NOR gates and four vertical NOR gates, with all transistors intact, that is shown in Figure 9-3.

We'll use this logic array to make one of the logic blocks we read about in Chapter 3. The logic block we'll make is the one that tells how many points your team scored in a race at the track meet. The truth table for this logic block looked like this:

Row	Status of your team's runner			Your team gets	
	Disqualifies	Comes in 1st	Comes in 2nd	2 points	1 point
1	Low	Low	Low	Low	Low
2	Low	Low	High	Low	High
3	Low	High	Low	High	Low
4	Low	High	High	High	High
5	High	Low	Low	Low	Low
6	High	Low	High	Low	Low
7	High	High	Low	Low	Low
8	High	High	High	Low	Low

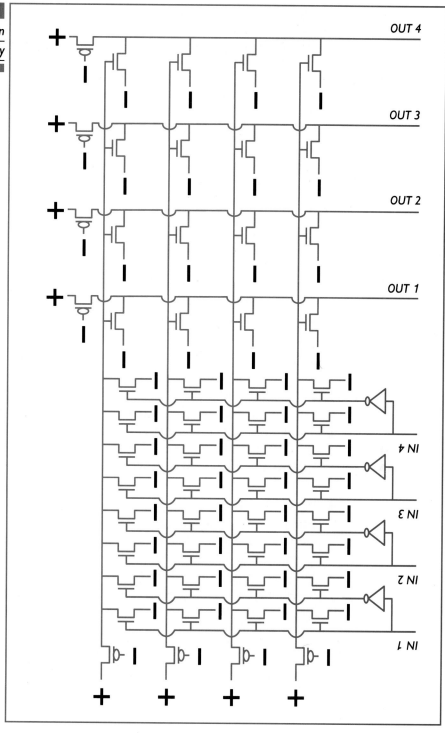

FIGURE 9-3

Example of an intact logic array

The first thing to notice about the logic block for this truth table is that it has only three inputs—corresponding to the columns for the runners' status. Therefore, we won't be using IN4 on the logic array, so we disconnect it from all of the horizontal NOR gates by removing all transistors that are connected to IN4.

Another thing to notice about the logic block for this truth table is that it has only two outputs—the columns for points. Therefore, OUT3 and OUT4 are unnecessary and we disconnect them by removing all transistors that are connected to OUT3 and OUT4. The logic array now looks like that shown in Figure 9-4.

Now, we'll turn the logic array into a logic block that follows the rules of the truth table.

First, let's work with the output that tells whether your team gets two points. We'll use OUT1 for this output. Look at the rows in the truth table in which this output is low. There are six of them: rows 1 and 2, and 5 through 8.

- Row 1 says that OUT1 should be at low voltage if IN1, IN2, and IN3 are at low. So, in horizontal NOR gate 1, we need to remove some transistors. When inputs are at low voltage, $\overline{\text{IN}}$ transistors are removed, and when inputs are at high voltage, IN transistors are removed. In this instance we need to take out $\overline{\text{IN1}}$, $\overline{\text{IN2}}$, and $\overline{\text{IN3}}$. Since this NOR gate is being used to generate OUT1, disconnect its output from OUT2, as shown in Figure 9-5.

- Row 2 of the truth table says that OUT1 should be at low voltage if IN1 and IN2 are at low and IN3 is at high. So, in horizontal NOR gate 2, remove the transistors for $\overline{\text{IN1}}$, $\overline{\text{IN2}}$, and IN3. Since this NOR gate is being used to generate OUT1, disconnect its output from OUT2, as in Figure 9-6.

- We could do this four more times for rows 5 through 8 but we would run out of horizontal NOR gates before we finished. There is a way to use just one horizontal NOR gate for these four rows of the truth table. Look at rows 5 through 8—notice that OUT1 should be at low voltage if IN1 is at high. If this is the case, it doesn't matter what IN2 and IN3 are. So, in horizontal NOR gate 3, remove the transistors for IN1, IN2, $\overline{\text{IN2}}$, IN3, and $\overline{\text{IN3}}$. Since this NOR gate is also being used to generate OUT1, disconnect its output from OUT2, as shown in Figure 9-7.

Now, let's work with the output that tells whether your team gets one point. We'll use OUT2 for this output. Again, look at the rows in the truth

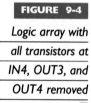

FIGURE 9-4

Logic array with all transistors at IN4, OUT3, and OUT4 removed

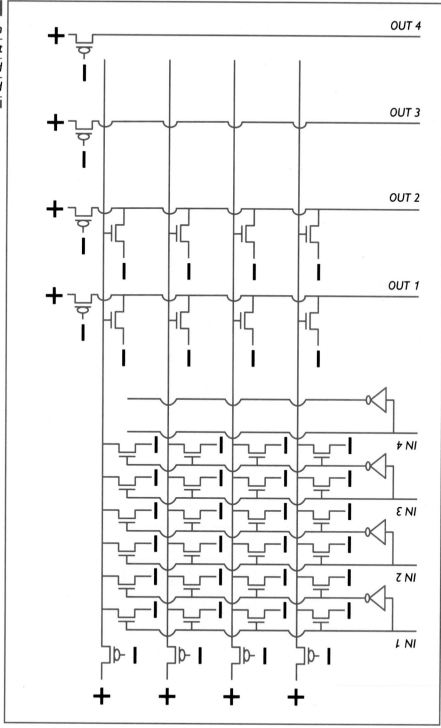

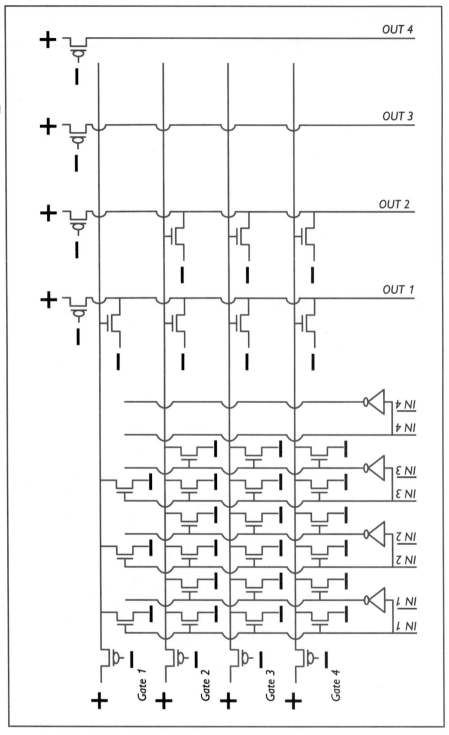

OUT 4

OUT 3

OUT 2

OUT 1

IN 4
IN 4

IN 3
IN 3

IN 2
IN 2

IN 1
IN 1

Gate 1

Gate 2

Gate 3

Gate 4

FIGURE 9-6

*Removing input
and output
transistors at
gate 2*

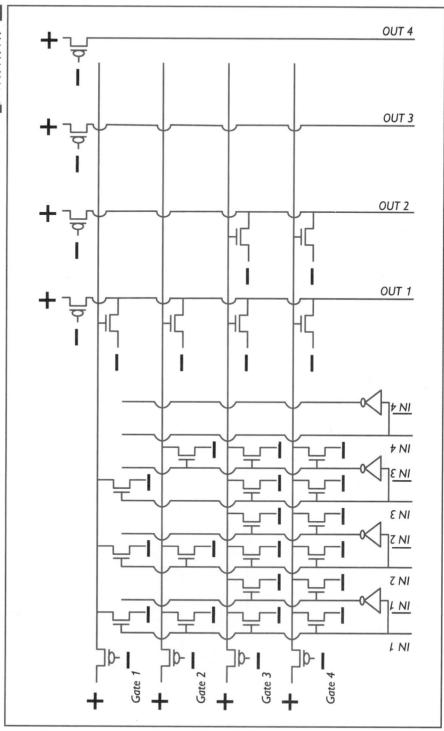

FIGURE 9-6

Removing input and output transistors at gate 2

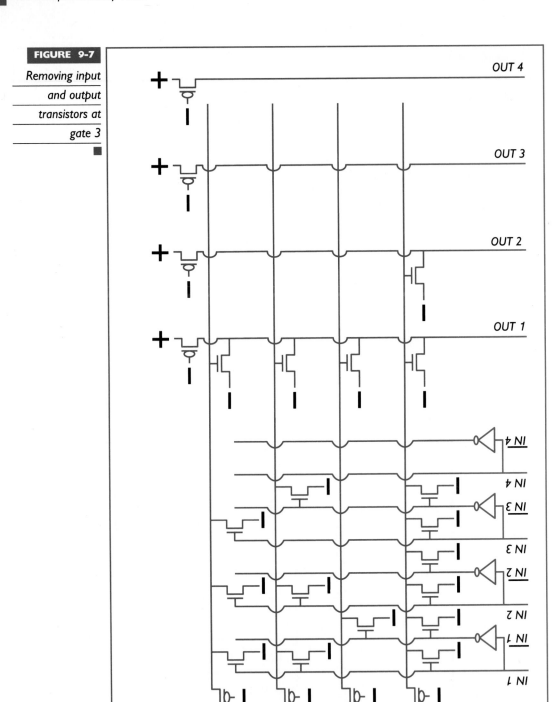

FIGURE 9-7

*Removing input
and output
transistors at
gate 3*
■

table for which this output is low. There happen to be six of them again: rows 1, 3, and 5 through 8.

- Row 1 says that OUT2 should be at low voltage if IN1, IN2, and IN3 are at low, which are the same conditions for OUT1 being at low. We could remove the transistors for $\overline{IN1}$, $\overline{IN2}$, and $\overline{IN3}$ in the horizontal NOR gate 4, and then disconnect its output from OUT1. But, there's no need to use up an extra horizontal NOR gate. We can use gate 1 to generate both OUT1 and OUT2. We do this by putting back the transistor that was removed at OUT2 when we were looking at the first row of the truth table for OUT1. Now there is an extra horizontal NOR gate to use, and the logic array looks like that shown in Figure 9-8.

- Row 3 of the truth table says that OUT2 should be at low voltage if IN1 and IN3 are at low, and IN2 is at high. So, in horizontal NOR gate 4, remove the transistors for $\overline{IN1}$, IN2, and $\overline{IN3}$. Since this NOR gate is being used to generate OUT2, disconnect its output from OUT1, as shown in Figure 9-9.

- It would seem that we have run out of NOR gates, even though we have four more rows of the truth table in which OUT2 is at low voltage. However, as with rows 5 through 8 before, we can use one of the horizontal NOR gates to generate both OUT1 and OUT2. This is done by reconnecting the output of gate 3 to OUT2. Now, whenever IN1 is at high voltage, both OUT1 and OUT2 will be at low voltage, as in Figure 9-10.

That's it. I've taken care of all the outputs, and looked at all rows where those outputs are at low voltage. You can make sure that this logic block works by tracing voltages for various inputs.

So, to make a logic block from a logic array, we repeat a few simple steps.

1. Disconnect unnecessary inputs to horizontal NOR gates by removing transistors connected to them.

2. Disconnect unnecessary outputs from vertical NOR gates by removing transistors connected to them.

3. For each output, do the following:

   - For every truth table row in which that output should be at low voltage, choose a horizontal NOR gate for that row. If an

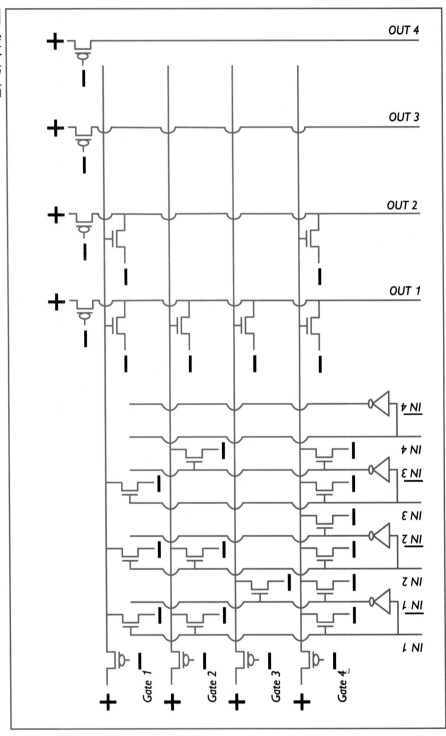

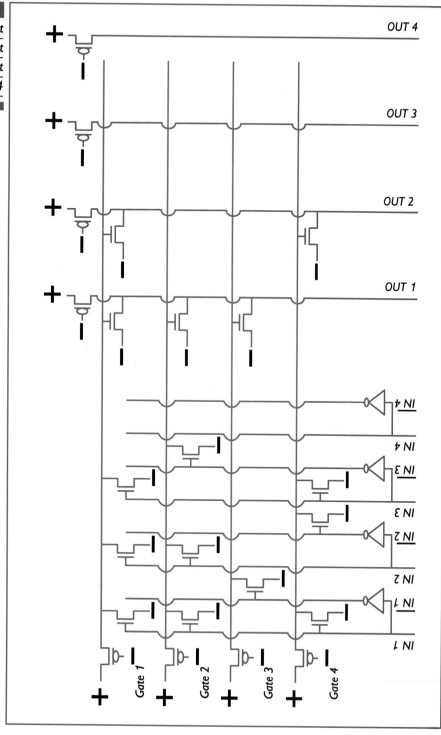

FIGURE 9-9

Removing input and output transistors at gate 4

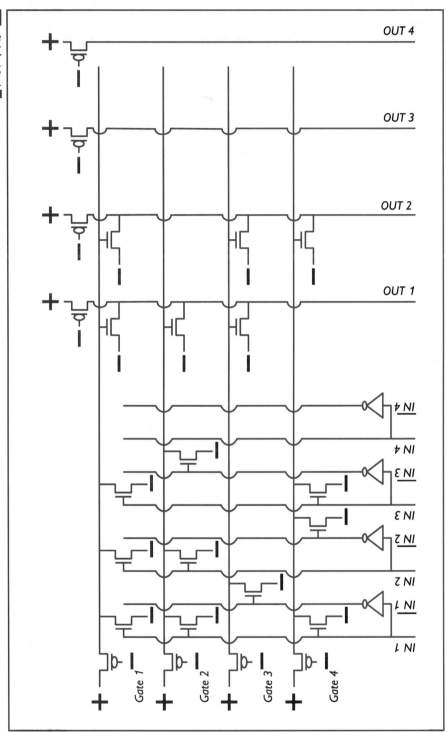

FIGURE 9-10

Replacing the
OUT2 transistor
at gate 3

■

input is at low voltage, remove the $\overline{\text{IN}}$ transistor. If an input is at high voltage, remove the IN transistor.

■ Go to the next row of the truth table in which that output should be at low voltage. When you have looked at all such rows, go to the next output.

4. When you have looked at all outputs, you are done.

PROGRAMMING LOGIC ARRAYS

Logic arrays are programmed by a process similar to burning ROMs. Powerful bursts of electrons are used to disconnect transistors from NOR gates. However, because programmable logic arrays are more complicated than ROMs, the transistors in them can't easily be destroyed from the input or output lines. So modern programmable logic arrays are sold with special programming circuitry. The programming circuitry cannot be used during normal operation of a programmed logic array. However, special programming devices can use this circuitry to disconnect transistors from NOR gates.

Review

■ An important feature of the NOR gate is that you can make NOT and NAND gates using only NOR gates.

■ NOR gates with multiple inputs and a single output can be made using pseudo-NMOS technology.

■ In pseudo-NMOS NOR gates, the presence or absence of transistors determines whether or not IN lines are inputs to the NOR gates.

■ A programmable logic array is an arrangement of IN lines, horizontal NOR gates, vertical NOR gates, and OUT lines.

■ Because programmable logic arrays contain many NOR gates, it is very easy to make logic blocks from logic arrays.

10

How Multiplication Can Be Done

I N this chapter, we will design a nybble multiplication machine. As you know, multiplication requires several steps that are done one at a time. It is very difficult to build one large logic block that multiplies two numbers and gives the answer immediately and directly. Therefore, the multiplication machine we are going to design will do multiplication one step at a time. As you will see by the end of the chapter, a finite state machine will be of great help in controlling this multiplication machine.

A REVIEW OF BINARY NUMBER MULTIPLICATION

I n Chapter 5, you learned how to do multiplication of numbers in binary number representation. It will be helpful to remember what multiplication of two four-bit numbers looks like on paper:

```
        XXXX
  ×   XXXX
      - - - - -
        XXXX
      XXXX
    XXXX
  XXXX
      - - - - - -
  XXXXXXX
```

There was also a list in Chapter 5 of four important things to remember about binary multiplication:

1. You multiply the multiplicand by each bit in the multiplier. Since the multiplier is four bits long, you will get four partial products.

2. Each partial product is either the multiplicand or zero. This is because each digit in the multiplier is either one or zero.

3. You shift each successive partial product one place to the left (except the first one) and then add them to get the product.

4. The number of bits in the product is, at most, the number of bits in the multiplicand plus the number of bits in the multiplier.

The first item in the list tells us that we need a way to multiply the multiplicand by each bit in the multiplier. The second item in the list tells us that this multiplication is very easy. If the bit is one, represented by high voltage, then the partial product is the multiplicand. If the bit is zero, or low voltage, then the partial product is zero. We will build a simple device to do this multiplication.

THE TWO-LINE SELECTOR

Let's start the design of our nybble multiplication machine with eight conductors. We'll eventually be putting the four left conductors at the voltages that represent the multiplier and the four right conductors at voltages that represent the multiplicand.

Now, look at Figure 10-1. It shows the logic diagram and the schematic symbol for a *two-line selector*.

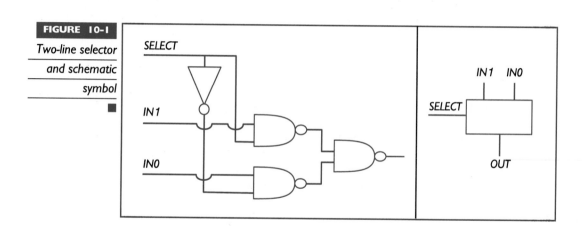

FIGURE 10-1

Two-line selector and schematic symbol ∎

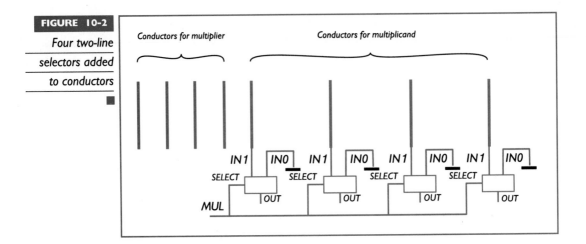

FIGURE 10-2

Four two-line selectors added to conductors

When SELECT is at low voltage, OUT is at the same voltage as IN0. It doesn't matter what voltage IN1 is. When SELECT is at high voltage, OUT is at the same voltage as IN1. It doesn't matter what voltage IN0 is.

If I add these selectors to the eight conductors of my multiplication machine, as shown in Figure 10-2 above, I can multiply a multiplicand by either one or zero.

The IN0 lines on these selectors are permanently set at low voltage. Now, when MUL is at low voltage, the OUT lines will all be at low voltage. When MUL is at high voltage, the OUT lines will be at the same voltages as the IN1 lines. So, if I want to multiply a multiplicand by one, I put MUL at high voltage. If I want to multiply a multiplicand by zero, I put MUL at low voltage. Either way, the correct partial product appears at the OUT lines.

Now, I can multiply a multiplicand by either one or zero. However, I need to be able to multiply the multiplicand by *each bit in the multiplier*, whether it is one or zero. To do this, I'll need to build a device using two-line selectors and some clocked D flip-flops.

THE FOUR-BIT SHIFT REGISTER

Figure 10-3 shows eight clocked D flip-flops connected together. A group of flip-flops that work together to store a number is called a *register*. The D line on the flip-flop at the far left is called IN. The Q line on the flip-flop at

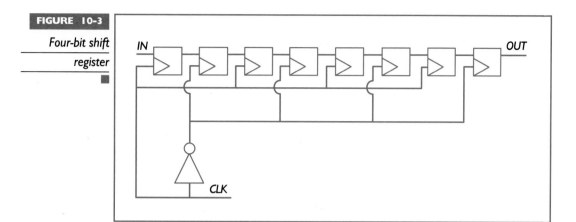

FIGURE 10-3

Four-bit shift
register

the far right is called OUT. The $\overline{Q}$ lines are not connected, so I won't show them from now on. The CLK line is connected directly to four of the flip-flops. It is also connected to the input of a NOT gate. The output of the NOT gate is connected to the other four flip-flops. So whenever the CLK input of one flip-flop is at high voltage, the CLK input of the adjacent ones is at low. Whenever the CLK input of one flip-flop is at low voltage, the CLK input of the adjacent ones is at high. This arrangement of adjacent flip-flops with CLK inputs is called a *four-bit shift register*.

To store voltages in the flip-flops, you have to put IN at those voltages one at a time, and you must alternate the voltage at CLK. The bits then move from the left flip-flop to the right flip-flop and finally start appearing at OUT. That's why it's called a four-bit *shift* register—it can shift the bits, one at a time left to right, to the OUT line.

Let's try using this register to store four bits of information—the number 1101. We'll have to put IN at the following voltages, one at a time: high, low, high, high. We'll also have to change the voltages on the CLK line. Remember, from the discussion of clocked D flip-flops in Chapter 7, that whenever the CLK line is at high voltage, the voltage at Q matches D. Whenever the CLK line is at low voltage, the voltage at Q stays, no matter what is at D. So, for each voltage at IN, we'll have to put CLK at high voltage and then at low voltage to shift the bit in. Figure 10-4 shows the sequence of voltages in the register as the number 1101 gets stored.

Notice what happens whenever a D flip-flop's CLK input is at high voltage: the voltage at D gets passed out and over to the input of the flip-flop to its right. However, the CLK input to this flip-flop is at low voltage, so the voltage doesn't get passed on to the *next* flip-flop. As you can see in the last sequence at the bottom of Figure 10-4, the number 1101 has been stored in the register.

Now suppose we leave IN at low voltage and continue making CLK alternate between high and low voltage. The stored voltage bits start shifting out on the OUT line. Figure 10-5 shows the voltages in the register as the stored number gets shifted out.

As you can see, every time CLK goes high, another bit from the number 1101 appears at OUT. This is why the four-bit shift register is useful in the multiplication machine. I can connect the register's OUT line to the MUL

Storing 1101 in

a four-bit shift

register

■

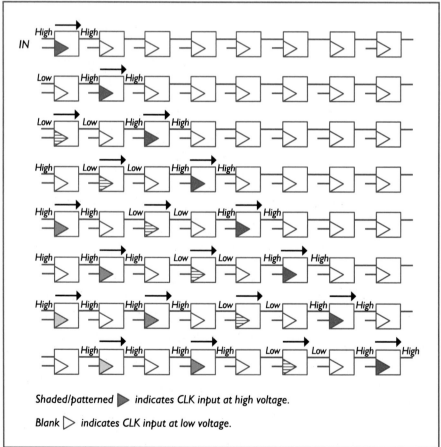

Shaded/patterned ▶ indicates CLK input at high voltage.

Blank ▷ indicates CLK input at low voltage.

FIGURE 10-5

Shifting 1101

out of a four-bit

shift register

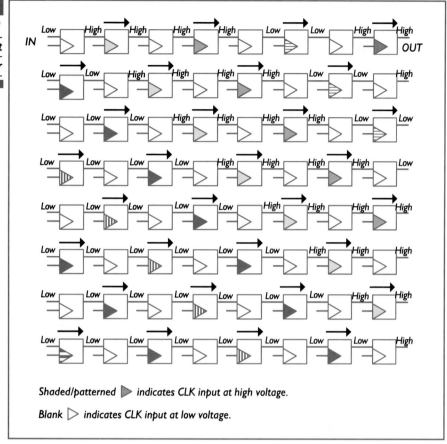

Shaded/patterned ▶ indicates CLK input at high voltage.

Blank ▷ indicates CLK input at low voltage.

line shown in Figure 10-2. If the multiplier is stored in the four-bit shift register, then as CLK alternates between high and low voltage, each bit of the multiplier will appear on MUL. The partial products will then appear on the four OUT lines.

There's still one thing to consider, though. It would be much more convenient to store the multiplier in the register all at once, instead of shifting it in one bit at a time. To do this, we add three two-line selectors, as shown in Figure 10-6.

Suppose we want to store 1101 in the register now. First, put INIT0 through INIT3 at the following voltages: high, high, low, high. Second, put IN/OUT at high voltage. This tells the register that we want to put data IN the register. Then make CLK go from low voltage to high. The register now looks like Figure 10-7.

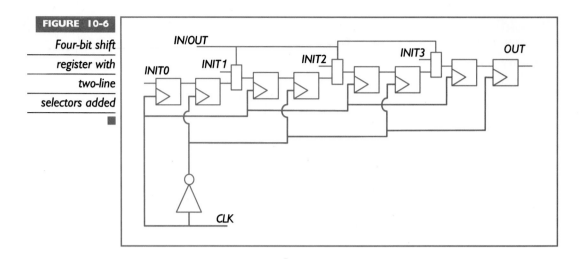

FIGURE 10-6

Four-bit shift register with two-line selectors added ∎

We'll be using this four-bit shift register in the design of our multiplication machine. We can now add it to what we already assembled in Figure 10-2. The results are shown in Figure 10-8. The INIT inputs have been connected to the conductors for the multiplier. This will allow us to store the multiplier in the register. The OUT output has been connected to MUL. As the bits of the multiplier are shifted out of the register, each will mulitply the multiplicand to generate a partial product.

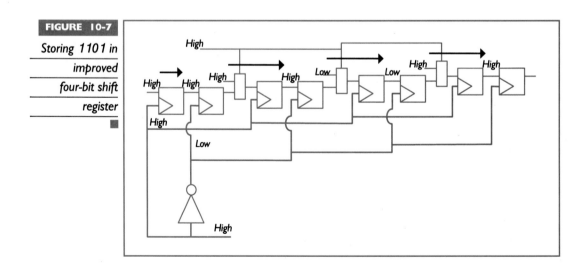

FIGURE 10-7

Storing 1101 in improved four-bit shift register ∎

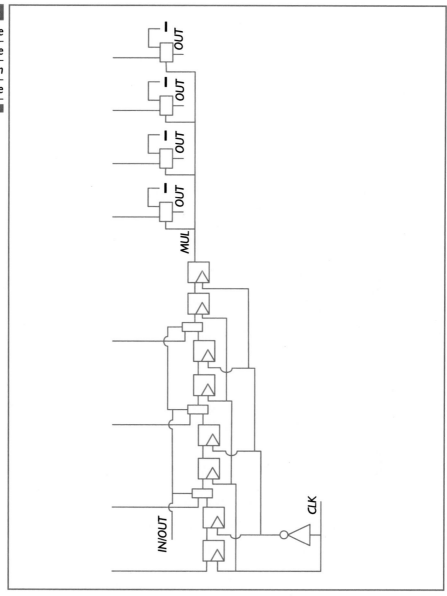

FIGURE 10-8

Assembling the
first part of the
multiplication
machine

THE NYBBLE
ADDER

A t this stage, the multiplication machine provides partial products. To make it do this,

1. Put the input conductors at voltages that represent the multiplier and the multiplicand.

2. Put IN/OUT at high voltage.

3. Make CLK go from low voltage to high voltage. The multiplier is now stored in the four-bit shift register.

4. Put IN/OUT at low voltage. This tells the shift register that stored data should be shifted out.

5. Make CLK continue alternating between low voltage and high voltage. The multiplier shifts out of the four-bit shift register one bit at a time and the partial products appear at the OUT lines one at a time.

As you know, to complete the multiplication, these partial products have to be shifted and added together. What kind of device can do this? To answer this question, we must be more specific about what we need to do to these partial products:

1. Add the first partial product to zero.

2. Shift the sum one bit to the right.

3. Add the second partial product to the shifted sum.

4. Shift the sum one bit to the right.

5. Add the third partial product to the shifted sum.

6. Shift the sum one bit to the right.

7. Add the fourth partial product to the shifted sum.

The first step may seem a bit unnecessary since adding the first partial product to zero has no effect on it. However, when we think of the first step in this way, it shows its similarity to the third, fifth, and seventh steps. This repetition of steps helps us build a simple device to do the adding and shifting.

The first thing to notice as we continue with our design is that we must add each four-bit partial product to some other number. So, we put a four-bit adder, like the one presented in Chapter 6, in our design by connecting it to the four OUT lines, as shown in Figure 10-9.

After each addition, the multiplication machine must remember the sum for the next step. As you know, computers can use flip-flops for memory. Therefore, we must add five clocked D flip-flops to the design, as shown in

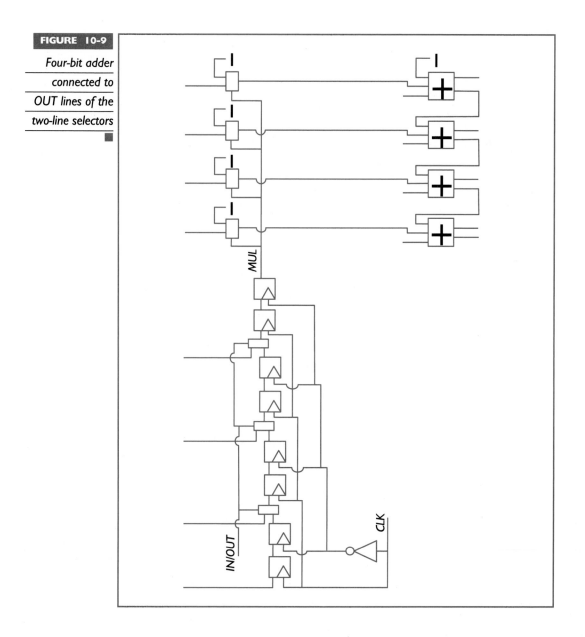

FIGURE 10-9

Four-bit adder connected to OUT lines of the two-line selectors

Figure 10-10. Five flip-flops must be added instead of four, because of overflow. Remember, the result of a four-bit addition can have up to five bits. The CLK inputs to these flip-flops are connected to the CLK inputs of the shift register. That way, whenever CLK goes to high, a new sum gets stored in the five flip-flops.

This sum needs to be shifted to the right and added to the next partial product. The best way to do this would be to connect the Q lines from the

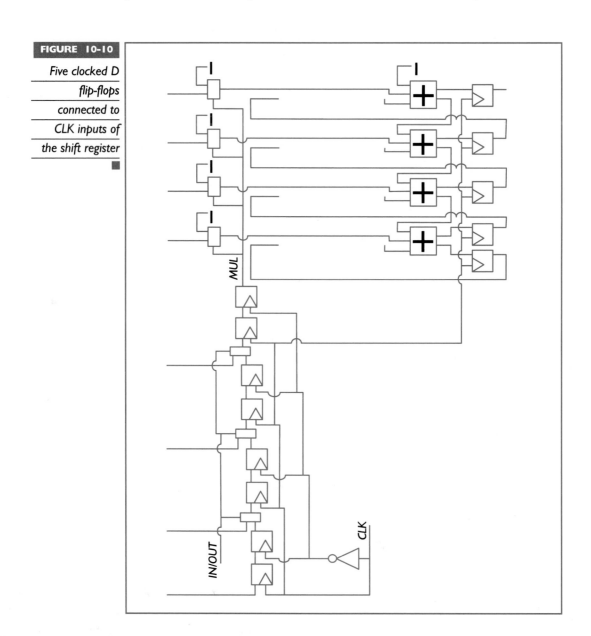

FIGURE 10-10

Five clocked D flip-flops connected to CLK inputs of the shift register

flip-flops back to the inputs of the adder. But there is a problem with this idea. As long as CLK is at high voltage, the sum stored in the five flip-flops will get added to the current partial product. This sum will get added to the partial product to generate a new sum, and so on. To prevent this from happening, we put four flip-flops at the inputs of the adder, as shown in Figure 10-11. We want the CLK inputs of these four flip-flops to be at high voltage when the CLK inputs of the other five flip-flops are at low voltage.

FIGURE 10-11

Four clocked D flip-flops connected to adder inputs

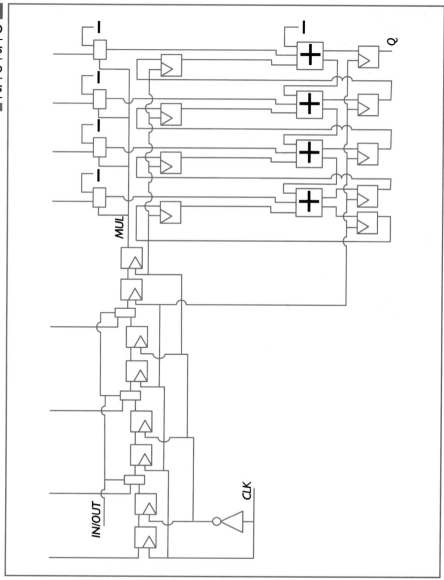

Conversely, we want the CLK inputs of the four flip-flops to be at low voltage when the CLK inputs of the five flip-flops are at high voltage. That way, even if the new sum is at the input to the four flip-flops, the old sum will remain at the outputs. To do this, we also connect the four flip-flops to $\overline{\text{CLK}}$.

Let's look at what happens now:

1. CLK goes to high voltage, $\overline{\text{CLK}}$ goes to low.

2. A bit from the multiplier gets shifted onto the MUL line.

3. The multiplicand is multiplied by this bit. The partial product is one of the inputs to the adder.

4. The adder adds the partial product to the previous sum.

5. The new sum is stored in the five lower flip-flops.

6. CLK goes to low voltage, $\overline{\text{CLK}}$ goes to high.

7. The new sum is shifted and is stored in the four upper flip-flops.

8. The next time CLK goes to high voltage, this new sum will be added to the next partial product.

So far, then, the multiplication machine can add and shift the partial products. However, there is nothing connected to the Q output of the last flip-flop at the lower right. As the final partial product gets generated, it gets shifted out of this flip-flop and is lost. We need to add another four-bit shift register to store the four least significant bits of the final partial product. This is shown in Figure 10-12.

There is one more problem we have to address. During the first addition, there is no "previous sum." We don't know exactly what is stored in the upper four flip-flops. Remember what we were supposed to do to the first partial product? We have to add a zero to it. This is easily done by adding four two-line selectors to the design, as shown in Figure 10-13.

Now, for the first addition step, a zero can be added to the first partial product. Finally, we have to put output conductors in the design. We should be able to read the final answer from these conductors. The largest product that can be produced is $1111 \times 1111 = 11100001$. So the product will never be more than eight bits long. We can connect five output conductors to the flip-flops in the second shift register and the remaining output conductors to three of the flip-flops in the lower row. This is shown in Figure 10-14.

FIGURE   10-12

Another four-bit

shift register

added

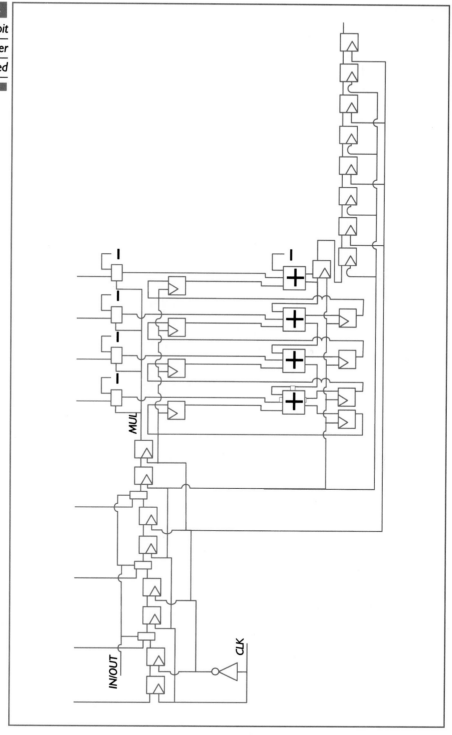

FIGURE   10-12

Another four-bit shift register added

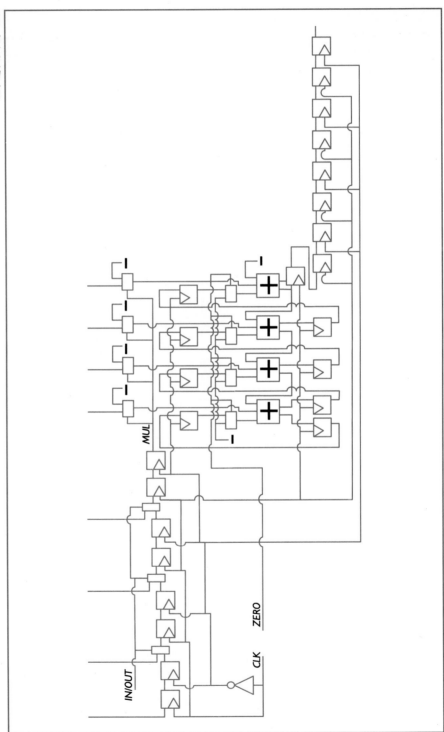

FIGURE 10-13

Another four
two-line
selectors added

FIGURE 10-14

Eight output
conductors
added to
complete the
multiplication
machine design

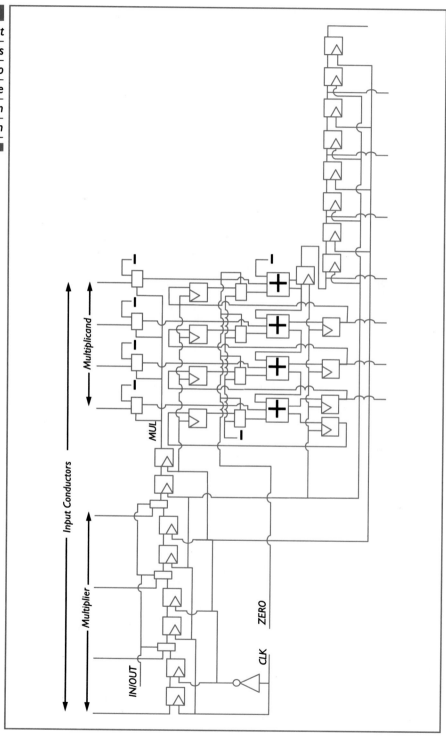

Our design is now complete. Here is what we have to do to multiply two four-bit numbers using our nybble multiplication machine:

1. Put the input conductors at the voltages that represent the multiplier and the multiplicand.

2. Put the IN/OUT line at high voltage.

3. Put the ZERO line at high voltage.

4. Put the CLK line at high voltage, then at low voltage.

5. Put the IN/OUT line at low voltage.

6. Put the ZERO line at low voltage.

7. Put the CLK line at high voltage, then at low voltage three more times.

The voltages at the output conductors now represent the result.

In the next chapter, we will see how most of this work can be eliminated by using a finite state machine.

Review

- The output of a two-line selector depends on whether SELECT is at high or low voltage. If SELECT is at low voltage, the output matches IN0. If SELECT is at high voltage, the output matches IN1.

- Using two-line selectors, a multiplicand can be multiplied by either one or zero.

- A group of flip-flops working together to store a number is called a register.

- A four-bit shift register can shift four bits from left to right. The shifts occur whenever the CLK input goes from low voltage to high. The bits are shifted into the register from the IN input and out through the OUT output.

- Two-line selectors can be used to store all of the bits of a number in a four-bit shift register simultaneously.

- A combination of four-bit shift registers, two-line selectors, and an adder can be used to make a multiplication machine.

11

How Finite State Machines Work

F I N I T E state machines help a computer perform step-by-step operations. In the last chapter, we designed a nybble multiplication machine. In this chapter, we'll design a finite state machine to control the nybble multiplication machine.

THE STATE DIAGRAM

To control the nybble multiplication machine, we need a device that puts conductors at high or low voltage at the right time. The conductors we are concerned with are IN/OUT, ZERO, and CLK. So the device must have three outputs to connect to these conductors. The voltages that these conductors are at must change for each step in the multiplication. So the output lines of the device must be at a certain voltage during each step. We say that the device must be in a certain *state* during each step. There is a finite (limited) number of steps and output combinations. So this device is called a *finite state machine*. When a finite state machine changes from one state to another, we say it has undergone a *transition*.

The device should be able to transition through eight states, one for each step of the multiplication operation:

State Number	Voltages			Description
	IN/OUT	ZERO	CLK	
0	1	1	0	Do nothing
1	1	1	1	Initialize shift register, add 1st partial product to zero
2	0	0	0	Prepare sum for 2nd addition
3	0	0	1	Add 2nd partial product to sum
4	0	0	0	Prepare sum for 3rd addition

State Number	Voltages			Description
	IN/OUT	**ZERO**	**CLK**	
5	0	0	1	Add 3rd partial product to sum
6	0	0	0	Prepare sum for 4th addition
7	0	0	1	Add 4th partial product to sum

The device should start out in state 0, doing nothing. When it receives a start signal, the device should transition through states 1 through 7, one at a time. After state 7, the product appears on the output lines. Then, the device should transition back to state 0, and await the next start signal. This tells us that the device should have two inputs: one to tell it to start the multiplication, and one to tell it to transition to the next state. We will call the first input START and the second input CLOCK.

The states of the device can be illustrated more clearly using a *state diagram* like the one in Figure 11-1. The circles represent the different states. If an output is at high voltage when the device is in a particular state, then the name of that output is printed inside the circle. If the output is at low voltage when the device is in a particular state, then the name of that output is not printed in the circle. The arrows represent possible transitions. The inputs that must be high to cause each transition are written near each arrow. If no input condition is specified, then the device undergoes the transition automatically when the CLOCK input goes high.

FIGURE 11-1

State diagram for multiplication machine

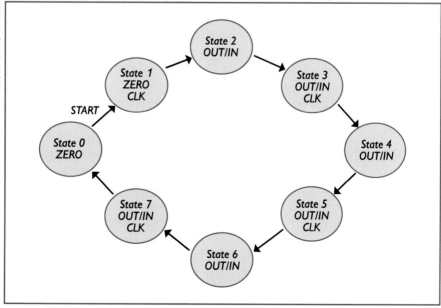

So, for the device to transition from state 0 to state 1, START must be at high voltage. Then, until the device transitions back to state 0, it doesn't matter what voltage START is at.

Let's build a logic block that transitions from state to state. The inputs to the logic block will be

1. The three-bit number of the current state, and

2. The START line.

The output of the logic block will be the number of the next state and the CLK, ZERO, and IN/OUT lines. The truth table for the logic block is shown here. Low voltage is represented by 0, and high voltage by 1. An asterisk (*) means that it doesn't matter whether START is at high or low voltage.

Current State	START	Next State	IN/OUT	ZERO	CLK
000	0	000	1	1	0
000	1	001	1	1	1
001	*	010	0	0	0
010	*	011	0	0	1
011	*	100	0	0	0
100	*	101	0	0	1
101	*	110	0	0	0
110	*	111	0	0	1
111	*	000	0	0	0

Figure 11-2 shows a programmable logic array, PLA, that has this as its truth table.

To move from state to state, it would seem natural to connect the Next State lines back to the Current State lines. However, if we actually did this, the PLA would jump from state to state uncontrollably. To control the transition of the PLA from state to state, we connect each Next State line to a clocked D flip-flop and each Current State line to a clocked D flip-flop. Then, we connect each Next State/Current State pair of flip-flops. This turns the PLA into a finite state machine, as shown in Figure 11-3.

Whenever CLOCK goes to high voltage, the Next State gets stored on the lines between each pair of flip-flops. When CLOCK goes to low voltage, the stored Next State becomes the new Current State. If CLOCK is continually alternated between high and low voltage, the finite state machine will transition from state to state in a controlled fashion.

How do we make sure the machine starts out at state 0? The best way is to make sure START is at low voltage, and that CLOCK alternates between low and high voltage several times. No matter what state the machine was

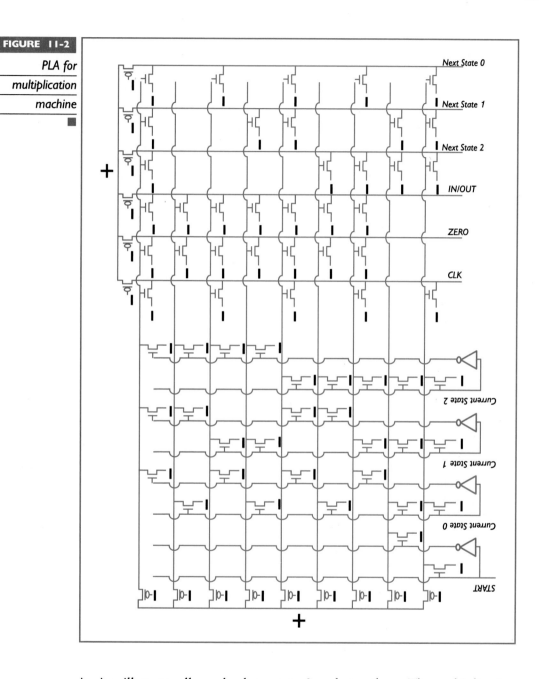

FIGURE 11-2

PLA for

multiplication

machine

in, it will eventually go back to state 0 and stay there. The multiplication machine will now be ready for a multiplication operation.

Figures 11-4 through 11-12 show the voltages at various points in the finite state machine as it transitions from state 0 through 7 and back to

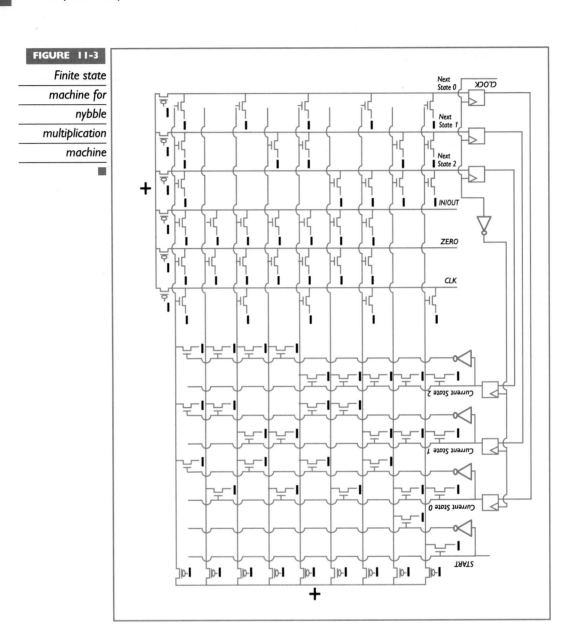

Finite state machine for nybble multiplication machine

■

state 0 again. The shaded boxes in the figures indicate the changes from state to state.

The outputs of the finite state machine can be connected to the inputs of the multiplication machine from the last chapter. The operation of the multiplication machine has now been greatly simplified:

FIGURE 11-4

Finite state
machine at
state 0

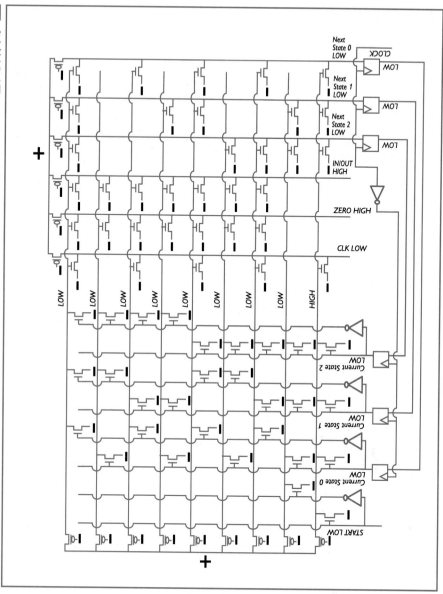

1. Put the multiplier and multiplicand on the appropriate input lines of the multiplication machine.

2. Keep START at low voltage and begin alternating the voltages at CLOCK.

FIGURE 11-5

State 1

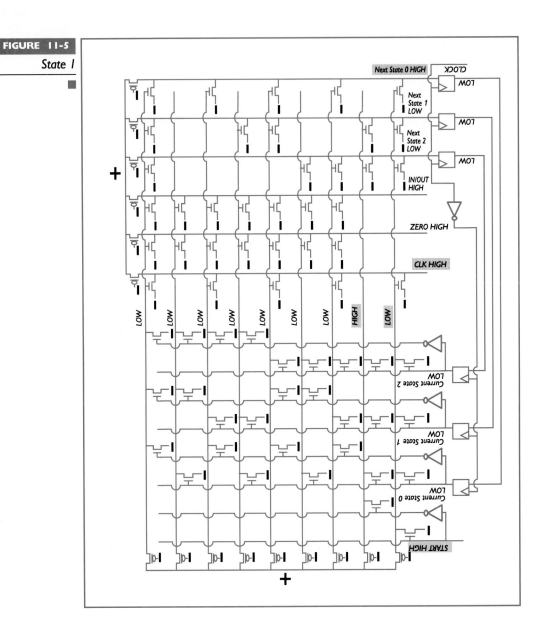

3. Put START at high voltage so that the finite state machine moves from state 0 to state 1. Then put START at low voltage.

4. After CLOCK has alternated voltages seven times, the product will be at the output lines of the multiplication machine.

FIGURE 11-6

State 2

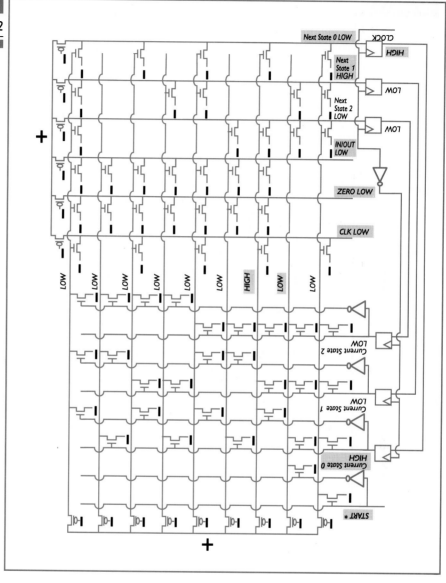

FIGURE 11-7

State 3

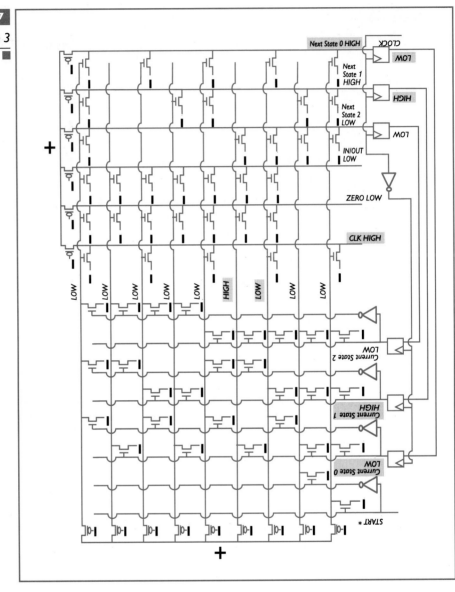

FIGURE 11-8

State 4

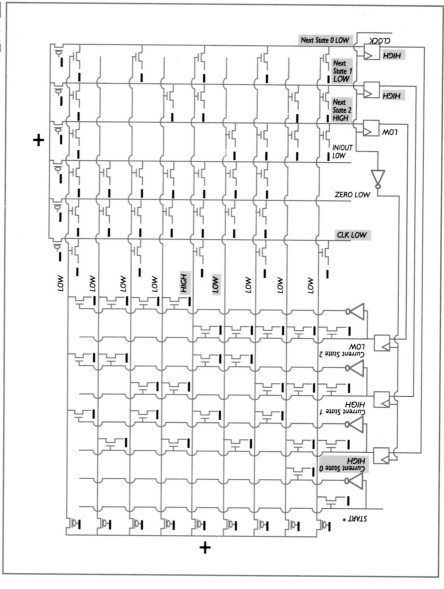

FIGURE 11-9

State 5

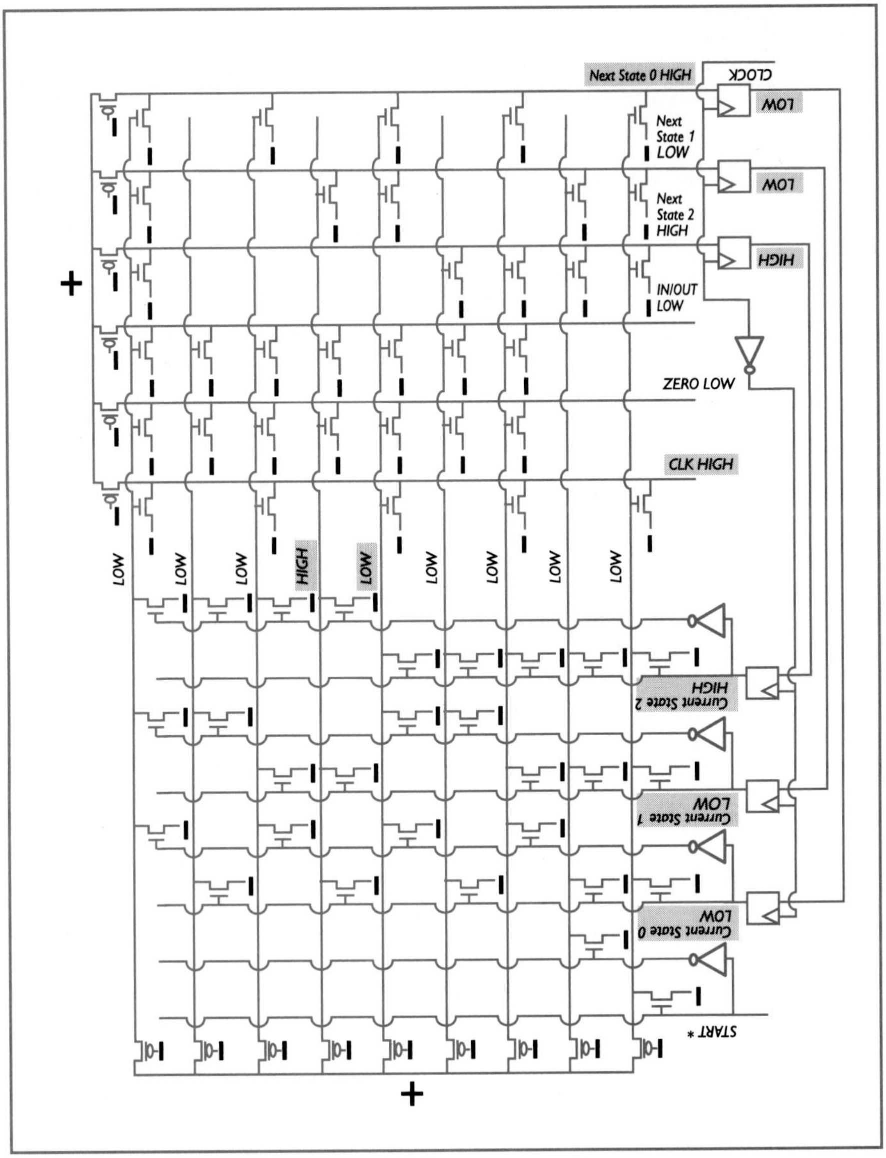

FIGURE 11-10

State 6

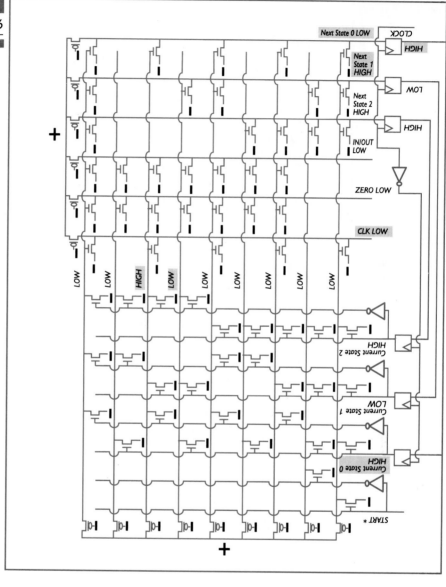

FIGURE 11-11

State 7

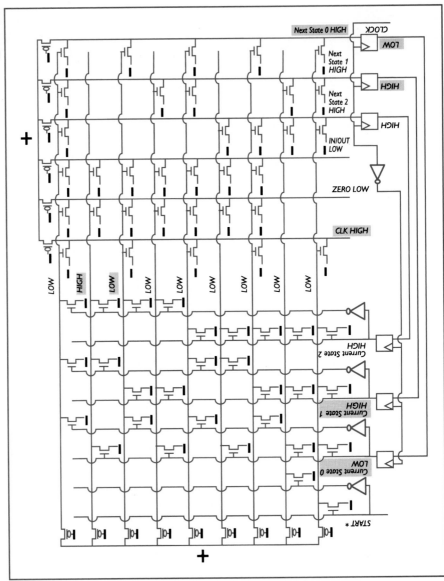

FIGURE 11-12

Back to state 0

■

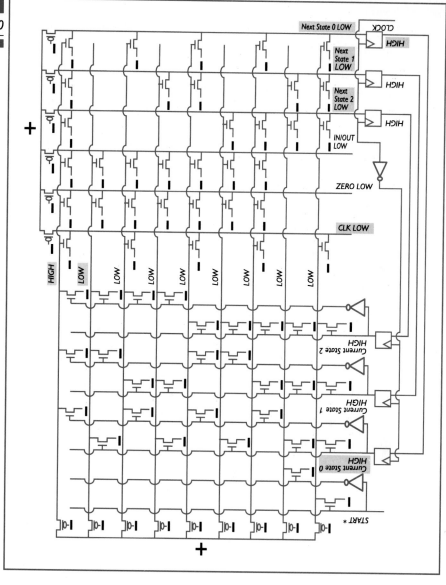

Review

- Finite state machines help a computer perform step-by-step operations.

- A finite state machine can be in one of a finite number of states. Its output lines are at a certain voltage in every state.

- The operation of a finite state machine can be illustrated using a state diagram.

- A finite state machine can be built from a logic block that has *current state* inputs and *next state* outputs. The logic block can be constructed from a programmable logic array.

- The addition of clocked D flip-flops prevents the finite state machine from transitioning uncontrollably.

- A finite state machine can control the nybble multiplication machine and make its operation simpler.

12

What a Microprocessor Does

I N this chapter, I am going to discuss the "brain" of every computer—the microprocessor. Even the simplest microprocessor is a very complicated device, so I'm not going to discuss it in great detail. However, the previous chapters have already taught you the basics of how a microprocessor works, and the last chapter combined much of what you have learned. Chapter 10 described how a device built out of transistors could process data. When we say "process data," we mean store, move, and utilize numbers represented by high and low voltages. In the nybble multiplication machine, flip-flops were used to *store* numbers. Shift registers were used to *move* numbers. The multiplication machine *utilized* the numbers we provided by multiplying them together.

PARTS OF A MICRO-PROCESSOR

I f you look inside a modern computer, you will see several small, flat, black boxes stuck to a green plastic board. Metal pins on these boxes are connected to each other by conductors embedded in the board. Inside these boxes are silicon chips. And built on the silicon chips are electronic devices, like the ones we looked at in previous chapters. The pins and conductors connect the smaller devices together to make one larger device—the computer.

Some of these boxes contain ROMs and RAMs. Some contain special devices like the nybble multiplication machine we discussed in Chapter 10. One box always contains a device called a microprocessor. A *microprocessor* is a small device that stores, moves, and utilizes data. It can only do simple things, like move numbers from one place to another, or perform simple mathematical operations on numbers. However, it does these things very fast. As always, the numbers are represented by high and low voltages.

६ ५ । ९ / ८ ।

In the last chapter, you saw how a finite state machine controlled other devices in the multiplication machine. It set conductors at high or low voltage at different times. Similarly, the microprocessor controls all other devices in the computer by setting conductors at high or low voltage. It can retrieve numbers stored in ROM or RAM, perform mathematical operations on them, and then store them back in RAM. Because the microprocessor controls all other devices in a computer, it is often called the "brain" of the computer.

Most microprocessors are composed of the parts shown in Figure 12-1.

THE ADDRESS BUS AND THE DATA BUS

A microprocessor performs operations on data. But where does it retrieve the data from? Where does it send data to? A microprocessor can retrieve data from, and send data to, two kinds of devices. The first kind are memory devices. In Chapter 8, you learned how data could be retrieved from RAMs and ROMs and how it could be stored in RAMs.

The second kind are I/O devices. I/O stands for *input/output*. They are called I/O devices because they provide input, in the form of numbers, to the microprocessor or receive output, also in the form of numbers, from the microprocessor. An example of an input device is a keyboard. A keyboard sends a code number to the microprocessor whenever a key is pressed. An

FIGURE 12-1

Parts of a microprocessor

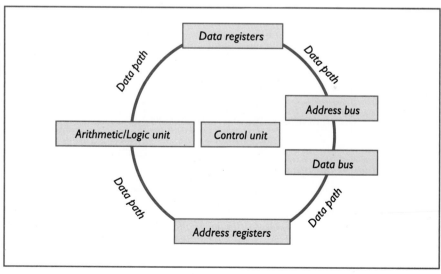

example of an output device is a printer. A printer prints a letter or number when the microprocessor sends it a code number. A microprocessor and some I/O devices are shown in Figure 12-2. I'll be talking more about I/O devices in Chapter 14.

The microprocessor exchanges data with I/O and memory devices in the same manner. The microprocessor has address lines, data lines, and a W/R line. These lines are connected to I/O and memory devices through pins and conductors.

In Chapter 9, you learned how data can be stored at, or retrieved from, a RAM address. The voltages of address lines must be set, which then causes the flip-flops at that address to become activated. Once these flip-flops are activated, data can be retrieved from them or stored in them.

In general, *any* device (not just a set of flip-flops) can be activated by setting the voltages of address lines. If a memory device is activated, then data can be retrieved from or stored at a memory location. If an I/O device is activated, then data can be sent to, or received from, that device. The voltage that the W/R line is at tells the memory or I/O device whether the microprocessor is retrieving data from it or sending data to it.

When the microprocessor wants to retrieve data, it puts the address lines at the appropriate voltages and puts W/R at low voltage. The memory or I/O device then puts the data on the data lines. When the microprocessor wants to send data, it puts the address lines at the appropriate voltages, puts

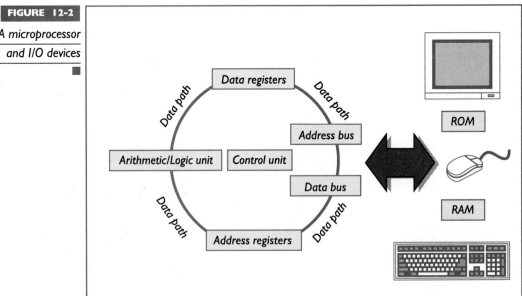

FIGURE 12-2

A microprocessor and I/O devices

the data on the data lines, and puts W/R at high voltage. The data is then received by the I/O device or stored in the desired location by the RAM.

A group of conductors that are used together is called a *bus*. The address lines are together called the *address bus*. The data lines are together called the *data bus*. If a bus consists of a certain number of conductors, then it is said to be that many bits wide. For example, a group of 32 conductors used as address lines is said to be 32 bits wide, and it is called a 32-bit address bus. A group of 16 conductors used as data lines is said to be 16 bits wide, and it is called a 16-bit data bus.

The sizes of a microprocessor's address bus and data bus are very important. The size of the address bus determines how many memory locations or I/O devices the microprocessor can access. For example, if the microprocessor has a three-bit address bus, it can only access eight memory locations or I/O devices. If the microprocessor has a 20-bit address bus, it can access over one million locations or I/O devices. The range of addresses a microprocessor can put on the address bus is called the *address space* of the microprocessor. The larger the address bus, the larger the address space of the microprocessor.

The size of the data bus determines how many bits of information the microprocessor can receive from memory locations or I/O devices simultaneously. For example, if the microprocessor has a four-bit data bus, it can receive at most one nybble of data at a time. Such a microprocessor could easily be connected to the RAM or ROM we looked at when we discussed memory in Chapter 8. If the microprocessor has a 16-bit data bus, it can receive two bytes of data simultaneously.

THE CONTROL UNIT

n the last chapter, we used a finite state machine to control a nybble multiplication machine. This finite state machine had three outputs, IN/OUT, ZERO, and CLK, that were connected to the rest of the nybble multiplication machine.

The finite state machine was able to control the multiplication machine by putting these outputs at high or low voltage at specific times. It was able to bring data into the multiplication machine, such as when the four-bit shift register was initialized. It was able to move data around in the multiplication machine, such as when each bit of the multiplicand was shifted out of the shift register. And it was able to produce new data, such as when partial products and the final product were generated.

The *control unit* in a microprocessor is a very complicated finite state machine. The outputs of the control unit are connected to other parts of the microprocessor, including the address and data buses. The control unit puts these outputs at high or low voltage at specific times in order to

■ move data in and out of the microprocessor,

■ move data among the various parts of the microprocessor along the *data path*, and

■ generate new data inside the microprocessor.

Each state of the control unit is a combination of outputs. Each different combination of outputs instructs the rest of the microprocessor to do something specific with the data. These combinations of outputs are called *microinstructions*.

Microprograms

The finite state machine from Chapter 11 had a single input, START. This input told the finite state machine when to transition from state 0 to state 1. It then transitioned through the sequence of states 1 through 7 and back to state 0 again. It then waited for START to go to high voltage, signaling the start of another multiplication operation.

The control unit has many different state sequences that it can move through. The input to the control unit is a number that tells it which state sequence to begin. For example, if the input is the number one, the control unit may move from state 0 to state 10, through the sequence of states 10 through 20, and then back to state 0. If the input is the number fifteen, the control unit may move from state 0 to state 6, through the sequence of states 6 through 18, and then back to state 0. Each state generates a microinstruction. So the control unit generates a different sequence of microinstructions for every sequence of states it transitions through.

A set of instructions is called a *program*. A set of microinstructions is called a *microprogram*. Therefore, each sequence of microinstructions that the control unit generates as it transitions through a sequence of states is called a microprogram. Each microprogram causes data to be processed in a different way. For example, one microprogram may cause two numbers to be retrieved from memory and added together. Another sequence of states may cause a zero to be stored in a specific memory location. You can think of the finite state machine we looked at in the last chapter as a simple control unit. It had only one microprogram consisting of eight microinstructions.

Where does the control unit get its input? The input to the control unit is a number. So you can probably guess that it retrieves this number from memory. Each input number is called a *machine language instruction*. Every time it completes a microprogram, the control unit retrieves another machine language instruction from memory. This instruction tells the control unit which state sequence to begin next. The microprocessor continually repeats the following two steps:

1. Retrieves a machine language instruction from memory.

2. Transitions through one of the state sequences (microprograms).

As you may have guessed, a set of machine language instructions is called a *machine language program*. Each machine language instruction causes the control unit to start a different microprogram. These ideas are diagramed in Figure 12-3.

FIGURE 12-3

Translating a machine language program into microinstructions

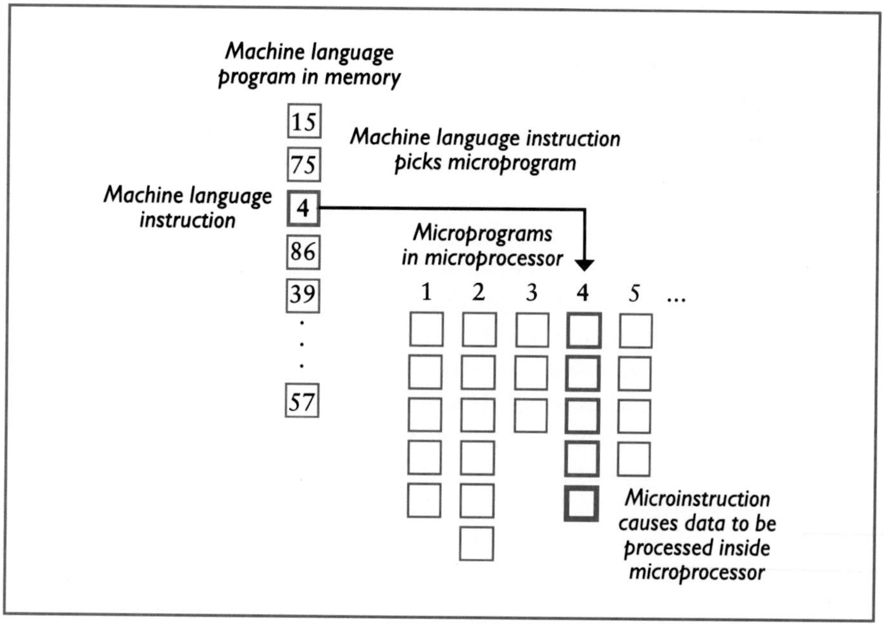

THE ARITHMETIC AND LOGIC UNIT

Another important part of the microprocessor is the *arithmetic and logic unit*, or *ALU*. The ALU can perform several different kinds of operations on data. It can add and subtract numbers, or check whether a number is positive, negative, or zero. Sometimes there are even large multiplication and division machines in ALUs. These allow the microprocessor to calculate products and quotients. The ALU can also perform logical operations, like those performed by NAND, NOR, and NOT gates, on individual bits in a number.

Usually, the ALU is built as a large logic array. The control unit uses some inputs to provide numbers to the ALU. The control unit uses other inputs to select operations to perform on the numbers. The results of the operations appear on output lines from the ALU. The control unit can then move the results along the data path to other parts of the microprocessor or out of the microprocessor.

ADDRESS AND DATA REGISTERS

Often, the microprocessor performs several operations on the same data. For example, it might perform several shift operations on a single multiplier, as the nybble multiplication machine did. Also, the microprocessor often generates data that it immediately uses. For example, it may generate partial products that it adds together.

Such data could be stored in main memory. However, every time the data was accessed, the microprocessor would have to put the correct address on the address lines. It would have to wait for the memory to put the data on the data lines. If the memory was large, this would waste a lot of time. It is more convenient to have some memory on the microprocessor itself. This memory takes the form of *address registers* and *data registers*. All microprocessors have some registers so they don't have to access outside memory every single time they require data or generate data.

The address registers in a microprocessor are the same size as the address bus. The control unit can quickly put addresses stored in address registers on the address bus. The control unit can also quickly increment or decrement addresses stored in address registers. This makes it easy for the microprocessor to access numbers that are at consecutive addresses.

The data registers in a microprocessor are usually the same size as the individual numbers stored in memory. The control unit can quickly move numbers from other parts of the microprocessor to the data registers, and from the data registers to other parts of the microprocessor.

The Program Counter

Usually, the microprocessor repeatedly retrieves machine language instructions from consecutive locations in memory. Figure 12-4 shows the sequence the microprocessor follows in retrieving instructions from consecutive memory locations.

All microprocessors have a special address register called the *program counter,* or *PC.* The PC always contains the address of the next location to retrieve an instruction from. Whenever the microprocessor retrieves an instruction from memory, it increments the value in the program counter.

FIGURE 12-4

Retrieving instructions from consecutive addresses

Memory	
Address	Content
1	Instruction 1
2	Instruction 2
3	Instruction 3
4	Instruction 4
5	Instruction 5
6	Instruction 6

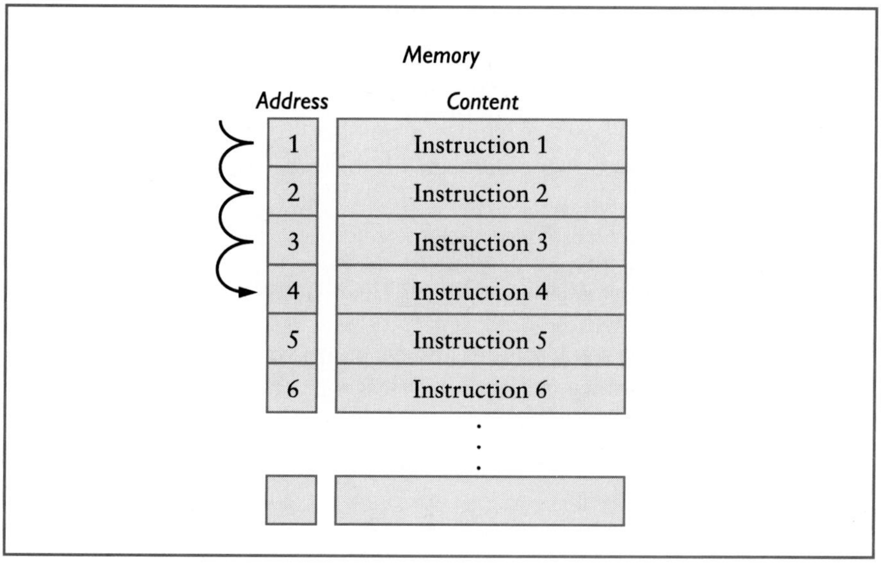

The Stack Pointer

Imagine a stack of boxes. From the floor up, the stack consists of one box after the other. The last box is said to be at the top of the stack. It is easy to put a box on top of the stack, and it is easy to remove a box from the top of the stack. It is hard to put a box into the middle of the stack, because the boxes above it must be lifted up carefully. It is hard to take a box out from the middle of the stack, because the boxes above it must be lifted down carefully.

When numbers are stored in a computer's memory, they can also be stored in the form of a stack. In a computer, a stack consists of numbers stored in one memory location after the other. The address following the address of the last number is called the "top of the stack." In a computer, it is easy to put a number on top of the stack, and it is easy to remove a number from the top of the stack. What makes it easy is a special address register called the *stack pointer,* or *SP.*

The computer usually has a section of memory that does not contain programs. Such a section of memory is called a *free block.* This memory can be used for temporary storage of numbers. The address of the first location in a free block of memory can be stored in the stack pointer. The stack pointer to "point" to that location. As shown in Figure 12-5, the stack pointer points to the top of the stack.

It is easy to put a new number on the top of the stack, because certain instructions push numbers on the stack. To *push* a number on the stack means to

1. Store a number at the address in the stack pointer, and then

2. Increment the stack pointer.

It is easy to remove a number from the top of the stack, because certain instructions pop numbers off the stack. To *pop* a number off the stack means to

1. Decrement the stack pointer, and then

2. Retrieve the number at the address in it.

The stack pointer always points to the first unused location in a free block of memory. All addresses less than the one in the stack pointer are occupied.

Stack pointer points to top of stack

■

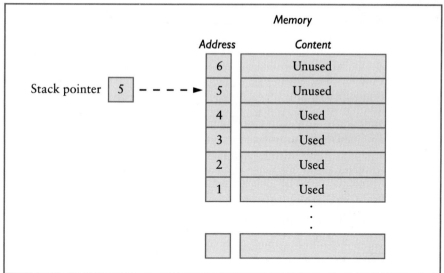

THE PROGRAM STATUS WORD

Another important register in the microprocessor is the *program status word,* or *PSW.* In the next chapter, you will learn how certain machine language instructions set or clear (reset) bits in the PSW. Other instructions make decisions based on whether these bits are set or cleared. So the PSW helps the microprocessor make decisions based on instructions that have been executed.

One of the bits in the PSW is called the *mode bit.* In modern microprocessors, the mode bit determines whether certain special instructions can be executed or not. If the mode bit is cleared, the microprocessor is allowed to execute most, but not all, of its instructions. If the mode bit is set, the microprocessor is allowed to execute all of its instructions.

Review

- To process data means to store, move, and utilize numbers.

- The microprocessor is often called the "brain" of the computer. This is because it controls all other devices in the computer.

- Microprocessors can retrieve data from and send data to memory and I/O devices.

- A group of conductors that are used together is called a bus.

- The size of a microprocessor's address bus determines its address space. The address space is the range of addresses the microprocessor can access.

- The size of a microprocessor's data bus determines how many bits of information the microprocessor can retrieve from memory or I/O devices at once.

- The control unit is a complicated finite state machine. The outputs of the control unit are connected to other parts of the microprocessor. The states of the control unit are called microinstructions. A sequence of microinstructions is called a microprogram.

- Every time it completes a microprogram, the control unit retrieves another machine language instruction from memory. This instruction tells the control unit which microprogram to begin next.

- The ALU allows the microprocessor to perform arithmetic and logical operations on data.

- The control unit can quickly take addresses stored in address registers and put them on the address bus. The control unit can also quickly increment or decrement addresses stored in address registers.

- The control unit can quickly move numbers from other parts of the microprocessor to data registers, and from data registers to other parts of the microprocessor.

- The program counter (PC) is a special address register in the microprocessor. It always contains the address of the next location to retrieve a machine language instruction from.

- The stack pointer (SP) is a special address register in the microprocessor. It always points to the first location in a free block of memory.

- The program status word (PSW) is a special register in the microprocessor. One of its purposes is to help the microprocessor make decisions.

13

What Machine Language Is

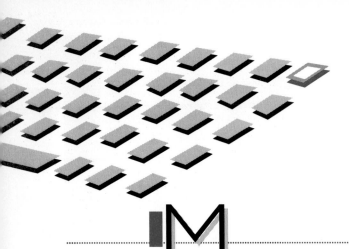

M

A C H I N E language can be very confusing if you don't have a good idea of how a microprocessor uses it. I want to start out by reviewing some simple ideas that you learned in previous chapters. You should keep these concepts in mind while you learn about machine language.

A memory stores numbers in the form of high and low voltages in binary number representation. The numbers in a memory are all of the same length, usually 8 to 32 bits. Each number is stored in a numbered location. The number of a location is called its address. The number stored in a certain location (at a certain address) is called the content of that location. We say things such as, "a fourteen is stored in the first location," "the address of the first location is zero," "a fourteen is stored at address zero," and "the content of the first location is fourteen."

A microprocessor is connected to memory by address and data buses and a W/R line. To retrieve a number from memory, the microprocessor

1. Puts the address of the number on the address bus, and

2. Puts W/R at low voltage.

The memory then puts the number on the data lines. To store a number in a certain memory location, the microprocessor

1. Puts the address of the location on the address bus,

2. Puts the number on the data bus, and

3. Puts W/R at high voltage.

The memory then takes the number from the data bus and the address from the address bus, and stores the number in the correct location.

A microprocessor has address registers and data registers. Address registers are the same size as the address bus, and are used to store addresses temporarily. Data registers are the same size as the data bus, and are used to store data temporarily.

The control unit in a microprocessor transitions through states to process data. Each state generates a microinstruction. The sequence of microinstructions that the control unit generates to perform an operation is called a microprogram.

Machine language instructions are numbers that tell the control unit which microprogram to generate. The microprocessor retrieves a machine language instruction from memory, generates the corresponding microprogram, and then retrieves the next instruction. This occurs continually. When the microprocessor is following a machine language instruction, we say that it is "executing" it. When a microprocessor is executing the instructions in a program, we say that it is "running" the program.

MACHINE LANGUAGE INSTRUCTIONS

Some machine language instructions are made up of just one number. The microprocessor can execute such instructions after retrieving just one number. Some machine language instructions are made up of two or more numbers. The microprocessor can complete the execution of such instructions only after retrieving all of the numbers, one at a time.

The first number in any machine language instruction is called the *operation code,* or *op-code.* The bits of the op-code give the microprocessor the following information:

- How many more numbers there are in the instruction (the *instruction length*)

- How to get data that the instruction may require (the *addressing mode*)

- What to do with the data (the *operation*)

The instruction length tells the control unit whether it has the entire instruction. If not, it retrieves numbers from the next few locations until it does have the entire instruction. Numbers that follow the op-code in a machine language instruction are called *operands.*

The instruction might not operate on any data. If the instruction does operate on data, the microprocessor must know where to get it. The addressing mode tells the microprocessor how to use the operands to get any data that the instruction may require. The data may be in the op-code itself, in the operands, in a data register, or in memory. If the data is in a data register, the operands tell the microprocessor which data register it is in. If the data is in memory, the operands tell the microprocessor what the address of the data is.

The third piece of information in the op-code, the operation, tells the microprocessor what to do with the data. It may tell the microprocessor to store the data in an address or data register, or store it in a memory location, or add it to other data, or something else.

To retrieve an instruction op-code from memory, the microprocessor puts the value stored in the program counter on the address bus. It then increments the program counter. The value in the program counter is now the address of the first operand of the instruction. If the instruction has no operands, then the value in the program counter is now the op-code of the next instruction. In either case, whenever an op-code or operand is retrieved from memory, the program counter gets incremented. So the value in the program counter is always the address of the next op-code or operand.

Not all numbers that can be stored in memory are valid machine language instructions. The set of numbers that a microprocessor can execute is called the *instruction set* of the microprocessor. Microprocessors manufactured by various companies differ in the features and capabilities they possess. So every type of microprocessor has a different instruction set. This means that a machine language program that runs on one microprocessor will not necessarily run on a different microprocessor.

JUMPING AND BRANCHING

It is not enough for the microprocessor to execute, in strict sequence, instructions stored at consecutive addresses. For example, suppose we wanted the microprocessor to execute the same five instructions over and over, continually. (If you think there's no need for this, watch a video arcade game while no one is playing it. It shows the same demonstration repeatedly, until someone pulls the plug!) If the microprocessor had to execute instructions sequentially, then this could not be done. Eventually, we would run out of memory in which to store our instructions.

The microprocessor usually retrieves instructions from consecutive locations in memory. Therefore, it needs a way to start retrieving instructions from a new address. Luckily, all microprocessors have an instruction that changes the address in the program counter. This instruction causes the microprocessor to begin retrieving instructions from a new and different memory location. It is called the *jump* instruction. The data that the jump instruction requires is the new address. When the microprocessor executes a jump instruction, it puts this new address in the program counter. Now, the microprocessor begins retrieving instructions from the new address. The next instruction it retrieves is the one at the new address, not the address following that of the jump instruction. Execution "jumps" to the instruction at the new address. The illustration shows the path the microprocessor takes during normal execution and during execution of a jump instruction. If we wanted the microprocessor to execute the same five instructions over and over, we would put a jump instruction and the address of the first instruction after the five instructions. The microprocessor would execute the five instructions in sequence. After executing the jump instruction, it would start executing the same five instructions again, continually.

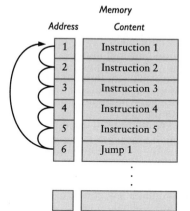

The data that the *loop* instruction requires is a number. Execution of a loop instruction causes the address in the program counter to be decremented by that number. The microprocessor then begins executing instructions it already executed once. If the microprocessor continues to execute the same instructions repeatedly without ever stopping, it is said to be in an *endless loop*. Here is the path the microprocessor takes through memory before and after executing a loop instruction.

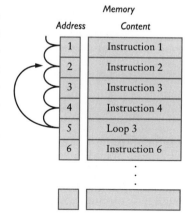

What if we wanted the microprocessor to execute five instructions only a certain number of times, instead of continually? How can we tell the microprocessor to jump to the first instruction a certain number of times, and then stop jumping to the first instruction? Let's be more precise about exactly what we want the microprocessor to do. It must keep track of how many times it has executed the five instructions. As long as it has not executed the five instructions the correct number of times, it must jump back to the first one. When it has executed the five instructions the correct number of times, then it can continue with other instructions.

Luckily, as you learned in Chapter 12, a microprocessor has a program status word (PSW) that helps it make decisions based on instructions that have been executed. Two of the bits in the PSW are named Q and N. These bits can be set or cleared by a *compare instruction*. The compare instruction takes two numbers as data. If the two numbers are *equal*, it sets the Q bit in the PSW at high voltage. If the first number is *less* than the second number, the compare instruction sets the Q bit at low voltage and the N bit at high. If the first number is *greater* than the second number, the compare instruction sets the Q bit at low voltage and the N bit at low voltage.

Every microprocessor also has a set of instructions called *branch* instructions. Like the jump instruction, the data that each branch instruction requires is an address. The address is known as the *branch address*. Each branch instruction checks bits in the PSW, to see if their values are one or zero (corresponding to high or low voltage). If the values of the PSW bits are what was expected, then the branch instruction causes the branch address to be loaded into the program counter, and execution continues from the instruction at the branch address. If the values of the PSW bits are not what was expected, then the branch instruction does nothing and execution continues from the instruction at the address following the branch instruction.

Suppose we want the microprocessor to execute a set of instructions one hundred times. We must put some extra instructions before and after the set. The instructions before the set put the value 100 in one of the data registers. The instructions after the set do the following:

1. Decrement the value in the same register,

2. Compare it to 0, and

3. Branch to the first instruction in the set if neither the Q nor the N bit is 1.

When the value in the data register gets decremented to zero, the compare instruction will cause the Q bit to be set, and the branch will no longer be taken. Figure 13-1 shows the execution of the branch instruction. The microprocessor can take one of two paths after executing the branch instruction. Which path the microprocessor takes depends on the contents of the data register.

The nybble multiplication machine in Chapter 10 was made up of simpler devices. Similarly, programs that perform large and complex tasks are always divided into parts that do simpler jobs. Each shorter part of a program is called a *subroutine*. For example, suppose you had a microprocessor with a simple arithmetic and logic unit (ALU) that could do addition, but couldn't do multiplication. You could write a machine language program that would instruct the microprocessor to do multiplication. The program might include

- one subroutine to find partial products,

- another subroutine to add them all up, and

- a third to display the final answer.

You might even want to use this multiplication program as a subroutine in a larger program. What if you wanted to use the same multiplication subroutine in different parts of the program? It would be wasteful to write separate copies of the same subroutine when the microprocessor could just jump or branch to the multiplication subroutine from different parts of the program. But how would it know where to jump back after it had finished executing the multiplication subroutine? The microprocessor needs a way to return to the part of the program it jumped from.

Luckily, every microprocessor has a pair of instructions that help it do this. These instructions use the stack pointer. They allow the microprocessor to jump to a subroutine from anywhere in a program, and return when the subroutine is finished. The instructions are called the *call* and *return* instructions.

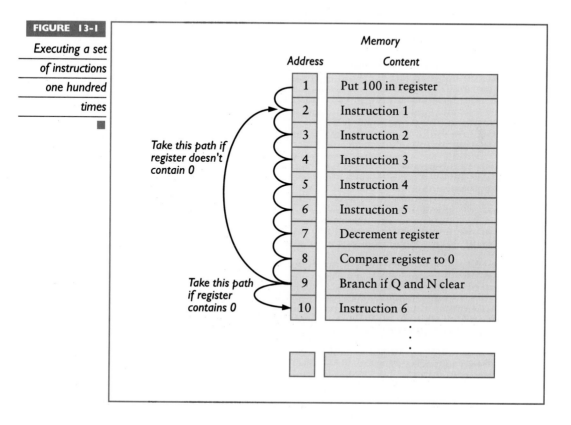

FIGURE 13-1

Executing a set of instructions one hundred times

The data that the call instruction requires is the address of the first instruction in the subroutine. When the call instruction gets executed, the microprocessor does two things:

1. It takes the current value in the program counter and pushes it on the stack. Remember, from earlier in the chapter, that the program counter contains the address of the instruction that *follows* the call instruction. This address is called the *return address,* because it is the address we want the microprocessor to return to when the subroutine is finished. So the return address gets pushed on the stack.

2. It loads the subroutine address into the program counter. Execution continues from the first instruction in the subroutine.

The last instruction in every subroutine is a return instruction. When the return instruction gets executed, the microprocessor pops the return address off the stack and puts it in the program counter. Execution then continues from the instruction following the call instruction. In this way, the microprocessor automatically jumps back to the same place in the program it jumped from.

This process can seem a little confusing. However, it is extremely useful when one subroutine calls another subroutine, which calls a third subroutine, and so on. Using the stack pointer and the call and return instructions, the microprocessor can return to the right parts of the program. Figures 13-2 through 13-5 show an example of the use of the call and return instructions.

ADDRESSING MODES

The addressing modes of a microprocessor determine how it uses its operands to get data. A microprocessor with many powerful addressing modes can process large amounts of data with just a few instructions. A microprocessor with a few weak addressing modes must execute many more instructions to process large amounts of data.

In this section, I am going to describe the addressing modes of the MC68000, a very popular microprocessor manufactured by Motorola Semiconductor Products, Inc. Similar addressing modes are used by all microprocessors.

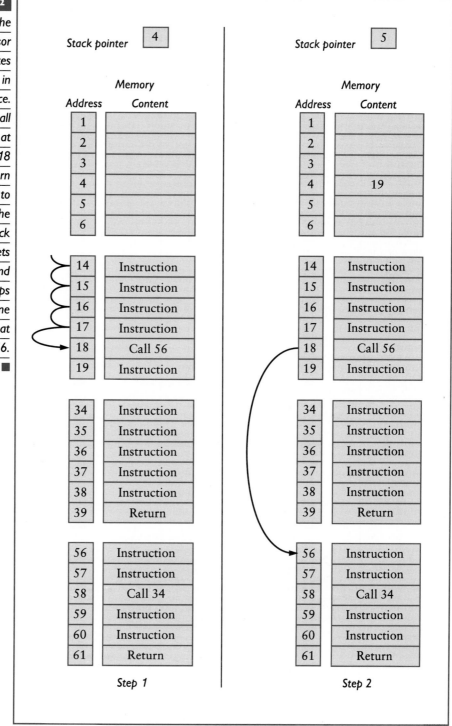

In step 1, the microprocessor executes instructions in normal sequence. In step 2, the call instruction at address 18 causes the return address (19) to be pushed on the stack. The stack pointer gets incremented, and execution jumps to the subroutine starting at address 56.

■

FIGURE 13-3

In step 3, the microprocessor continues executing instructions in normal sequence. In step 4, the call instruction at address 58 causes the return address (59) to be pushed on the stack. The stack pointer gets incremented, and execution jumps to the subroutine starting at address 34.

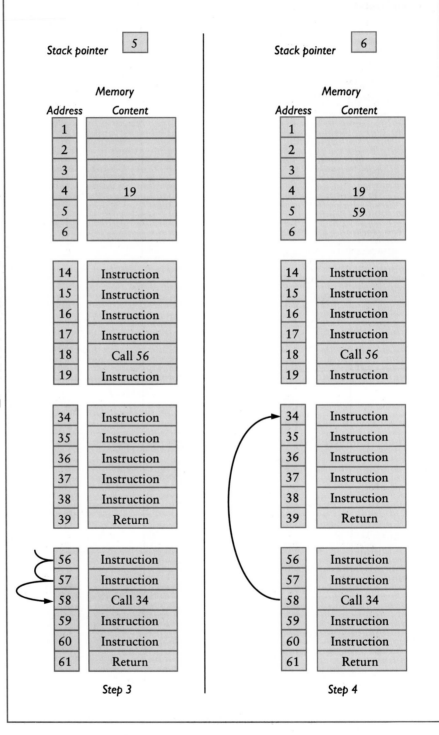

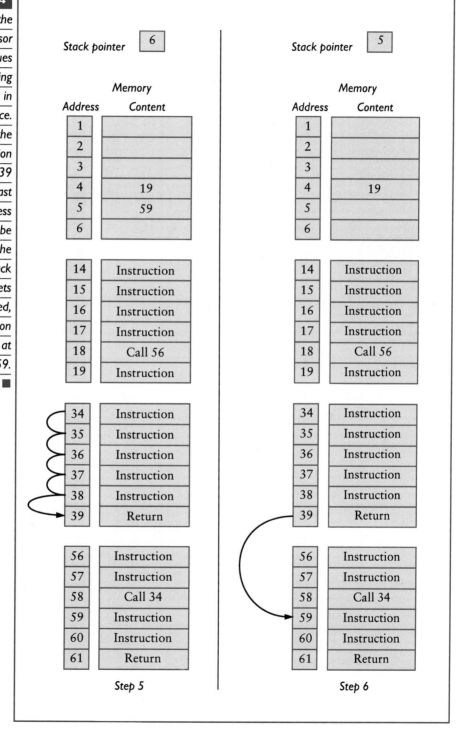

FIGURE 13-4

In step 5, the microprocessor continues executing instructions in normal sequence. In step 6, the return instruction at address 39 causes the last return address (59) to be popped off the stack. The stack pointer gets decremented, and execution continues at address 59.

FIGURE 13-5

In step 7, the microprocessor continues executing instructions in normal sequence. In step 8, the return instruction at address 61 causes the first return address (19) to be popped off the stack. The stack pointer gets decremented, and execution continues at address 19.

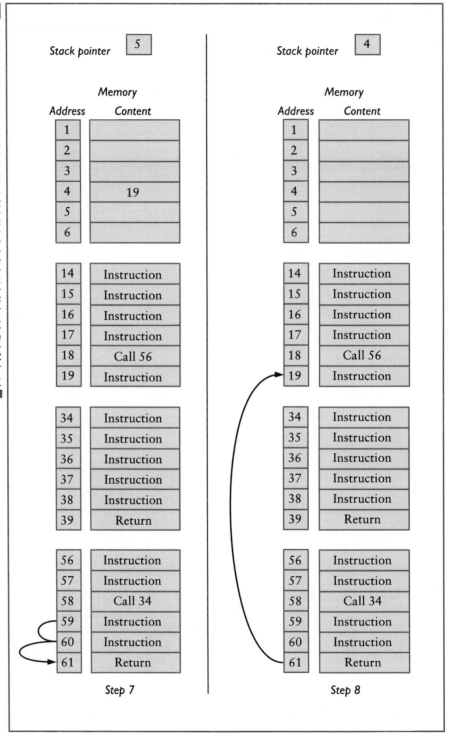

Immediate

Immediate addressing mode tells the micro-processor to find the data in the instruction itself. Suppose the microprocessor retrieves the op-code for an immediate instruction. This tells the control unit that the first operand it retrieves will be the data. Immediate addressing mode is illustrated here.

This addressing mode is useful if the data is known when the machine language program is put in the computer's memory.

Memory

Address	Content
1	Op-code
2	Data
3	
4	
5	
6	

Instruction (brackets rows 1 and 2)

Register Direct

Register direct addressing mode tells the microprocessor to find the data in an address or data register. Suppose the microprocessor retrieves the op-code for a register direct instruction. This tells the control unit that the first operand it retrieves will be the number of an address or data register. It then retrieves the data from that register. Register direct addressing mode is illustrated here.

When it is going to use a number repeatedly, the microprocessor can keep the number in an address or data register. This addressing mode can then be used to quickly retrieve the number.

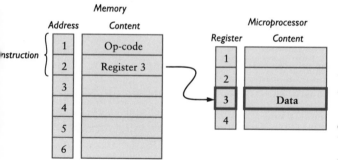

Memory

Address	Content
1	Op-code
2	Register 3
3	
4	
5	
6	

Instruction (brackets rows 1 and 2)

Microprocessor

Register	Content
1	
2	
3	Data
4	

Absolute

Absolute addressing mode tells the microprocessor that the *address* of the data is in the instruction itself. Suppose the microprocessor retrieves the op-code for an absolute instruction. This tells the control unit that the first operand it retrieves will be the address of the data. The microprocessor then retrieves the data from that address. Absolute addressing mode is shown in this illustration.

This addressing mode is useful if the data is to be stored in memory *and* its address is known when the program is put in memory.

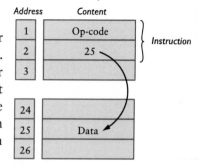

Memory

Address	Content
1	Op-code
2	25
3	
24	
25	Data
26	

Instruction (brackets rows 1 and 2)

Address Register Indirect

Address register indirect addressing mode tells the microprocessor that the address of the data is in an *address register.* Suppose the microprocessor retrieves the op-code for an address register indirect instruction. This tells the control unit that the first operand it retrieves will be the number of an address register. The control unit then retrieves the address of the data from the address register. It then retrieves the data itself from that address. Address register indirect addressing mode is illustrated here.

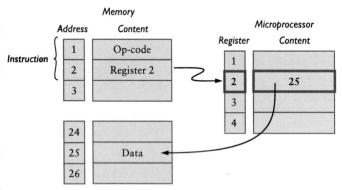

Sometimes, large amounts of data are stored in memory. The address of a particular piece of data may not be known when the program is put in memory—the microprocessor may have to calculate the address of the data. This addressing mode is useful in such a case. The address of the data can be calculated, and then stored in an address register. Address register indirect addressing mode can then be used to retrieve the data.

Predecrement and Postincrement

These addressing modes are just like address register indirect. In *predecrement* addressing mode, the content of the address register is decremented before it is put on the address bus. Predecrement addressing mode is illustrated in Figure 13-6. In *postincrement* addressing mode, the content of the address register is incremented after the data is retrieved. Postincrement addressing mode is illustrated in Figure 13-7.

Sometimes, large amounts of data are stored in consecutive memory locations. These addressing modes are useful in processing such data. The address of the first or last number can be stored in an address register. Postincrement or predecrement addressing mode can be used to retrieve this number. When a number is retrieved, the address register automatically contains the address of the next number. The same instruction can be used over and over again until all the numbers have been processed.

STARTUP

A s soon as a computer is turned on, special electrical circuits begin to alternate a CLK line between high and low voltage. This process is called

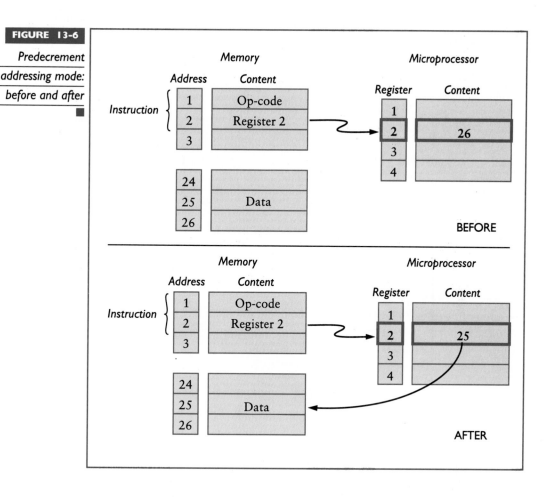

FIGURE 13-6

Predecrement
addressing mode:
before and after

startup. The CLK line is connected to most of the chips in the computer, including the microprocessor. In Chapter 11, the CLOCK line made the finite state machine transition from state to state. Similarly, the CLK input makes the microprocessor's control unit transition from state to state.

The microprocessor needs to start from some initial state each time the computer is turned on. It has a special input called RESET for this purpose. When RESET goes to high voltage, information that was stored in the data and address registers may be lost. The microprocessor stops what it was previously doing and begins retrieving machine language instructions from address 0. In this way, it starts over "from scratch."

Usually, the machine language program that starts at address 0 is stored in ROM. That way, the instructions that the microprocessor starts with are not lost when the computer is turned off. This program is called the *startup program.* It usually tells the microprocessor to test other devices in the computer. The startup program also instructs the microprocessor to bring

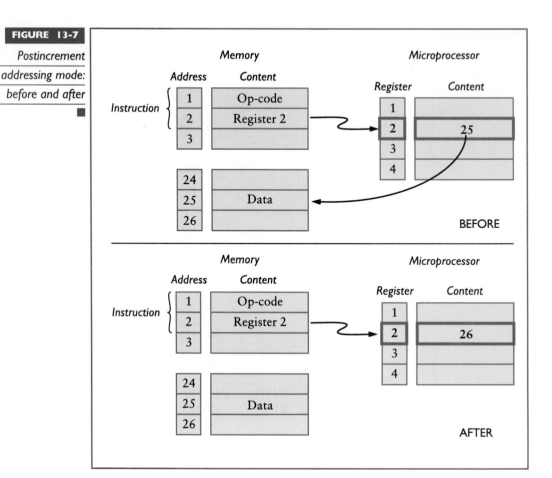

FIGURE 13-7

Postincrement
addressing mode:
before and after
■

several important programs into RAM. These include the computer's *operating system, interrupt service routines, exception handlers,* and *system
service routines.* The last instruction in the startup program can instruct the
microprocessor to jump to the first instruction of a new program.

INTERRUPTS

nput devices, such as a keyboard or a mouse, collect data from outside
the computer. Such devices need the microprocessor to process the data they
collect. We say that such devices require microprocessor *service.* Input
devices need a way to interrupt what the microprocessor is currently doing.
They are connected to a microprocessor's *interrupt* lines.

When an input device wants to interrupt the microprocessor, it puts one of the interrupt lines at high voltage. This is called an *interrupt request*. When an interrupt line goes to high voltage, the microprocessor

1. Completes the execution of the current machine language instruction,

2. Pushes the program counter on the stack, and

3. Writes a new address into the program counter.

This new address is called an *interrupt vector*. The interrupt vector is a fixed address that depends on which interrupt line went to high voltage. The microprocessor expects that a machine language subroutine starts at that address. This subroutine is expected to instruct the microprocessor to process the data that the device has collected. Such a subroutine is called an *interrupt service routine*. At the end of an interrupt service routine is a return instruction. Once the microprocessor has finished running the interrupt service routine, it continues from the point it was interrupted.

In a sense, an interrupt service routine is a special kind of subroutine. It gets called not by a call instruction, but by an interrupt line going to high voltage.

Let's assume that an input device, the keyboard, is connected to the microprocessor's first interrupt line, INT1, and that the microprocessor is busy running a program. When a person presses a key, the keyboard puts INT1 at high voltage and puts a code number that corresponds to the key in a register. The microprocessor completes the current instruction and pushes the program counter on the stack. It sees that the device connected to INT1 requested an interrupt, and puts a 100 in the program counter. (If the device connected to INT2 had requested an interrupt, it would have put a 200 in the program counter.) This causes the microprocessor to start running the interrupt service routine that starts at address 100. This routine tells the microprocessor to retrieve the key code from the register and take some action on it. Eventually, the microprocessor finishes running the interrupt service routine. It pops the return address off the stack and continues where it left off in the program.

Exceptions

Sometimes, something unusual happens while the microprocessor is executing an instruction. Then, the microprocessor must interrupt itself. This special kind of interrupt is called an *exception*. For example, what if a program keeps pushing numbers on the stack until the address of the top of the stack no longer fits in the stack pointer? This is called *stack overflow*. What if a program keeps popping numbers off the stack until the stack pointer reaches zero? This is called *stack underflow*. What if the microprocessor has a divide instruction, and the program attempts to divide a number by zero? These are all examples of *exceptional conditions*.

When an exception occurs, the microprocessor

1. Stops executing the current machine language instruction,

2. Pushes the program counter on the stack, and

3. Loads an exception vector into the program counter.

The *exception vector* is a fixed address that depends on what kind of exceptional condition occurred. The microprocessor expects that a machine language subroutine starts at that address. This subroutine is expected to instruct the microprocessor to handle the exception. Such a subroutine is called an *exception handler*. At the end of an exception handler is a return instruction.

When an interrupt request occurs, the microprocessor can complete an instruction before calling the interrupt service routine. However, when an exceptional condition occurs, the microprocessor cannot always complete the instruction it is executing. In this case, execution continues from the instruction *following* the one that produced the exceptional condition.

In a sense, an exception handler is a special kind of subroutine. It gets called neither by a call instruction nor by an interrupt request, but by an exceptional condition in the microprocessor.

PROTECTED INSTRUCTIONS

Some instructions in a microprocessor's instruction set have important and yet possibly dangerous consequences. For example, an instruction that puts a value in the stack pointer is risky. It might point the stack pointer to memory that is being used. Then, push instructions would cause occupied memory locations to be overwritten. An instruction that puts a brand new value in the PSW is also risky. It can drastically change decisions made by subsequent branch instructions. In general, instructions that drastically affect the operation of the computer are dangerous.

In modern microprocessors, such instructions are *protected*. Under normal circumstances, the microprocessor is not allowed to execute them. The mode bit in the PSW determines whether protected instructions can be executed or not. Only programs written by people who have in-depth knowledge of the computer system are allowed to contain protected instructions.

When the microprocessor is RESET, it starts out in unprotected mode. Then, the mode bit in the PSW is set, and the startup program is allowed to execute protected instructions. It does everything necessary to set up the microprocessor for normal operation. This includes loading interrupt service routines, exception handlers, and system calls into RAM. The startup program then clears the mode bit in the PSW. After that, if the microprocessor tries to execute a protected instruction, an exceptional condition will occur. The protected instruction will not be completed.

When exceptional conditions occur, it is usually necessary to drastically change the microprocessor's operation. So, exceptional conditions automatically cause the mode bit in the PSW to be set. This means that exception handlers are allowed to contain protected instructions. However, programmers who write exception handlers are very careful to always include an instruction to clear the mode bit before the end of each exception handler.

So, while the microprocessor is in protected mode, its operation is typically unaffected. However, an attempt to execute a protected instruction, including one that changes the mode bit in the PSW, causes an exceptional condition. The microprocessor executes the exception handler, and then continues execution with the instruction following the protected instruction.

SYSTEM CALLS

The startup program contains protected instructions, but it clears the mode bit before allowing other programs to run. Interrupt and exception handlers contain protected instructions, but they are only executed when an interrupt or exception occurs. They also clear the mode bit before allowing a normal program to continue running. If the program attempts to execute a protected instruction itself, an exception occurs, and the instruction never completes. It would seem that a normal program can execute protected instructions only when an interrupt or an exception occurs.

Sometimes, while it is running a normal program, the microprocessor must execute protected instructions, and the computer needs a way to guarantee that precautions will be taken before executing them. Most modern microprocessors have an instruction that helps guarantee this. This is the *system call* instruction. The system call instruction requires as data a single number, called the *system call number*. The system call instruction sets the mode bit, and causes a system call vector to be loaded into the program counter. The *system call vector* is a fixed address that depends on the system call number. The microprocessor expects that a machine language subroutine starts at that address. This subroutine is written by programmers who know the computer well, and is expected to safely perform a possibly dangerous task that requires protected instructions. Such a subroutine is called a *system service routine*. It takes all necessary precautions before executing protected instructions. The last thing the system service routine does is clear the mode bit. Once the microprocessor has finished running the system service routine, it returns to the instruction following the system call.

In a sense, a system service routine is a subroutine that is allowed to contain protected instructions. It gets called neither by a call instruction, nor by an interrupt request line going to high voltage, but by the system call instruction.

Review

- Machine language instructions are numbers that tell a microprocessor what to do.

- The microprocessor retrieves a machine language instruction from memory, performs the action it is supposed to, and then retrieves the next instruction. This occurs continually.

- When the microprocessor is following a machine language instruction, we say that it is executing it. When a microprocessor is executing the instructions in a program, we say that it is running the program.

- The first number of any machine language instruction is called the op-code. The op-code specifies the instruction length, the addressing mode, and the operation.

- The program counter (PC) always contains the address of the next location to retrieve a machine language instruction from.

- A jump instruction causes a new address to be put into the program counter. Execution continues from the new address in the PC.

- A loop instruction causes the program counter to be decremented by a number. Execution continues from the new address in the PC.

Review (continued)

- A compare instruction takes two numbers as data and compares them. It records the result of its comparison in the program status word.

- A branch instruction checks the values of bits in the program status word (PSW). If the bits are set or cleared as expected, then the branch instruction causes a new address to be put into the program counter. Execution continues from the new address. If the bits are not set or cleared as expected, then nothing happens. Execution continues from the instruction following the branch instruction.

- The stack pointer (SP) is an address register in the microprocessor. It contains the address of the top of the stack. The stack is a set of numbers in consecutive memory locations.

- The call instruction causes the address in the PC (the return address) to be pushed on the stack. It then loads its data into the PC. Execution continues from the new address in the PC.

- The return instruction pops a return address off the stack. It then loads the return address into the PC. Execution continues from the return address.

- In immediate addressing mode, the number following the op-code in the instruction is the data.

- In register direct addressing mode, the number following the op-code in the instruction is the number of a register. The data is in the register.

- In absolute addressing mode, the number following the op-code in the instruction is the address of the data. The data is in memory at that address.

- In register indirect addressing mode, the number following the op-code in the instruction is the number of an address register. The number in the register is the address of the data. The data is in memory at that address.

- Predecrement addressing mode is like register indirect addressing mode, except that the value in the address register is decremented before being put on the address bus.

- Postincrement addressing mode is like register indirect addressing mode, except that the value in the address register is incremented after the instruction is executed.

Review (continued)

■ A startup program is stored in ROM, so that it is always available. It causes the microprocessor to bring other programs into RAM for execution.

■ Input devices collect data from outside the computer. They interrupt the microprocessor's normal processing by setting interrupt lines to high voltage.

■ An interrupt service routine is a special kind of subroutine. Instead of being executed by a call instruction, an interrupt service routine is executed when an interrupt line goes to high voltage.

■ An exception handler is a special kind of subroutine. Instead of being executed by a call instruction or by an interrupt line going to high voltage, an exception handler is executed when an exceptional condition occurs in the microprocessor.

■ A system service routine is a special kind of subroutine that can contain protected instructions. Instead of being executed by a call instruction or by an interrupt line going to high voltage, a system service routine is executed by the system call instruction.

14

How I/O Devices Work

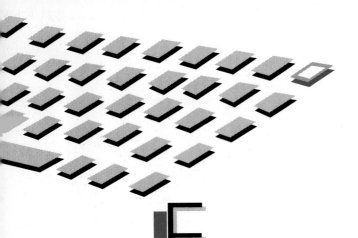

EVEN a computer with a very powerful microprocessor is useless unless it can receive information from people, and provide information in a form they can understand. In this chapter, I am going to talk about devices that allow a computer to communicate with the outside world. Such devices, which were briefly introduced in Chapter 12, are called *input/output*, or *I/O devices*. If you think of the whole computer as one large device, these devices allow it to accept input and produce output.

A computer can store nothing but high and low voltages. In binary number representation, high and low voltages can represent numbers. But what if the computer needs to communicate using letters and punctuation marks as well as numbers? The computer must have a code in which a number represents a letter, punctuation mark, or other symbol. In other words, it needs a code in which a number represents a *character*. One such code that most modern computers use is called the American Standard Code for Information Interchange, or *ASCII*. In ASCII, a seven-bit number is used to represent uppercase and lowercase letters, numerals, punctuation marks, and other common symbols. The following table shows ASCII numbers and the character each one represents.

Code	Character	Code	Character	Code	Character
32	SPACE	33	!	34	"
35	#	36	$	37	%
38	&	39	'	40	(
41	)	42	*	43	+
44	,	45	-	46	.
47	/	48	0	49	1
50	2	51	3	52	4
53	5	54	6	55	7
56	8	57	9	58	:
59	;	60	<	61	=
62	>	63	?	64	@
65	A	66	B	67	C
68	D	69	E	70	F
71	G	72	H	73	I
74	J	75	K	76	L
77	M	78	N	79	O
80	P	81	Q	82	R
83	S	84	T	85	U
86	V	87	W	88	X
89	Y	90	Z	91	[
92	\	93	]	94	^
95	_	96	'	97	a
98	b	99	c	100	d
101	e	102	f	103	g
104	h	105	i	106	j
107	k	108	l	109	m
110	n	111	o	112	p
113	q	114	r	115	s
116	t	117	u	118	v
119	w	120	x	121	y
122	z	123	{	124	|
125	}	126	~		

As you can see, some numbers are not used. This is because there are more seven-bit numbers than there are commonly used characters. Some computers use the extra numbers to represent less commonly used symbols like the British pound sign, arrows, or mathematical symbols.

KEYBOARDS

Typically, a person communicates with a computer using a keyboard. A *keyboard* is an input device with a group of buttons, called keys, that are labeled with letters and numbers. A person types on it just like a typewriter, and can provide the computer with new information quickly and easily. A typical computer keyboard is illustrated here:

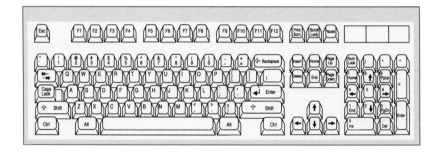

Just like typewriters, computer keyboards also have SHIFT, CAPS LOCK, BACKSPACE, TAB, RETURN, punctuation mark, and other symbol keys. Most computer keyboards also have a separate *numeric keypad*. This is a small cluster of number keys to the right or left of the letter keys. For typing a lot of numbers, the numeric keypad is faster and more convenient to use than the number keys in the row above the letter keys.

Computer keyboards also have special keys that are not found on typewriters. These can include

- Function keys (F1, F2, F3, etc.)

- Arrow keys (⬅, ➡, ⬆, ⬇)

- A control key (CTRL)

- An escape key (ESC)

- An "alternate" key (ALT)

- Editing keys (INS, DEL, HOME, END, PGUP, PGDN)

These keys can be used to give special instructions to the computer and will be discussed in Chapter 16.

The keys are usually made of plastic and slide up and down on posts, as shown here. There is a spring around each post that pushes the key up when it is not being pressed down. Sometimes there is a simple mechanism inside the post that causes the key to click when it is pressed. Fast typists like to hear or feel this click when they are using the keyboard as it indicates to them that they didn't accidentally miss a key.

The keys are not arranged in straight columns, but each key is assigned a row and a column number. One way for the microprocessor to know which key is pressed is for the keyboard to tell it two numbers. Let's look at a simple circuit that detects when a key is pressed and provides its row and column numbers.

Figure 14-1 shows a pseudo-NMOS circuit which I will call a *switch*. The dotted arrows show that the two output conductors, ROW OUT and COLUMN OUT, are normally at high voltage. There are direct conducting paths from high-voltage terminals, through PNP transistors, to both of them. A switch that looks like this is said to be "open."

Now suppose that a circular conductor is placed as shown in Figure 14-2. This turns on both NPN transistors. As the dotted arrows show, there is now a conducting path from a low-voltage terminal, through the NPN transistors, to both outputs. As with other pseudo-NMOS circuits, the outputs are effectively at low voltage. A switch that looks like this is said to be "closed."

Figure 14-3 shows sixteen switches connected together in a *switch array*. Once the correct ROW or COLUMN line goes to low voltage, we need to determine its number. A logic block that does this is called an *encoder*. An encoder is the opposite of a decoder. If you give a decoder a number, it puts the correct output line at high voltage. If you put an input line at low voltage, an encoder gives you its number. The following is a truth table for an encoder, and the schematic diagram for an encoder is shown in Figure 14-4.

IN0	IN1	IN2	IN3	OUT0	OUT1
1	1	1	0	0	0
1	1	0	1	0	1
1	0	1	1	1	0
0	1	1	1	1	1

We can use one encoder to tell us the row number of the key, and one encoder to tell us the column number.

The circuit shown in Figure 14-5 could be used in a computer keyboard. A switch could be placed under each key. If the key were depressed, the switch under it would close. The row and column number of the key could

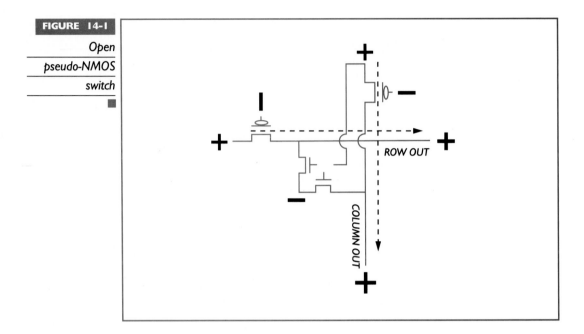

FIGURE 14-1

Open

pseudo-NMOS

switch

be moved from the output lines of the encoders into registers. The pressing of the key could cause an interrupt line to go to high voltage. The interrupt

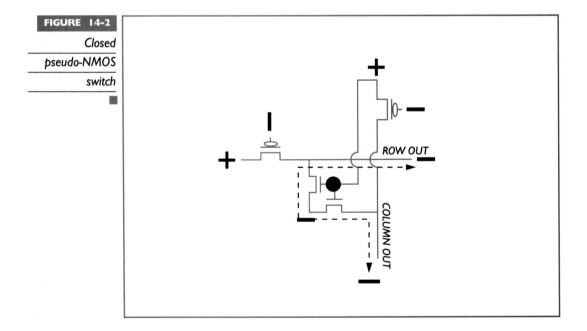

FIGURE 14-2

Closed

pseudo-NMOS

switch

FIGURE   14-3

Switch array

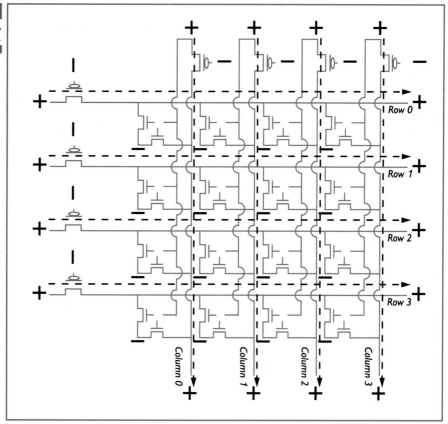

FIGURE   14-3

Switch array

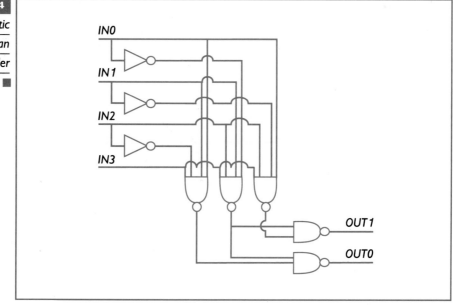

FIGURE   14-4

Schematic
diagram of an
encoder

IN0

IN1

IN2

IN3

OUT1

OUT0

service routine for the keyboard would instruct the microprocessor to read the row and column numbers of the key out of the registers. Then, the microprocessor could take some action depending on which key was pressed.

We've seen how a microprocessor could get information from outside the computer through a keyboard using some simple circuits. In reality, key-

FIGURE 14-5

Encoders used in

a switch array

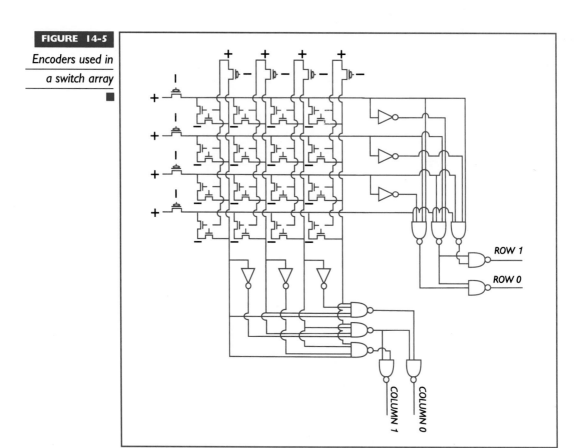

board circuits are more complicated. They can tell a microprocessor when multiple keys are pressed and when a key has been held down for some time.

MONITORS

n this section, I am going to talk about how a computer can display words and pictures on an output device called a *monitor*. Monitors operate much like televisions. A monitor can also be called a video display unit (VDU), a video monitor, or a cathode-ray tube (CRT). The *cathode-ray tube* is an important electrical device on which monitors (and televisions) are based. We'll see what it does in a moment.

The glass screen on which computer images are displayed is coated on the inside with a chemical called *phosphor*. Phosphor is usually black. That's why, when your monitor is off, the screen is black. But if a burst of electrons hits a piece of phosphor, it glows briefly. The more powerful the burst of electrons, the brighter the phosphor glows.

Behind the coated glass screen is the CRT. This device shoots a beam of electrons at the phosphor screen. As you learned in Chapter 1, electrons don't travel easily through air. Because of this, the CRT must be built inside a sealed compartment from which all air has been removed. Electrons are shot from the CRT, travel through the vacuum, and hit the phosphor, making it glow.

Four metal plates are placed around the beam of electrons that travels between the CRT and the phosphor screen. When these plates are put at different voltages, they cause the beam of electrons to point in different directions. By putting the four plates at the right voltages, the beam of electrons can be directed at any spot on the phosphor screen. When the voltages change, the beam moves quickly to a new spot on the screen. The strength of the beam also can be changed quickly. This makes some spots of phosphor glow brightly, while others are dim or black. The following illustration shows the devices which are inside the sealed compartment.

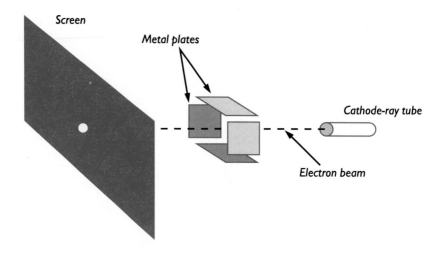

In a monochrome monitor, the screen is uniformly coated with just one kind of phosphor. The phosphor glows in a single color—usually white, green, or amber—when it is hit by a beam of electrons. By varying the strength of the beam, a darker or lighter shade of the color can be made to appear on the screen.

Color monitors are built in different ways. One way to display color images is to place tiny dots of three different kinds of phosphor on the screen. One kind glows bright or dim *red,* depending on the strength of the electron beam that hits it. Another glows bright or dim *green.* The third glows bright or dim *blue.* The dots are arranged in triangles, as shown in the following illustration.

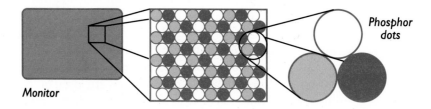

For this type of color monitor, three electron beams are used. One beam hits only red dots, another hits only green dots, and the third hits only blue dots. When the dots in a single triangle are hit by beams of different strengths, the glowing colors mix. A small spot on the screen glows in one of many different colors—including black and white.

Raster Scanning

To draw an image that fills the entire screen, every triangle or spot of phosphor must be made to glow at the right color or brightness. The beams start at the top left of the screen and move to the right. Their strengths change to make some dots glow brightly and leave other dots black. When the beams reach the right side of the screen, they are turned off. The beams are redirected to the left side, turned on, and then moved to the right again. A

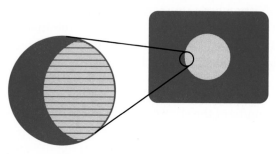

line appears under the one just drawn. This continues until the whole screen is filled with lines of colored spots that make up a picture. Displaying an image as a series of horizontal lines is called *raster scanning.* Such a picture can be drawn on the screen almost instantly. As soon as the phosphor stops glowing from the first picture, another image is drawn on the screen. Image after image is drawn so fast that the human eye perceives a picture that remains steady on the screen.

If an image is drawn over and over again, with slight variations in each version, the illusion of movement can be created. This is just like drawing a similar picture on every page in a pad of paper. When you quickly flip through the pages, the picture looks like it is moving, as you see here.

For a computer to draw a picture on a monitor, it must first have the picture in memory. To store a picture in memory, the computer divides the image into a grid of tiny squares. Each square is called a *picture element,* or *pixel* for short. For each pixel, a number is stored in memory that depends on what color the pixel is. If a pixel were bright white, a large number might be stored in its memory location. If a pixel were black, a small number might be stored in its memory location. If the pixel were some other color, a different number would be stored in its memory location. A picture might be divided into a grid that is 1,024 pixels high and 1,024 pixels wide. Such a picture would take up 1,048,576 memory locations (1,024 × 1,024). The section of memory where a picture is stored is called *video memory.* How does a picture get stored in video memory in the first place? Normally, a program must instruct the microprocessor to draw the picture by writing the correct numbers in video memory locations.

A special *video circuit* constantly retrieves the numbers from video memory and sends signals to the three CRTs in the monitor. These signals change the strengths of the electron beams at the right times in order to draw a proper picture. For example, suppose the video circuit retrieves the number that corresponds to the color blue. It increases the strength of the beam that hits blue dots and decreases the strength of the other beams. This causes a blue spot to appear on the screen. Suppose it retrieves the number that stands for the color purple. It increases the strengths of the beams that hit red and blue dots and decreases the strength of the beam that hits the green dots. This causes a purple spot to appear on the screen. Suppose it retrieves the number that stands for the color black. It turns off all of the CRTs. This causes a spot on the screen to remain black. Eventually, whatever was stored in video memory gets turned into black, white, and colored dots on the screen. If the right numbers are stored in video memory, this will be a useful picture. If the right numbers have not been stored in video memory, this will be just a bunch of black, white, and colored dots.

The more complicated a picture is, the larger the video memory must be. For example, if a picture consists only of black pixels and white pixels, each pixel needs only one bit of storage in video memory. If a picture consists of gray or colored pixels, more information is needed about each pixel, and this information takes up more memory.

The number of pixels that a picture is divided into is called the *resolution* of the picture. A computer that displays high-resolution pictures uses lots of pixels. It can show smooth curves and lots of intricate detail. However, such pictures take up a lot of memory. A computer that displays a low-resolution picture uses a small number of pixels. Such a picture takes up less memory, but looks blocky and blurred.

Vector Scanning

Vector scanning is another way simple pictures can be drawn on a computer screen. Horizontal lines are not drawn in a sequence from the top to the bottom of the screen. Instead, the electron beams are moved like pencils, drawing horizontal, vertical, and curved lines in different places on the screen.

In this case, the numbers stored in video memory are instructions on what to do to the electron beams. One number may say to turn a beam on. Another may say to turn a beam off. Another may say to move the beams to the right or left, or up or down. A computer that uses a vector scanning monitor has a special video circuit. It retrieves these numbers and causes the electron beam to follow the instructions. In this way, the computer can draw a picture on the screen.

Electron-Beam Lithography

The video circuit we discussed in the section on vector scanning can draw lines on phosphor with an electron beam. A similar circuit can eliminate the need for glass masks in VLSI.

In Chapter 4, I talked about the process of masking in VLSI. From that chapter, you know that ultraviolet light is passed through glass masks. The ultraviolet light polymerizes specific areas of a photoresist coating. It is very important that precise areas of the photoresist be polymerized. These areas will determine the shapes of layers of substances that will be used to build a circuit on a silicon chip.

Certain chemicals that are resistant to acid can be polymerized by a beam of electrons. These chemicals can be used in place of photoresist. In this process, areas of photoresist are not polymerized using ultraviolet light and a glass mask. Instead, specific areas of these chemicals are polymerized by aiming a beam of electrons at them.

With this method, engineers don't need to draw precise pictures on glass masks. They just store instructions on drawing these pictures in the memory of a computer. A video circuit similar to that used for vector scanning can follow these instructions. It properly aims a thin electron beam at the chemical coating. Precise areas of the coating are then polymerized.

This process is called *electron-beam lithography*. Electron-beam lithography allows engineers to build even smaller circuits on silicon chips than they could using the masking process.

JOYSTICKS

The joystick is probably the simplest input device used with a computer. You most likely have used a joystick, such as the one pictured here, to play a video game.

A joystick consists of a stick in a base. The upper end of the stick can be moved in different directions. A joystick usually has at least one button, which is located either on the base or on the stick itself.

Look at Figure 14-6. It shows a pseudo-NMOS circuit with five switches and five output lines labeled LEFT, RIGHT, UP, DOWN, and BUTTON. A circuit similar to this can be found in the base of a joystick. The circle represents the end of the stick that is in the base. Normally, the conductors in the switches don't touch each other. The switches are open, and the output lines are all at high voltage.

FIGURE 14-6

Pseudo-NMOS circuit for a joystick

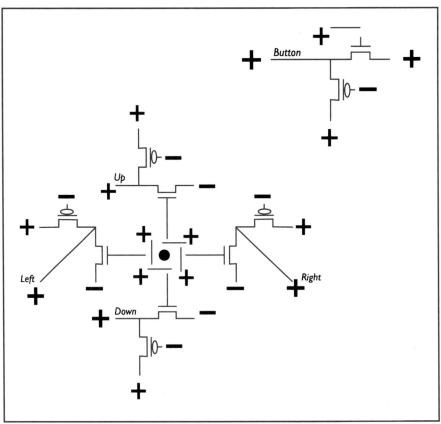

If the joystick is moved, its other end moves in the opposite direction and bends one or two of the conductors in the base. (The switches are placed in the base so that the correct one closes when the joystick is moved.) Switches close, and the output lines for the closed switches go to low voltage. Four of the switches respond to joystick movement, and the fifth responds to the button being pressed. If it is moved down, the down switch is closed. If it is moved left, right, or up, the left, right, or up switches are closed. If it is moved diagonally down and to the left, then both the down and the left switches are closed at the same time. By checking the voltage at the OUT lines, you can tell which of eight directions the joystick is being moved in. Figure 14-7 shows the result when the joystick is moved to the lower right and the button is pressed.

The voltages that the output lines are at can be stored in a register. When a joystick is connected to the computer, the computer can access this register. By checking the bits in the register, the microprocessor can tell which position the joystick is in. It can also tell whether or not the button is being pressed.

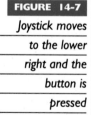

FIGURE 14-7

Joystick moves to the lower right and the button is pressed

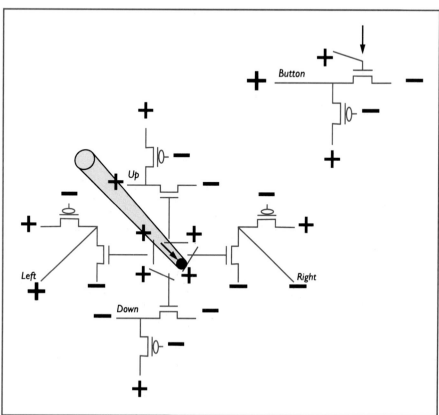

THE MOUSE

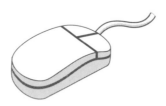

One way to make a computer easier to use is to make its input devices easier to use. Since people are very good at pointing at objects, engineers developed a simple input device, a mouse, that lets people use their pointing ability to operate the computer.

Usually, when computer users refer to a mouse, they mean the input device shown here. This device rests on the work surface and is connected to the computer by a wire. Protruding slightly from the underside of the mouse is a ball. The person using the mouse can move it across a surface, causing the ball to roll. Inside the mouse, two tiny rollers are held against the ball. One roller spins when the ball moves forward and backward, and the other when it rolls left and right. Special circuits in the mouse tell the computer how fast each roller is spinning, and in which direction. By comparing the speed and direction of the spinning rollers, the computer can determine the speed and direction in which the mouse moves across the work surface.

Normally, the computer uses this information to draw an arrow on the monitor. The arrow moves as the mouse moves, and the computer keeps track of its position on the monitor. A person can use the mouse to point the arrow at pictures or text displayed on the monitor by the computer. A mouse also has one or more buttons that operate just like joystick buttons. By pointing at an object and then pressing the button, a person can instruct the computer to do something.

PRINTERS

A printer can be connected to a computer to allow it to display information on paper. The microprocessor can then send input, in the form of numbers, to the printer. How the printer eventually uses these input numbers depends on what kind of printer it is. In this section, I am going to talk about two kinds of printers: line printers and laser printers.

Line Printers

In a line printer, the paper is held between hard rollers which move the paper up and down. A line printer also has a print head which moves back and forth horizontally across the paper. The print head is what actually marks the paper. By moving the paper up and down, and by moving the print head back and forth, the printer can make a mark almost anywhere on the paper, as shown here.

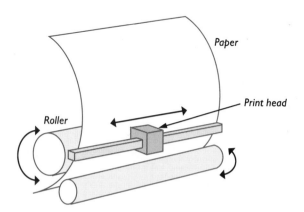

Line printers interpret their input numbers as ASCII letters, numerals, and punctuation marks. A line printer stores these numbers in a small memory until it has a whole line of characters. Then it moves the print head from left to right across the paper, printing the characters indicated by the ASCII numbers. If the microprocessor wants the line printer to start printing special characters, it can send one of the unused ASCII numbers. This allows the computer to print **bold**, *italic*, or underlined characters. When one line has been printed, the line printer moves the paper up by a fixed amount of space. The print head is now positioned below the line that was previously printed and the printer then waits for another line of ASCII numbers to be sent by the computer. When it has the next line, it moves the print head back across the paper, right to left, printing the characters indicated by the ASCII numbers.

Each type of line printer uses a different type of print head. The kind of print head a line printer uses helps to determine

- How expensive the printer is

- How fast it prints

- How good the printed characters look

- How many different kinds of characters can be printed

Daisy Wheel

The simplest kind of print head is the *daisy wheel*. A daisy wheel has several spokes. At the end of each spoke is a hard block with the raised image of a character, as shown here.

An inked ribbon is located between the wheel and the paper. In order to print a character, the wheel is rotated until the block with the desired character comes up next to the ribbon. (The printer uses the input numbers to determine how much to rotate the daisy wheel.) The block is then struck against the ribbon and the paper so that the character is transferred to the page, as shown here.

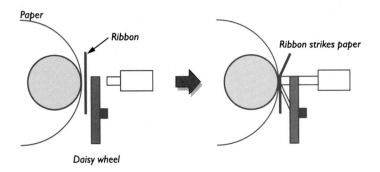

The advantages of a daisy wheel printer are

- It's inexpensive.

- It prints "letter quality." This means that the printed letters look the same as if they had been printed by a typewriter.

The disadvantages of a daisy wheel printer are

- It's slow, because for each character to be printed, the daisy wheel must be rotated so that that character is in line with the ribbon.

- It's noisy, because of the way a block strikes the paper every time a character is printed.

■ It can only print the characters that are on that particular daisy wheel. Because of this, a daisy wheel printer cannot draw pictures. If foreign languages, mathematical symbols, or other special characters are to be printed, then the daisy wheel must be replaced.

Dot-Matrix

The most popular kind of line printer is the *dot-matrix* printer. A dot-matrix printer prints characters as a grid of dots—like pixels. The head of a dot matrix printer has between 9 and 27 pins which can be moved in and out, as shown here.

An inked ribbon is located between the head and the paper, just as in a daisy-wheel printer. To print a character, the head moves along the ribbon, the pins dart out at the right time to mark small dots on the paper. A dot-matrix printer determines which character to print from its input numbers. Then, it determines which pins to move and when to move them.

You read that a video circuit draws pictures on the monitor with rows of pixels. Similarly, dot-matrix printers can be programmed to draw pictures on paper with rows of dots. The computer just needs to tell the printer to move pins in or out at the right times. This feature can be used to draw special characters like Greek letters or mathematical symbols.

If a print head that has a large number of pins is used, the resolution of characters is increased. The printer can create well-formed characters with tiny details. A good printer can print characters at near letter-quality. The characters look almost like typewritten characters.

The advantages of a dot-matrix printer are

■ A simple one is inexpensive.

■ It can print readable text very fast.

■ It can print near letter-quality text.

■ It can print special characters.

■ It can draw pictures.

The disadvantages of a dot-matrix printer are

■ It's noisy, because of the way the pins strike the ribbon.

■ Near letter-quality printing is slow, because the printer must print a large number of dots to produce well-formed, detailed characters.

Ink-Jet

Ink-jet printers are very similar to dot matrix printers. Instead of several pins striking the back of an inked ribbon, the head of an ink-jet printer has several holes which squirt ink directly onto the paper.

The advantages of ink-jet printers are the same as those of dot-matrix printers. Other advantages of an ink-jet printer are

- It's quieter than the other line printers.

- It can print text that is closer to letter-quality.

- Some can apply ink of different colors.

The disadvantage of an ink-jet printer is

- It's more expensive than other line printers.

Laser Printers

Laser printers print an entire page at once, rather than one line at a time. They work in much the same way as a copying machine; however, the information is "copied" from the printer's memory instead of from a printed paper. Most laser printers contain a sophisticated microprocessor that can understand complex programs sent from the computer. Instead of printing the ASCII characters, the laser printer interprets them as programs to be executed. For example, suppose the following program was sent to a laser printer in the form of ASCII numbers. It would print two concentric circles on a page. A line printer, on the other hand, would probably just print the program itself:

```
/doOneCircle
{ 0 0 100 0 360 arc stroke } def

/doAnotherCircle
{ 0 0 50 0 360 arc stroke } def

300 500 translate doOneCircle

25 0 translate doAnotherCircle

showpage
```

The laser printer has a large memory similar to the video memory of a computer. As it interprets the program instructions, the printer's microprocessor "draws" a picture in this large memory. The "showpage" instruction at the end of the program tells the microprocessor that it is finished drawing a page. When it receives this instruction, the microprocessor begins transferring the page from its memory to paper.

Inside the laser printer is a circuit similar to a video circuit. Instead of directing a beam of electrons against a phosphor screen, this circuit directs a laser beam back and forth against a rotating cylinder. The cylinder is covered with a substance called *selenium*. When spots of selenium on the cylinder are hit by the laser beam, they go to high voltage. A black chemical called *toner* is poured against the selenium. The toner sticks to the spots that are at high voltage and it slips away from other areas. When the cylinder is pressed against paper, any toner that was stuck to it transfers to the paper. This is shown in the following illustration. So a picture is drawn on the rotating cylinder in much the same way one is drawn on a computer screen. This picture eventually appears as black spots on the paper. With a fine, carefully controlled laser beam, a high-resolution picture can be printed.

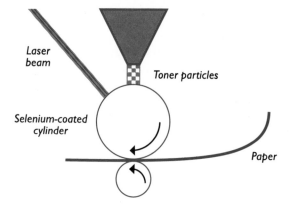

The advantages of a laser printer are

- It's faster than other printers, because it prints an entire page at once.

- It's quieter than other printers, because no parts strike against other parts.

- It produces extremely high-quality, professional-looking text

- It prints anything—regular and special characters as well as pictures.

The disadvantages of a laser printer are

■ It's very expensive.

■ It usually prints only black-and-white images.

■ Complicated pictures may take a long time to print.

Review

■ I/O devices allow a computer to communicate with the outside world.

■ ASCII is one code that represents a character using a seven-bit number.

■ Computer keyboards usually have numeric keypads and other special keys that are not found on typewriters.

■ An encoder is the opposite of a decoder. If you put an input line of an encoder at low voltage, the encoder puts the number of that line on its output lines.

■ In a keyboard, encoders can be used with a switch array to provide the row and column numbers of a key when it is pressed.

■ Inside a monitor, a CRT shoots a beam of electrons at a phosphor screen. The direction of the beam is controlled by metal plates. When the beam hits a spot of phosphor, it causes the spot to glow.

■ In a monochrome monitor, the screen is coated with just one kind of phosphor. By varying the strength of the electron beam, darker and lighter shades of that phosphor's color can be made to appear on the screen.

■ One way to create color images is to put on the screen three kinds of phosphor that glow red, green, or blue. By using a separate electron beam for each kind of phosphor, many different colors can be made to appear.

■ A video circuit retrieves numbers from video memory and sends signals to the CRT. The signals change the intensity of electron beams as they move back and forth, and up and down over the screen. In this way, the computer can cause letters, numbers, and pictures to appear on the screen.

■ Drawing a picture with horizontal lines of glowing phosphor is called raster scanning.

■ Moving the electron beams like pencils, to draw horizontal, vertical, and curved lines in different places on the screen is called vector scanning.

■ Electron-beam lithography is the use of electron beams instead of ultraviolet light in the masking process to polymerize chemicals.

■ A pseudo-NMOS circuit can be used to get input from a joystick.

Review (continued)

- A printer allows a computer to display information on paper.

- A line printer has rollers that move paper up and down, and a print head that can move back and forth across the paper. The print head can make a mark almost anywhere on the paper.

- A daisy wheel print head has several spokes. At the end of each spoke is a hard block with the raised image of a character. The block is struck against an inked ribbon and the paper so the character appears on the page.

- A dot-matrix print head has several pins that can move in and out independently. The pins strike a ribbon and the paper to make visible dots.

- An ink-jet print head has several tiny nozzles that squirt ink directly on the paper to make visible dots.

- Instead of printing the ASCII characters sent from the computer, a laser printer interprets them as instructions on how to draw pictures.

- Inside a laser printer, a circuit similar to a video circuit directs a laser beam against a rotating cylinder. Spots of selenium on the cylinder then go to high voltage, and a black chemical called toner sticks to them. When the cylinder is pressed against paper, the toner sticks to the page.

15

How a Computer Uses Storage Devices

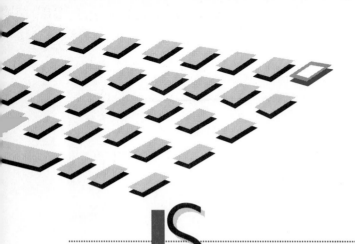

STORAGE devices allow a computer to store an unlimited amount of information quickly and permanently. They also allow the computer to change the information it has stored. This information can be used later, perhaps by other computers. I'll start out by explaining why computers need storage devices.

THE STORAGE HIERARCHY

As you know, a computer stores information in the form of high and low voltages. These voltages represent numbers. These numbers may, in turn, represent ASCII characters. To perform operations on numbers, a microprocessor must be able to access them quickly. So, numbers that a microprocessor is operating on are usually stored in registers. Just one or two microinstructions can perform an operation on numbers stored in registers.

There are three problems with this. First, what if a large amount of data must be processed? A large number of registers could be built on the microprocessor; however, this would be wasteful, since the microprocessor is only going to be using one or two of them at a time. Second, how will the data get into the registers in the first place? Registers are like small RAMs. As you know, when the computer is turned off, data stored in RAMs is lost. So, when the computer is turned on, the microprocessor's registers don't contain anything meaningful. Third, when the data has been used to generate a result, what should be done with the result? If it is stored in registers, then it will be lost when the computer is turned off.

The solution to some of these problems is to use memory—RAM and ROM. There are advantages and disadvantages to using memory instead of registers. One advantage is that large amounts of data can be stored in memory, and brought into the microprocessor when needed. The results can also be stored in memory. One disadvantage is that when data is stored in memory, several microinstructions are required to operate on it. Separate microinstructions are required

- to set the address and W/R lines, so the data stored in memory appears on the data lines,
- to move the data from the data lines into the microprocessor,
- to operate on the data, and
- to move the result from the microprocessor to the data lines, so it gets stored in memory.

You may remember from Chapter 8 that large memories need large decoders, which are slow. If the memory is very large, it takes a relatively long time for it to store and retrieve data. So it takes much more time to operate on data that is in memory than it does to operate on data that is in registers. However, the microprocessor often uses the same data over and over again. If this data is kept in registers, then the microprocessor won't waste a lot of time accessing memory.

There are still two problems here. First, if a computer constantly requires new and different data, and constantly generates new and different results, there still will never be enough memory to store it all. Second, any information stored in RAM is lost when the computer is turned off. This means that any results that a computer generates and stores in RAM will be lost.

You may also remember from Chapter 8 that information can be stored permanently in ROMs. However, it takes a long time to store even a little bit of data in a ROM, because it has to be burned in. And once information is stored, it can't be changed easily.

A computer needs to be able to store an unlimited amount of information permanently. There must be a method for storing data that is faster than burning ROMs and that allows the stored information to be changed. Storage devices are the solution to these problems.

Storage devices are I/O devices. You may remember from Chapters 12 and 14 how a microprocessor communicates with I/O devices. When the microprocessor puts the address of an I/O device on the address lines, that device becomes activated. If the microprocessor is sending data to the I/O device, it puts it on the data lines. If the microprocessor is receiving data from the I/O device, it gets it off the data lines. In this manner, the microprocessor can send instructions and data to the I/O device and receive data from it.

There is one disadvantage to using storage devices: many instructions are required to store and retrieve data from them. Separate instructions are required

- to control the devices,
- to tell them to put data in RAM or in the microprocessor, and
- to tell them to get data from RAM or the microprocessor.

So it takes much more time to operate on data that is stored by storage devices than it does to operate on data that is stored in memory or registers. Remember, though, that the microprocessor often operates on the same data over and over. Also, not all results that the microprocessor generates need to be stored permanently. Such data and results can be kept in memory or registers. Then the microprocessor won't waste a lot of time accessing storage devices.

Registers, memory, and storage devices are all parts of a microprocessor's *storage hierarchy*. The storage hierarchy is an arrangement of methods for storing data. This hierarchy is shown here:

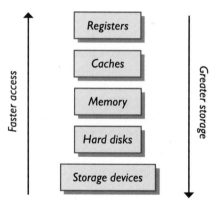

The fastest method is at the top, and the slowest method is at the bottom. However, only a little bit of data can be stored using the fastest method. An unlimited amount of data can be stored using the slowest method. (We'll be discussing caches and hard-disk drives later in this chapter.)

Computer engineers need to keep the storage hierarchy in mind when they build computers. For example, suppose a microprocessor has lots of registers. They will take up space on the chip that could be used for something more important. If a microprocessor has too few registers, it will be slow, because it will keep having to access memory.

FILES

A *file* usually consists of pages of information about a particular subject. In an office, you might find files on customers or files on business transactions. In a police station, you might find files on known criminals. In a kitchen, you might find a recipe file. The information in a file is kept together and stored under a name. This name might be the name of a customer or criminal, a type of business transaction, or the name of a food ingredient. Files are usually stored by name in alphabetical order, so that the information on a particular subject can be retrieved by a person quickly.

Similarly, a computer stores information on a particular subject in a file. A computer might store a written document in a file of ASCII characters. A computer might store a file of numbers related to a business transaction. A computer always stores program files: files of numbers that are machine language instructions.

Each computer file also has a name. However, unlike office files, computer files are stored so that they can be retrieved quickly by a computer. Exactly how they are stored depends on what device is used to store them—they are not always ordered alphabetically.

TAPE DRIVES

Computers can store large amounts of information on magnetic tape. The cassette tape you put in your stereo to listen to music is an example of a magnetic tape. In fact, some computers have the ability to store and retrieve data on cassette tapes, using regular cassette tape players. An unlimited amount of data can be stored, just by using more and more tapes.

Magnetic tape is usually made out of plastic that is covered with a thin layer of *iron oxide*. (Iron oxide is rust!) If you have played with magnets, you know that metal things can be made into magnets by touching them to other magnets. For example, if you touch a paper clip to a magnet, the paper clip will attract other metal objects. This is illustrated here:

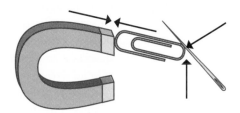

If you touch a small paper clip to a very powerful magnet, the paper clip will become magnetized—turned into a magnet. It will attract other metal objects even when it is not touching the powerful magnet. This is shown here:

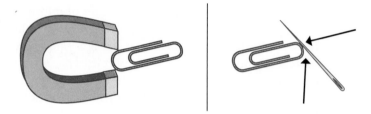

Normally, a paper clip will become demagnetized over time. However, the iron oxide on magnetic tape can be permanently magnetized or demagnetized using a tape recorder.

When a tape recorder is used to record sounds, the magnetic tape slides against a recording head. The *recording head* magnetizes and demagnetizes sections of iron oxide as the tape moves by. The recording head is connected to the microphone of the tape recorder. Inside the microphone is a piece of thin plastic that vibrates when sounds hit it. These vibrations are converted into high and low voltages. These high and low voltages are sent through a wire to the recording head. The recording head magnetizes the tape when the wire is at high voltage, and demagnetizes the tape when the wire is at low voltage. So the sound vibrations get stored as magnetized and demagnetized areas of iron oxide on the tape. This process is illustrated here:

When a tape recorder is used to play sounds, the events occur in reverse order. The magnetic tape slides against a playing head. The *playing head* detects the magnetized and demagnetized areas of iron oxide as the tape moves by. The playing head is connected to a speaker by electrical wire. When the playing head detects a magnetized area, it puts the wire at high voltage. When the playing head detects a demagnetized area, it puts the wire at low voltage. The speaker converts these high and low voltages into sound vibrations. This process is shown in the following illustration.

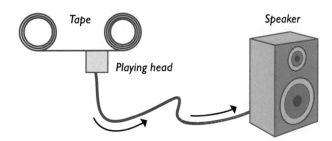

A tape recorder used by a computer is often called a tape drive. When a computer uses a tape drive to store information, it doesn't need a microphone. A simple I/O device connects the computer directly to the recording head of the tape drive. The microprocessor sends data to the I/O device, which sends the high and low voltages to the tape drive. The high and low voltages get stored on a tape as tiny magnetized and demagnetized sections of iron oxide.

To retrieve information stored on tape, a similar I/O device can connect the playing head of the tape drive to the computer. The magnetized and demagnetized areas of iron oxide get converted to high and low voltages. The I/O device interprets them as numbers and sends them to the microprocessor or stores them in RAM.

You can record a new song over an old song on a cassette tape and the old song gets erased forever. Similarly, when a computer stores data on a tape, any data that was previously stored there gets erased. If the information stored on a tape needs to be changed, it can be recorded over with new information.

There are some disadvantages to using a tape drive to store information on cassette tapes:

- A tape drive is very slow.

- If the computer needs information that is stored at the end of the tape, it must retrieve all of the information on the tape until the desired information is found. The computer could tell the tape drive to fast-forward the tape, but the information may go by too fast, and the computer may miss it.

- A small amount of data takes up quite a bit of tape.

One way to get around these problems is to use special high-speed tape drives and tapes. These devices are as tall as people and use tape that is stored on large, flat spools. Such machines can move tape very fast. This allows a computer to find information anywhere on a tape quickly and accurately.

Also, large amounts of information can be stored in just a small section of the tape.

There are still problems with large tape machines and tape:

- Such large tape drives cannot be used with desktop computers.

- Because it stores so much information, this kind of tape is very delicate. Special care must be taken to keep it clean and protected. A weak magnet can erase information stored on the tape without even touching it. A bit of dirt, dust, or moisture on the tape can cause a large amount of important information to be lost.

- Information at the end of the tape can be found quickly, but the tape must be fast-forwarded. Thus, it still takes longer to find information at the end of the tape than to find information at the beginning of the tape.

- Suppose some data needs to be added at the beginning of the tape or in the middle of the tape. Then, all of the data after it needs to be moved over. This process can take a long time.

A computer should be able to store information in such a way that any one piece can be retrieved as quickly as another piece. And, a computer should be able to insert new data without having to move other data over.

FLOPPY-DISK DRIVES

The solution to these problems is to store information on magnetic *floppy disks* instead of tapes. Floppy disks are made out of the same flexible material as magnetic tape, but they are thicker, and round. Magnetic floppy disks come in many different diameters. The most popular disk sizes are 5 1/4-inch and 3 1/2-inch.

A computer uses a special machine called a *floppy-disk drive* to store and retrieve data using floppy disks. The floppy-disk drive is connected to an I/O device called a disk controller. The *disk controller* controls the floppy-disk drive according to instruction codes sent by the microprocessor. It transfers data between the floppy disk, the microprocessor, and memory. Inside the floppy-disk drive is a sensitive head that is used both to record on and to "play" from the disk. The delicate head is well protected inside the disk drive. The disks themselves are kept inside protective sheaths, as shown here.

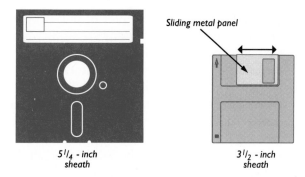

5¹/₄ - inch
sheath

Sliding metal panel

3¹/₂ - inch
sheath

So large amounts of information can be stored safely on a tiny section of a disk. The sheaths for 5 1/4-inch disks have an oval hole in them to expose the disk for reading and writing. The sheaths for 3 1/2-inch disks have a metal panel that moves aside to expose the disk.

When the floppy disk is inserted into the floppy-disk drive, a clamp holds it firmly in place. The head moves to a position just above the disk's exposed surface. The clamp can rotate the disk within the sheath, and the head can move back and forth. In this way, the head can be positioned over any part of the disk. The following illustration shows a view of the 5 1/4-inch floppy disk, clamp, and head.

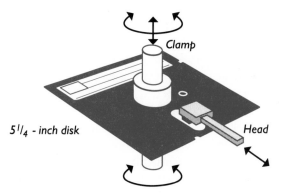

Clamp

5¹/₄ - inch disk

Head

The computer must prepare a disk before storing information on it. This preparation is called *formatting*. The computer sends instructions to the disk controller to divide the disk into concentric rings, or *tracks*. The tracks are then divided into *sectors*, as shown in this illustration. The sectors in every track are numbered, and the sector number is recorded at the beginning of each sector. (The number is stored as a series of magnetized and demagnetized areas of the disk, just like on tape.) The disk controller can position the head over any track by

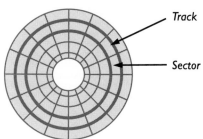

Track

Sector

moving it in toward the center or out away from the center of the disk. It can position the head over any sector by rotating the disk until the correct sector number passes under the head. The disk continues to rotate while data is read from or written to that sector.

Unlike tapes, floppy disks have no "beginning" and "end." How long it takes for a given sector to pass under the head depends on where the head was previously positioned. On the average, it takes an equal amount of time to position the head over any sector. A fixed amount of information, usually around 500 bytes, can be stored in each sector of the disk. This is called the *sector size.*

Every formatted disk has a special sector or sectors where the computer stores the directory. The *directory* tells the computer where on the disk information is stored, much as a table of contents tells readers where to find information stored in a book. When a computer wants to find information quickly, it goes to the directory sector(s).

All computers of the same model store the directory in the same sector(s) on every disk. So a disk formatted by one computer can be read by another computer that is the same model. However, computers manufactured by different companies use different sectors to store the directory. Or, sometimes they store other kinds of information in the directory. Suppose you move a disk from the disk drive of one computer to the disk drive of a different model computer. The second computer may not be able to use the disk. This is either because it looks for the directory in the wrong place, or it expects different information to be stored in the directory.

The *sector map* is part of the directory on any disk. It tells the computer whether each disk sector is empty or contains data. The sector map is usually a very long number. It consists of groups of bits: one group for every disk track, and one bit in each group for every sector in the track. If the bit is 1, then the computer can tell that the sector contains data. If the bit is 0, then the computer can tell that the sector is empty. Since a newly formatted disk contains no files, the bits in its sector map are all 0.

Suppose the memory of a computer contains a file stored as numbers and ASCII characters. The computer can perform the following actions to store the file on a disk:

1. Instruct the disk drive to position the head over the directory sector.

2. Read the sector map into memory that is not being used.

3. Find an empty sector by looking for a 0 in the sector map bits.

4. Instruct the disk drive to move the disk head over the empty sector.

5. Send the file data to the disk drive. The disk drive stores the data in the sector.

6. Because the sector now contains data, correct the sector map by replacing the 0 with a 1.

7. Instruct the disk drive to move the disk head over the directory sector.

8. Send the updated sector map to the disk drive. The disk drive stores the new sector map in the directory. The next time the sector map is retrieved from the directory, the computer will be able to tell that the sector already contains data.

If the file is too big to fit in one sector, the computer must split the file into pieces for two or more empty sectors. If the file is successfully stored in one or more sectors, the computer writes the name of the file in the directory. The name is stored as ASCII numbers, of course. After the name, the computer writes the track and sector numbers in which the file is stored. The computer may store other information about the file, such as the date and time it was written. In this way, the computer can store files on the disk until all sectors are full.

To retrieve or erase a file from the disk, the filename must be in the computer's memory. The computer performs the following actions to retrieve a file from the disk:

1. Instruct the disk drive to position the head over the directory sector.

2. Read the directory into memory that is not being used.

3. Look for the name of the file in the directory.

4. Find out which sectors the file is stored in.

5. Instruct the disk drive to position the head over the first sector.

6. Retrieve the data from the sector.

7. Instruct the disk drive to position the head over the next sector. Continue reading data until the whole file is in memory.

The computer can erase a file very easily. It just needs to find the sectors that the file is stored in, and mark them empty in the sector map. It must then write spaces (ASCII number 32) over the filename in the directory. For all practical purposes, the file has been erased. If the computer tries to retrieve the erased file, it will be unable to find the filename in the directory. The next time the computer wants to store a file on the disk, it will find from the sector map that the erased file's sectors are empty and it will record the new file over the old file's sectors. Unlike files stored on a tape, files stored on a disk don't need to be "moved over" to make room for new files.

Often, the computer reads a file from the disk and then changes it in memory. There are now two versions of the file: an old one on disk, and a new one in memory. To replace the old version with the new version, the computer can erase the old version and then write the new version. A safer way to replace the old version is to write the new version first, and then erase the old version. That way, if something goes wrong, there is always at least one version of the file stored safely on the disk.

CACHES

A modern computer has a large memory, and it takes a relatively long time to store numbers in it and retrieve numbers from it. In a modern computer, the difference in time between a register access and a memory access is very great, so this type of computer needs more storage methods in its storage hierarchy. A device called a cache fits between registers and memory in the storage hierarchy presented earlier in this chapter. A *cache* is a small, fast memory. A cache stores more data than can be stored in registers, but it is slower than registers. A cache stores less data than can be stored in memory, but it is faster than memory. Modern caches are highly complex devices, but I'll give you a basic idea of how they work.

A cache is connected to the address and data buses of the microprocessor. The cache has its own address and data buses that are connected to the main memory, as shown in Figure 15-1. Inside the cache is a small, fast memory, one part of which stores addresses. Another part of the memory stores the data in those addresses. When the microprocessor reads data from a certain address for the first time, the cache gets it from main memory for the microprocessor. *It also automatically records the address in its address memory and the data in its data memory.*

FIGURE 15-1

Cache connected to microprocessor and main memory

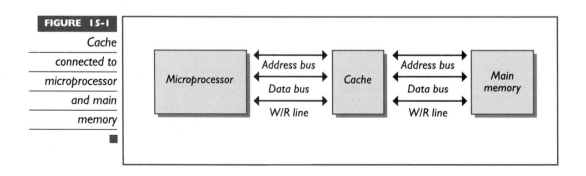

Figure 15-2 shows an example of this. The microprocessor has put 25000 on the address bus. It has put the W/R line at low voltage. The cache puts 25000 on the address bus to the memory. It puts the W/R to the memory at low voltage. After some time, the memory puts the data, 18, on the data lines to the cache. The cache stores the address and data in its memory and then puts 18 on the data lines to the microprocessor.

When the microprocessor reads data that is not stored in the cache, a *cache miss* is said to have occurred. Cache misses are bad, because the cache must get the data from the slow main memory for the microprocessor.

If the microprocessor requests data from address 25000 again, the cache notices that the address is in its address memory. It takes the corresponding data out of its data memory and provides the data to the microprocessor. It never needs to access main memory! This is shown in Figure 15-3. So the microprocessor gets the data in far less time than if it had accessed main memory.

When the microprocessor reads data that happens to be stored in the cache, a *cache hit* is said to have occurred. Cache hits are good, because the cache can provide data to the microprocessor very quickly.

Eventually, the cache's memory fills up with records of addresses and data that the microprocessor has requested. The next time a cache miss occurs, the cache replaces one of these records with a new record. If the microprocessor then reads from the address that has been replaced, a cache miss will occur again.

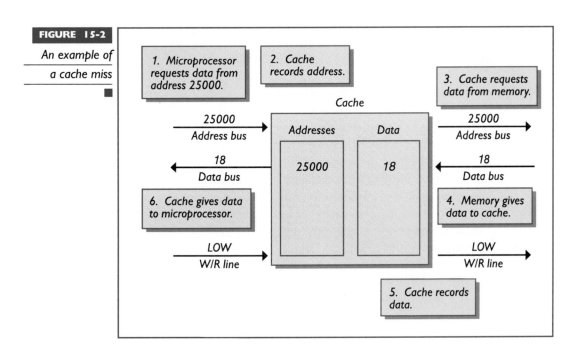

FIGURE 15-2

An example of a cache miss

FIGURE 15-3

*An example of
a cache hit*
■

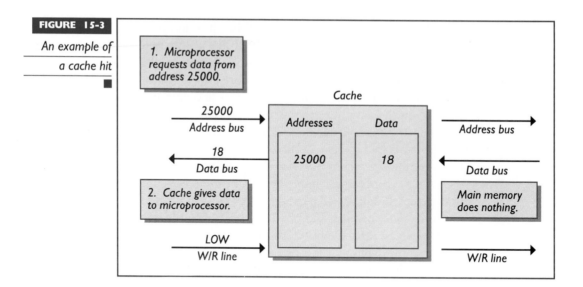

I've described what happens when a microprocessor reads data in a computer with a cache. You might be wondering what happens when the microprocessor writes data in a computer with a cache. Two things can happen, depending on what kind of cache is in the computer.

The first kind of cache is a *write-through* cache. It first checks whether the address being written to is in its address memory. If so, it updates the data in its data memory. Then, it immediately writes the data to main memory. This takes some time. However, while the cache is busy writing to memory, the microprocessor can do other work. The only problem is if the microprocessor immediately writes data a second time. Then, the microprocessor must wait for the cache to complete the first write to memory.

The second kind of cache is a *write-back* cache. It first checks whether the address being written to is in its address memory. If so, it updates the data in its data memory. However, it does not write the data to main memory. So, if the microprocessor immediately writes data a second time, the cache is ready. Note that, in this case, the main memory contains data that is out of date. It was supposed to contain new data, but the new data is being held in the cache. The cache didn't write the new data to memory. If the microprocessor is the only device that accesses the memory, this is not a problem. All accesses take place through the cache, and the cache makes sure the microprocessor gets the latest data. However, in some computers, other devices like disk drives and video circuits also access memory. They don't go through the cache. If another device accesses main memory, it will get data that is out of date.

One solution to this problem is for the microprocessor to *flush* the cache. A cache flush tells the cache to write all of its data to main memory and to clear its own memory. Now the main memory contains the latest data. However, subsequent memory accesses will result in cache misses.

HARD-DISK DRIVES

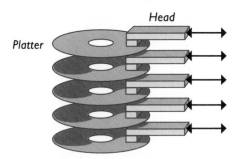

Head

Platter

A hard-disk drive is a storage device that fits between memory and other storage devices in the storage hierarchy. Like other storage devices, hard-disk drives store a large amount of data permanently. The amount of data a hard-disk drive can store is limited, but it can store and change it much faster than other storage devices.

A hard-disk drive stores data on a set of hard round platters similar to disks. It has several heads to read data from and write data on the platters, as shown here. So a hard-disk drive can store far more information than a floppy-disk drive can store on a single floppy disk. The platters are coated with a material that allows them to store much more information than iron oxide allows. However, this material is especially delicate. So the platters and heads are permanently encased in a protective chamber that contains no air. New platters cannot be inserted in a hard-disk drive the way new floppy disks can be inserted in a floppy-disk drive. This is why a hard-disk drive can store only a limited amount of information.

Because the chamber contains no air and is well protected, the platters can spin much faster than a floppy disk spins. The heads can move more rapidly than the head in a floppy-disk drive. This is why a hard-disk drive can store and change information faster than a floppy-disk drive.

Review

- Storage devices are I/O devices. They allow a computer to store information quickly and permanently.

- Storage devices allow a computer to change the information it has stored.

- Registers, caches, memory, hard-disk drives, and other storage devices form a computer's storage hierarchy.

- At one end of the storage hierarchy are microprocessor registers. Just

Review (continued)

one or two microinstructions can quickly perform an operation on data stored in registers. However, a microprocessor usually does not have a large number of registers.

■ In the middle of the storage hierarchy is memory. Several microinstructions are required to operate on data stored in memory. Memories can be very large, but are still limited in size.

■ At the other end of the storage hierarchy are storage devices. Several instructions are required to operate on data stored in storage devices. An unlimited amount of data, however, can be stored using storage devices.

■ A computer stores data about a particular subject in files.

■ Computers can store an unlimited amount of data on tapes and disks by using more and more tapes or disks.

■ A computer can store data by converting high and low voltages into magnetized and demagnetized areas on tapes and disks.

■ Information stored at the end of a tape takes longer to access than information stored at the beginning.

■ To insert new data in the middle of a tape, the data following it must be moved over.

■ Information stored on a tape will be erased if the tape comes into contact with a magnet, dust, or moisture.

■ Information stored anywhere on a disk takes about the same time to access.

■ Data on a disk does not need to be moved over to insert new data.

■ The head of a disk drive is well protected inside the drive. A floppy disk is protected inside its sheath.

■ A computer must format a disk to prepare it for storage. The computer divides the disk into tracks and numbered sectors, and writes the directory in one of the sectors.

■ The sector map is a set of bits in the directory. Each bit indicates whether a sector is empty or contains data.

■ A cache is a small, fast memory that fits between registers and main memory in the storage hierarchy.

■ A hard-disk drive is a fast storage device that fits between memory and other storage devices in the storage hierarchy. A hard-disk drive can store a large but limited amount of information on a set of platters similar to disks.

16

How the Parts of a
Computer System Work Together

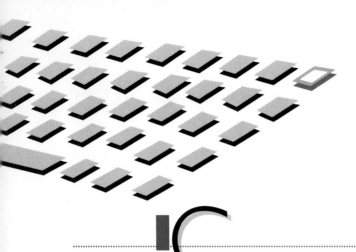

ONGRATULATIONS! You now know basically how every part of a computer works. In this chapter, I am going to review how these various parts work together to do useful things. In later chapters, I'll be discussing the ingenious ways in which programs are written for modern computers. This will help you understand why computers have become such powerful and versatile tools.

PARTS OF A
COMPUTER
SYSTEM

All computers have a microprocessor, memory, storage devices, and I/O devices. The microprocessor is the most important device, because it processes data and controls the other parts of the computer. The microprocessor continually retrieves instructions from memory that tell it where to get data, how to operate on it, and where to store the results.

The events that occur inside a computer are determined completely by the microprocessor. At the same time, what the microprocessor does is determined completely by the program it is running. That's why, when we say that a program is doing something, or that the computer is doing something, we really mean that the program is instructing the microprocessor to do it. When we say that the computer knows something, we really mean that some information is in the computer's memory. When we say that the computer knows how to do something, we really mean that a program can instruct the microprocessor to do it.

In the previous chapter, you saw that a microprocessor can perform operations directly on data in its registers. It can also perform operations on data in memory and on data stored on disks and tapes, but it must bring the data into memory or registers first. Once it has data, it can produce results and store them in registers, in memory, or on disks and tapes. The same thing applies to instructions. A microprocessor can execute instructions that are in memory. It also can execute instructions that are stored on disks and tapes, but it must bring them into memory first.

The person who operates a computer is called the *user*. The computer and the user communicate through I/O devices. A microprocessor accesses an I/O device the same way it accesses a memory location. It puts an address on the address lines, which activates the I/O device. The microprocessor can send instruction codes and data to the I/O device by writing them to this address. It can receive data from the I/O device by reading from this address. For example, writing instruction codes to a disk controller can position a disk drive head over a particular track and sector. Writing data to it can cause the data to be written on that track and sector. Reading data from it can cause data to be read from that track and sector. Writing data to an output device, like a printer, can cause characters to appear on paper. By reading data from an input device, such as a keyboard, the microprocessor can tell which key is being pressed.

EDITORS

The parts of a computer work together to help the user accomplish tasks. To illustrate this, let's look at a type of program called an *editor*. An editor allows a user to create and modify files.

In Chapter 14, you saw how a keyboard could put a code in a register whenever a key was pressed. The microprocessor could read the code from the register and make decisions based on it. An editor includes instructions that tell the microprocessor to get input from the keyboard in this manner. Whenever the programmer presses a key, the microprocessor reads the keyboard code. Suppose the user has pressed a letter or number key. In this case, the microprocessor stores the ASCII number in RAM. Once this number is in RAM, the video circuit can display the character on the monitor. In this manner, whatever the programmer types appears on the monitor.

So far, the computer behaves much like an everyday typewriter. But there is more to an editor than that. As the user continues typing, the computer keeps track of the position on the screen where the letters are placed. When the letters reach the edge of the screen, the computer can start printing them at the left edge of the next line. Unlike most typewriters, a computer running an editor can tell when to start a new line. To show the user where letters will appear next, the computer displays a blinking line or a box, called a *cursor*. This process is illustrated in Figure 16-1.

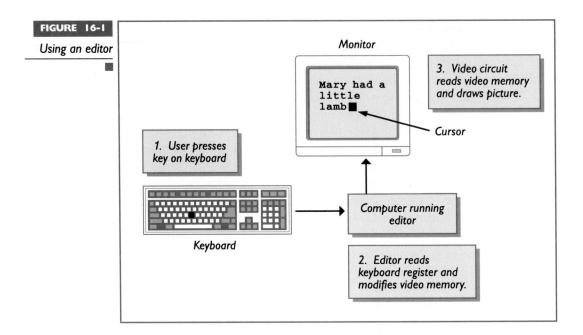

FIGURE 16-1

Using an editor

Monitor

Mary had a
little
lamb■

← Cursor

3. Video circuit
reads video memory
and draws picture.

1. User presses
key on keyboard

Keyboard

Computer running
editor

2. Editor reads
keyboard register and
modifies video memory.

If the user presses a special key or key combination, the microprocessor detects it when it reads the keyboard register. In this case, the computer must take some special action. For example, suppose the user presses the DELETE key after typing the phrase that is shown in Figure 16-1. Instead of displaying a character on the screen, the microprocessor must erase the last character that the user typed. It accomplishes this by replacing the cursor code in RAM with a 32, the ASCII number for space, and then displaying the cursor where the b used to be (used to b?), as shown here. The cursor is now in the position where subsequent typed characters will appear. In this manner, the user can correct mistakes while typing.

Mary had a
little lam■

Other keys, usually the arrow keys, tell the computer to move the cursor to the left or right, to the previous line, or to the next line. In this manner, the user can tell the computer to start displaying characters at different positions on the screen. Often, an editor gets input from a mouse as well as the keyboard. The user can move the mouse to point an arrow at a new position on the screen. When the user presses a mouse button, the cursor moves to that position. This is faster than pressing the arrow keys to move the cursor.

With the keyboard or the mouse, the user can *select* characters that have already been typed. This tells the computer that some special action is going to be performed on these characters. For example, they may be moved to a new location, copied, or erased. Normally, the computer will display these characters either boldfaced, underlined, or surrounded by a highlighted box. That way, the user can see exactly which characters are selected. Meanwhile, the computer makes a record of the selected characters. For example, one memory location could point to (contain the address of) the first character selected, while another points to the last character selected.

If characters are to be erased, the microprocessor can quickly replace the codes for the selected characters with the codes for spaces. Figure 16-2 illustrates memory and the monitor screen before and after characters are erased. The arrows indicate that some memory locations point to the first and last characters that have been selected. The selected characters are underlined on the screen. If the characters are to be copied, the microprocessor can quickly copy their ASCII numbers to other locations in memory. This is illustrated in Figure 16-3. If the characters are to be moved, the microprocessor can copy them and then replace the originals with spaces. This is illustrated in Figure 16-4. As new codes are put in RAM, the characters that appear on the screen change according to the user's wishes. Characters disappear, or appear in new places.

In response to user input, every editor can save the ASCII numbers it has recorded in a file. This means there is a permanent record of whatever the user typed. By giving the correct input while an editor is running, the user can

- retrieve the contents of old files,

- modify them, and

- save the modified contents back to the storage device.

With an editor, a user can create large, complicated files containing ASCII numbers. Such files are called *text files*.

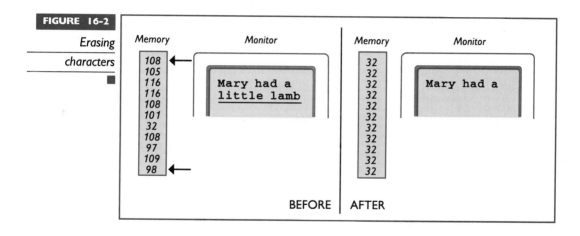

FIGURE 16-2

Erasing characters

BEFORE | AFTER

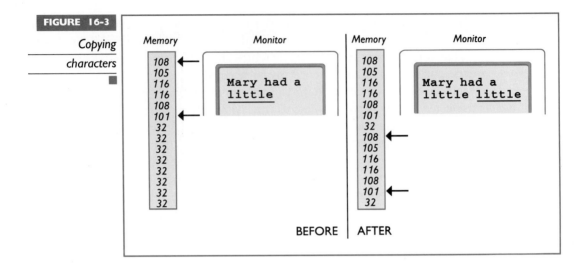

FIGURE 16-3

Copying

characters

■

TYPES OF COMPUTER SYSTEMS

Computers come in all shapes and sizes. But each of them has the parts that I listed at the beginning of this chapter: a microprocessor, memory, I/O devices, and storage devices.

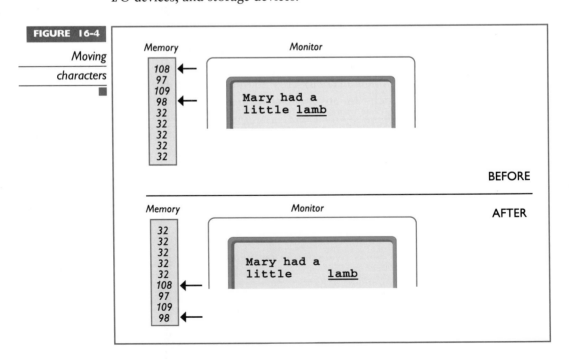

FIGURE 16-4

Moving

characters

■

Calculators

A calculator is a very simple computer. Its input device is a small keyboard. Its output device is the small display where numbers appear. Some calculators also have a printer that prints numbers and mathematical symbols on paper. A calculator runs a simple program stored in ROM. This program

- instructs the calculator to find out which keys are pressed,

- tells it which calculations to perform when keys are pressed, and

- tells it what to display on the screen.

Even the simplest calculator has a small RAM that can store a single number. More complicated calculators have larger RAMs that can store many numbers and programs written by the user. The most sophisticated calculators can store data on magnetic cards.

Personal Computers

The type of computer you might find in a person's home, or in a small business office, is called a personal computer. This is because it is usually used by just one person at a time. The input devices for a personal computer generally include a large keyboard with a numeric keypad, and a mouse. The output devices for a personal computer generally include a color monitor and a small dot-matrix printer. A personal computer can run a wide variety of programs. These programs help the user with various tasks such as writing letters and reports, managing money, and drawing. A personal computer usually has a hard-disk drive for storing programs and other files. It also includes a drive for storing files on floppy disks. Floppy disks can be used to move files from one personal computer to another. New programs and files can be purchased on floppy disks and copied to the hard disk. Cassette tape drives are also available for personal computers, but generally, they are too slow to be useful.

Workstations

Often, large numbers of people work on computers together and exchange files frequently. It is inconvenient to exchange files using floppy disks. Luckily, computers can be connected to each other with wires, and can exchange files with each other electronically. A group of computers communicating with each other over wires is called a *network*. A network of four computers is shown in Figure 16-5. Each one includes a keyboard, a monitor, and a box containing the microprocessor, memory, and a floppy-disk drive.

Not every computer in a network has to have a printer or a disk drive. Instead, when a user wants to print a file, he can instruct his computer to send the file to a computer in the network that is connected to a printer. That computer will print the file. Similarly, the user can store his files on, and retrieve files from, the disk drives of other computers in the network. Some computers do nothing but print files that are sent to them by other computers. Other computers do nothing but store files for other computers. Such computers are called *dedicated servers,* because they do nothing but provide a single service to other computers. The computers that use these services are called *clients.* Figure 16-6 shows a network of four computers. Two are clients. One is a dedicated file server. Another is a dedicated print server. The clients have a keyboard, a monitor, and a box containing the microprocessor and memory. They are operated by users. One server has a box connected to a large hard-disk drive. The hard-disk drive stores files for the clients. The print server has a box connected to a printer. It prints files for the clients.

The computers in a network are called *workstations.* A workstation generally has a very fast microprocessor and a large amount of RAM. It might also have a small hard-disk drive, so it doesn't need to contact a dedicated server for every file. The input devices for a workstation usually include a keyboard and a mouse. The output device usually consists of a monochrome monitor.

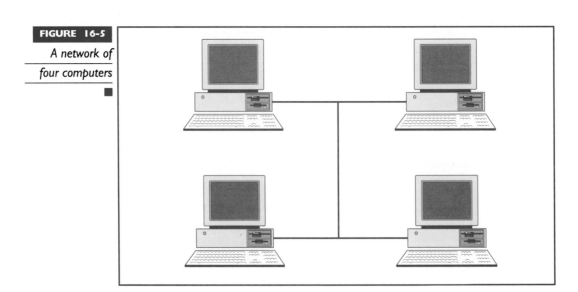

FIGURE 16-5

A network of

four computers

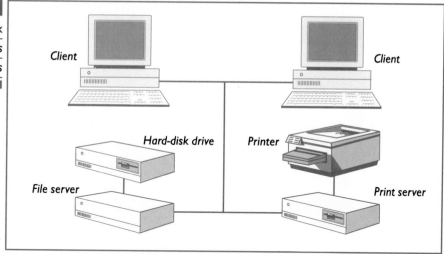

A network including clients and servers

Client · Client · Hard-disk drive · Printer · File server · Print server

Mainframe Computers

Believe it or not, there are still some computers that take up entire rooms. This is not because they use vacuum tubes, as you read in Chapter 4. It is because they have very fast, powerful microprocessors and many hard-disk drives to store tremendous amounts of data. They may be connected to several different kinds of printers. Such computers are called *mainframe* computers. Many users can access a single mainframe computer at once.

Users communicate with mainframe computers using workstations or simple terminals. A *terminal* is just an I/O device that includes both a keyboard and a monitor. It has a very simple microprocessor, and a small memory. This allows it to display what the user types, send information to the mainframe, and receive information from the mainframe. Mainframe computers and terminals are used by banks, libraries, airlines, and other businesses that store and process large amounts of data in a central location.

HARDWARE, FIRMWARE, AND SOFTWARE

The parts of a computer that you can touch are called *hardware*. This includes the microprocessor, memory chips, and I/O devices. However, hardware is useless without programs to instruct a computer how to use it.

The programs that a computer runs are called *software*. You can't really touch a program. It consists only of numbers that are represented as high and low voltages. Some people use the word *firmware* to mean software that is encased in hardware: programs that are stored in ROMs.

MIPS, MFLOPS, AND HERTZ

People need a way to tell how fast and powerful a computer is. One measure of a computer's power and speed is how many simple instructions its microprocessor can execute in one second. By simple instructions, we mean instructions that load data from memory, store data in memory, and perform addition or subtraction of whole numbers, etc. Most modern microprocessors can execute millions of simple instructions per second. So, the unit for measuring their speed is *MIPS* (millions of instructions per second). The microprocessors in personal computers can perform 5 to 10 MIPS, while those in workstations can perform 50 MIPS or more.

A microprocessor is not always executing simple instructions, though. When computers perform difficult mathematical calculations, they must use floating-point numbers (numbers with fractional parts). Most modern microprocessors have special instructions to perform mathematical operations on floating-point numbers. Another measure of a computer's power and speed is how many floating-point instructions it can execute in one second. The unit for measuring this is MFLOPS, or millions of floating-point operations per second. Some very powerful microprocessors can perform up to 40 MFLOPS.

People often try to measure the power of a computer by its microprocessor's clock rate. The clock rate is how often the CLK input to the microprocessor goes from low to high voltage. This rate is measured in *hertz* (abbreviated as Hz), or *cycles per second*. Modern microprocessors run at a rate between 20 and 200 million cycles per second (20 to 200 megahertz, or 20 to 200MHz). This means that the CLK input to the microprocessor cycles (goes from low to high voltage) 20 to 200 million times in one second. However, this is not always a reliable measure of a microprocessor's power. Some microprocessors can execute an entire instruction in just one cycle. Others take tens or even hundreds of cycles to execute just one instruction. Remember the nybble multiplication machine from Chapter 10? It took eight cycles to perform a single multiplication operation. So a microprocessor that runs at a high clock rate is not necessarily faster or more powerful than a microprocessor that runs at a slower clock rate. For example, Intel Corporation's 80386 microprocessor, which can run at 33MHz, is not as powerful as their 80486 microprocessor running at 25MHz. The 80486 executes more instructions in one second than the 80386.

WHEN SOMETHING GOES WRONG

By now you can appreciate how complicated a computer is. Millions of transistors work together in a computer at lightning-fast speed. A program running on the computer has to account for

- user input,

- the control of storage devices, and

- the handling of interrupts and exceptions.

However, computers are not perfect, and sometimes something goes wrong.

The most common thing that happens when something goes wrong in a computer is called a *freeze,* a *hang,* or a *system crash.* The computer stops generating output and accepting input. The image on the monitor is frozen, and typing on the keyboard no longer has any effect. The only thing that can be done is to turn the computer off and on again. A system crash can be very frustrating for the user. For example, suppose a user has been typing a large file using an editor for several hours. If a system crash occurs, the user has no way to instruct the editor to save the file permanently. The only thing to do is to turn the computer off and start all over again.

A system crash can be caused by a defective part in the computer. More commonly, it is caused by a defective program. The program fails to take some event into account, like an erroneous input by the user, or a problem with one of the I/O devices. Or, it may accidentally overwrite memory locations that are being used to store important data. As a result, it gets into an infinite loop and stops accepting input or updating the screen.

A much more serious kind of crash is a *disk crash.* A disk crash is when the head of a hard-disk drive crashes into the surface of the platter spinning under it. This results in the permanent destruction of files on the disk. Turning the computer off and on again will not work if the computer uses the hard disk during startup.

MODELING AND SIMULATION

Have you ever built a model car or plane? It may not have worked like a car or plane, but it looked a lot like the real thing. You may even have learned something about cars and planes, just by building models and studying them.

Models can also be built in computers. A computer model is a program that shows you how something in the real world looks or works. Computer models are often called *simulations*. If you know how something works, you can program a computer to share that knowledge with other people. Sometimes, models can also be instructional to the people who programmed them. Complicated machines from the real world can be simulated in a computer, because computers can rapidly perform difficult calculations. For example, a simulation can show people what happens during a car crash without actually wrecking real cars.

A very popular kind of computer simulation is a *flight simulator*. Programmers who fly, and know very well how planes work, can write mathematical equations to describe how cockpit controls affect the plane's motion. A flight simulator shows a user the inside of an airplane cockpit, complete with controls and the view through the cockpit windows. The user can manipulate the simulated cockpit controls using the keyboard or a joystick. The computer changes the picture to show the movement of the cockpit controls and calculates the motion of the plane. It keeps track of how the view from the cockpit changes and displays this on the monitor. The computer calculates the sizes and shapes of buildings and mountains and displays these as well. The user feels like he is actually flying the plane. The computer can even determine when the plane crashes, and show an explosion on the screen. A user can learn a great deal about flying a plane without ever leaving home (or risking an air catastrophe)!

Review

- All computers include a microprocessor, memory, storage devices, and I/O devices.

- When we say that a program is doing something, or that the computer is doing something, we really mean that the program is instructing the microprocessor to do it.

- A user and a computer communicate through I/O devices.

- An editor allows a user to create and modify ASCII files.

- An editor reads input from a mouse or keyboard. Based on the input, it modifies the contents of memory locations. The video circuit displays the text file that is in memory on the screen so the user can view it.

- With the appropriate keyboard or mouse input, the user of an editor can

  Add text to a file.

  Erase text from a file.

  Move text around in the file.

  Save the file on a disk.

  Edit files stored on a disk.

- A group of computers communicating and exchanging files over wires is called a network.

- Dedicated file servers are computers that do nothing but store and manage files for clients in the network.

- Dedicated print servers are computers that do nothing but print files for clients in the network.

- A terminal is an I/O device with a keyboard and a monitor. It has a simple microprocessor and just enough memory to communicate with mainframe computers.

- The parts of a computer you can touch are called hardware.

- The programs that a computer runs are called software.

- The speed and power of a computer can be measured in MIPS (millions of instructions per second) or MFLOPS (millions of floating-point operations per second).

- A program that shows how something works is called a model or simulation.

17

How Computers Are Programmed Using Languages

I N this chapter, I am going to describe various computer languages. I will explain how a computer can translate programs written in other languages into machine language.

LOW-, INTERMEDIATE-, AND HIGH-LEVEL LANGUAGES

I t takes a long time for a person to write a machine language program. The person writing the program, the *programmer,* must determine the number or numbers in every instruction. Each number depends on the op-code, the operands, and the addressing mode of the instruction. It is not difficult to determine the numbers, but it takes a long time to write just a few instructions. Once the programmer has the complete instructions, he or she must put them into memory for the microprocessor to execute. It is hard for a person to read a machine language program and find out what it does. This is because it consists of nothing but numbers.

The programmer's job would be much easier if the operation and the operands could be written in words. If someone else could translate the words into machine language instructions, the programmer would save a lot of time. A program written in words would also be easier to read and understand. It would also be helpful if there were some fast way to put the machine language instructions in memory.

A computer can do simple tasks rapidly and accurately, so it is ideal for translating words into machine language instructions. Once this is done, a computer can quickly put the instructions in its own memory. Instead of writing programs in machine language, the programmer can write them in an *intermediate-level* or a *high-level language.* Then, the computer can translate them into machine language. Machine language is considered a low-level language because machine language instructions don't need to be translated. The microprocessor interprets them directly. Programs written in intermediate-level and high-level languages consist of words. A microprocessor cannot interpret these words directly, so the words must be translated into machine language instructions. The computer itself can translate such programs by running other programs called *assemblers*, *compilers*, and *interpreters*.

Statements and Directives

In the English language, statements are groups of words. Every statement says one thing. "The bird is in the tree" is an example of a statement. "is in the tree" is not a statement, because it is missing words. "is the The bird tree in" is not a statement, because even though all the words are present, they are not in the right order. In both cases, the person reading the words cannot correctly interpret them.

Similarly, in high-level languages, statements consist of groups of words. Every statement tells the computer to do something. If words are missing from the statement, or if the words in a statement are not in the right order, then the computer cannot interpret them.

We can make statements that tell a person how to interpret other statements. You probably know of the "opposite" game, where a person might say, "Today is opposite day. It is freezing cold outside." When you hear the first statement, you know that you must interpret the second statement in an unusual way. In this case you would interpret the second statement as meaning that it is really very hot outside. In another type of game, you might hear something such as, "Kantimping means sailing. I had a great time kantimping on the bay today." When you hear the first statement, you know that you must interpret the second statement in an unusual way. In this case, you would interpret the second statement as meaning, "I had a great time sailing on the bay today." In computer languages, a statement that helps to interpret other statements is called a *directive*.

Assembly Language

Assembly language is an intermediate-level language. Unlike a low-level language, it consists of words that cannot be directly interpreted by a microprocessor. Each assembly language statement tells the microprocessor to execute just one machine language instruction. That is why it is not considered a high-level language. Most high-level language statements tell the microprocessor to execute several machine language instructions.

There are two types of words in assembly language: mnemonics and symbols. *Mnemonic* means "assisting the memory." Each mnemonic corresponds to a machine language operation. Mnemonics assist the memory because it is easier for a programmer to remember a word than to remember the op-code for an operation. The programmer must write the correct mnemonic for a particular operation. *Symbols* stand for numbers. The programmer can use any symbol for any number. However, the programmer must write a directive that tells the computer which number the symbol stands for. The programmer must write this directive before using the symbol.

Every machine language instruction includes an op-code, an addressing mode, and operands. Every assembly language statement conveys the same information—the mnemonic specifies the op-code and numbers or symbols specify the operands. The addressing mode can be specified in different ways. Sometimes, the programmer types an extra word to specify it. Sometimes, the programmer types special characters to specify it. For example, the programmer might type a register number followed by a plus sign (+). This would specify postincrement addressing mode using that register.

The following illustration shows part of an assembly language program. It contains two directives and seven statements. You can see references to the stack pointer (SP) and data registers (D1, D2). Each statement tells a Motorola 68000 microprocessor to execute one instruction.

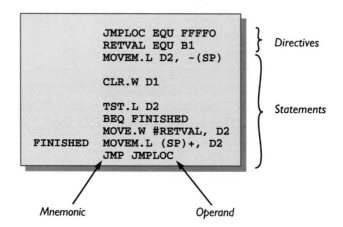

```
                    JMPLOC EQU FFFFO
                    RETVAL EQU B1            }  Directives
                    MOVEM.L D2, -(SP)

                    CLR.W D1

                    TST.L D2                    Statements
                    BEQ FINISHED
                    MOVE.W #RETVAL, D2
    FINISHED        MOVEM.L (SP)+, D2
                    JMP JMPLOC
```

Mnemonic   Operand

After a programmer writes a program, he needs some way to put the program where the microprocessor can access it. If it is a machine language program, the microprocessor must access the program to run it. If it is an intermediate-level or high-level language program, the microprocessor must access the program to translate it into machine language. The programmer can use an editor to put a program in a place where the microprocessor can access it.

An editor is almost always provided with every computer, so that users can create files. Every programmer writes the words of an intermediate- or high-level language program using an editor. The program is stored as ASCII numbers in a text file or in memory. However, the microprocessor should not execute these character codes. Each statement of the assembly language program is a command to execute a single machine language instruction. However, the ASCII numbers of the assembly language program are not the same as the machine language instruction numbers. If the microprocessor were to execute the numbers in the ASCII program file, it would not do what the program instructs it to do. The statements in the assembly language program file must be translated into machine language instruction numbers. Then, the microprocessor can execute these instructions.

To translate the assembly language program into machine language, the computer must run a program called an assembler. The *assembler* translates the character codes of assembly language statements into machine language instructions. If the assembly language program is in a text file, then the microprocessor brings it into memory. It then compares the character codes in the file with the character codes of assembly language words that it knows. In this way, the assembler "reads" the words. As the assembler reads an assembly language statement, it constructs the machine language instruction for that statement. When it reads the mnemonic, it knows the op-code. When it reads the numbers or symbols, it knows the operands. When it reads other words and characters in the statement, it knows the addressing mode. When it has the complete machine language instruction, the assembler can put the instruction in memory or write it to a file. If the microprocessor executes these instructions, it does what the programmer wanted it to do. The actions of an assembler are illustrated in Figure 17-1.

The assembler uses some memory to hold a symbol table. The *symbol table* contains the character codes of symbols followed by the numbers they stand for. A symbol table in memory is shown in this illustration. (The actual characters are shown instead of the ASCII numbers.) Initially, the symbol table is an unoccupied free block. The assembler knows no symbols. When the assembler reads a directive, it adds an entry to the symbol table. It writes the character codes of the symbol in the free block. Then it writes the number that the symbol stands for. If the assembler ever reads a word that is not a mnemonic, it checks whether the word is a symbol. It goes through the symbol table and compares the character codes of the word with the charac-

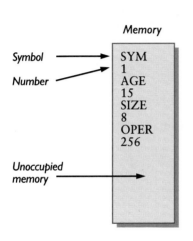

Memory

Symbol

Number

SYM
1
AGE
15
SIZE
8
OPER
256

Unoccupied memory

FIGURE 17-1

Assembler actions

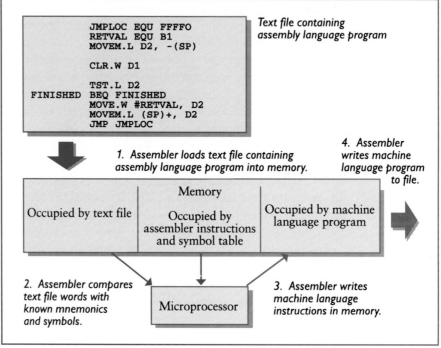

```
        JMPLOC EQU FFFF0
        RETVAL EQU B1
        MOVEM.L D2, -(SP)

        CLR.W D1

        TST.L D2
FINISHED BEQ FINISHED
        MOVE.W #RETVAL, D2
        MOVEM.L (SP)+, D2
        JMP JMPLOC
```

Text file containing assembly language program

1. Assembler loads text file containing assembly language program into memory.

4. Assembler writes machine language program to file.

Memory

Occupied by text file

Occupied by assembler instructions and symbol table

Occupied by machine language program

2. Assembler compares text file words with known mnemonics and symbols.

Microprocessor

3. Assembler writes machine language instructions in memory.

ter codes of the known symbols. If it finds a match, then it reads the number that the symbol stands for. It normally uses this number as one of the operands in an instruction.

An assembler contains very specific instructions to translate assembly language statements into machine language instructions. If the statements don't make sense, then the assembler prints a message on the computer screen. This message is called an *error message*. It tells the programmer that a mistake was made when the program was typed. The assembler can often figure out what kind of mistake the programmer made. It can tell the programmer

- if a word or character is missing,

- if there is a word or character that doesn't belong,

- if one of the operands is too large or too small,

- if a symbol was used before a directive specified what number it stood for, and

- other similar mistakes.

You might be wondering how editors and assemblers are written. After all, they are programs too! How can you write an editor program if you don't have an editor to write it with? How can you assemble an assembler program if you don't have an assembler to assemble it with? This is a lot like the "Which came first, the chicken or the egg?" question.

People who programmed the first computers wrote text files without editors. They typed on a special typewriter that produced punched cards. Each pattern of holes on the card was a code for a different character. Then, they fed the cards into a special input device. This device scanned the patterns and wrote the ASCII numbers of the characters in a file. The first assemblers had to be written in machine language. It was a difficult and time-consuming process, but it had to be done. Of course, once a simple assembler and editor were written, they could be used to write better assemblers and editors.

As you recall from Chapter 13, different microprocessors have different instruction sets. So, today, there is an assembler for every different microprocessor. Whenever someone invents a new microprocessor, an existing assembler is modified. It must be adapted to understand new mnemonics and to produce machine language instructions for the new microprocessor. The modified assembler runs on one microprocessor, but it produces machine language instructions for a different microprocessor. Such an assembler is called a *cross-assembler*.

COMPILERS

Writing programs in assembly language is much easier than writing them in machine language. The programmer only needs to know one easy-to-remember, easy-to-read mnemonic for each machine language instruction. The assembler takes care of the time-consuming task of figuring out the op-code, the addressing mode, and the operands of each instruction.

However, writing in assembly language is still quite difficult. This is because a single assembly language statement corresponds to a single machine language instruction. One machine language instruction can perform a simple operation on numbers in memory or in registers. However, to perform complex tasks, such as counting the number of words in a file, finding the square root of a number, or translating an assembly language program, many machine language instructions are required. Therefore, the programmer must write many assembly language statements.

In some languages, each statement gets translated into several machine language instructions. Such languages are called *high-level languages*. They allow a programmer to write a complete program with just a few simple statements. The statements get translated into a machine language program that might consist of hundreds of instructions.

Three examples of high-level languages are Pascal, C, and FORTRAN. The Pascal language is named after Blaise Pascal, a 17th century mathematician. C is the third revision (after A and B) of a language similar to Pascal. FORTRAN stands for formula translation. It was originally used to program computers to solve difficult mathematical problems.

Below are three programs. One is written in Pascal, one in FORTRAN, and one in C. They all do the same thing: they print a message, calculate the sum of the numbers from one to 100, and then print the sum. Here is the Pascal program:

```
program PascalExample(output);
     { An example Pascal program }
var index: integer; sum: integer;
begin
    writeln('The sum of the numbers from 1 to 100 is ');
    sum := 0;
    for index := 1 to 100 do
        sum := sum + index;
    writeln(sum);
end.
```

Here is the C program:

```
#include <stdio.h>
main() {
    int index, sum = 0;
    printf("The sum of the numbers from 1 to 100 is ");
    for (index = 1;  index <= 100;  index++)
        sum += index;
    printf("%d\n", sum);
    exit(0);
}
```

Here is the FORTRAN program:

```
    INTEGER INDEX, SUM
    PRINT *, 'The sum of the numbers from 1 to 100 is '
    SUM = 0
    DO 100 INDEX = 1, 100
        SUM = SUM + INDEX
```

```
100 CONTINUE
    PRINT *, SUM
    STOP
    END
```

A program that translates a high-level language into machine language is called a *compiler*. Often, a compiler will translate a high-level language program into an assembly language program. Then, an assembler will translate it into machine language. The ASCII file containing the high-level language program is the input to the compiler. The ASCII assembly language file is the output of the compiler and the input to the assembler. The output of the assembler is a file containing the machine language program, ready for the microprocessor to execute. This process is illustrated in Figure 17-2.

Compile-Time and Run-Time Errors

Sometimes, the compiler finds errors in the high-level language file. These errors are called *compile-time errors*. The programmer did not write the program correctly, so the compiler cannot translate it. If a program contains compile-time errors, the programmer must modify the text file using an editor.

Sometimes, a newly written program can be compiled and run, but it produces unexpected results. This is called a *run-time error*. It means that there was a difference between what the programmer *intended* the computer to do and what he *instructed* it to do. The computer cannot tell what the programmer really wanted it to do. It can only execute the program. So the computer cannot find run-time errors. The programmer must be extremely careful when writing a program. He must instruct the computer to do everything that he wants done—no more, no less.

For example, suppose the programmer wanted to instruct the computer to multiply two numbers and then print the result. Suppose that while typing the program, the programmer accidentally typed the plus sign instead of the multiplication sign. The compiler generates assembly language instructions to perform addition instead of multiplication. The assembler likewise generates machine language instructions to perform addition instead of multiplication. Finally, the microprocessor executes these instructions and produces the sum of two numbers. The compiler, the assembler, and the microprocessor all did exactly what the programmer instructed them to do. However, the result was not what the programmer expected. He must run the editor and examine the text file to see if he made any mistakes. If he is lucky, he will find the mistake quickly and be able to change it. Then, he must run the compiler and the assembler again to produce the machine

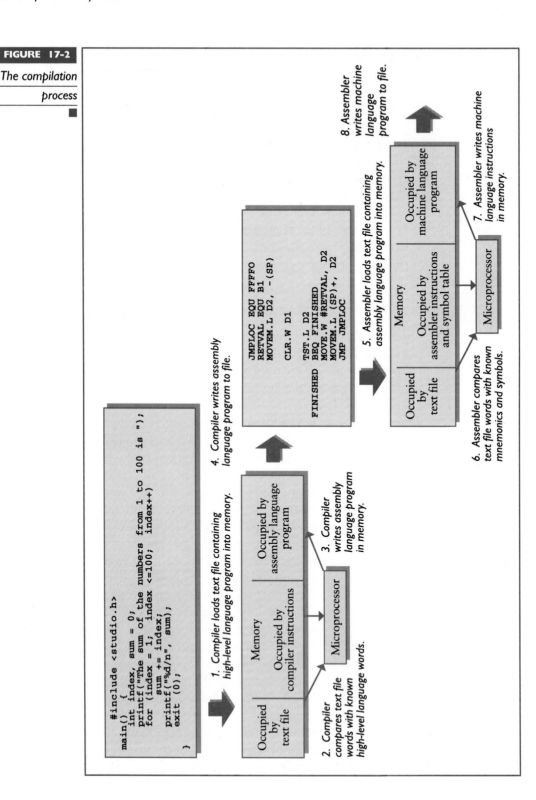

FIGURE 17-2

The compilation

process

```
#include <studio.h>
main() {
    int index, sum = 0;
    printf("The sum of the numbers from 1 to 100 is ");
    for (index = 1; index <=100; index++)
        sum += index;
    printf("%d/n", sum);
    exit (0);
}
```

1. Compiler loads text file containing high-level language program into memory.

Memory

Occupied by text file

Occupied by compiler instructions

Occupied by assembly language program

Microprocessor

2. Compiler compares text file words with known high-level language words.

3. Compiler writes assembly language program in memory.

4. Compiler writes assembly language program to file.

```
JMPLOC EQU FFFF0
RETVAL EQU B1
       MOVEM.L D2, -(SP)

       CLR.W D1

       TST.L D2
       BEQ FINISHED
       MOVE.W #RETVAL, D2
       MOVEM.L (SP)+, D2
FINISHED  JMP JMPLOC
```

5. Assembler loads text file containing assembly language program into memory.

Memory

Occupied by text file

Occupied by assembler instructions and symbol table

Occupied by machine language program

Microprocessor

6. Assembler compares text file words with known mnemonics and symbols.

7. Assembler writes machine language instructions in memory.

8. Assembler writes machine language program to file.

language file. Finally, he must make the microprocessor execute the machine language file.

INTERPRETERS

A programmer must take the following steps before the computer actually runs a high-level language program:

1. Run an editor and write the text file containing the high-level language program.
2. Run a compiler to produce the assembly language file.
3. Run an assembler to produce the machine language program file.
4. Make the microprocessor execute the machine language program.

If the programmer changes the program because of a run-time error, every step must be repeated. This is inconvenient and time-consuming. Beginning programmers write programs that have many compile-time and run-time errors. It is especially frustrating for them. However, there are languages that don't require a separate editor, compiler, and assembler. They are called *interpreted languages*. The program that is used to translate these languages is called an *interpreter*.

Just as a human interpreter can translate statements from one language to another while someone is speaking, so can an interpreter program translate high-level language statements into machine language as they are being typed in. An interpreter is like an editor with a built-in compiler and assembler. The programmer can type a statement and then press the RETURN key. This tells the interpreter to translate the statement into machine language and execute it immediately. If there is a compile-time error, the interpreter prints an error message immediately. If there is a run-time error, the programmer sees the results immediately. Either way, the result occurs immediately after the programmer types the statement, and it is much easier for a programmer to catch mistakes and correct them.

Of course, it is also inconvenient to retype every statement every time you want the microprocessor to run a program. So, interpreters have a way to store statements as a complete program. The program can be stored in memory or on disk. If the program is stored on disk, the programmer can then type a command to bring the program into memory. Once the program is in memory, the programmer can type another command to run the program from start to finish. The interpreter takes each statement of the program one at a time, translates it, and executes it. A program runs slowly in this manner. This is because the microprocessor spends a lot of time translating a statement before it executes it.

If the program contains no errors, it is a waste of time to translate it every time it is run. That's why most interpreters have a way to compile an interpreted-language program. The programmer can test statements using the interpreter, and quickly catch any errors. Then, he can put the statements in a program, and make sure the whole program works correctly. While he is still finding errors in the program, he won't mind that it runs slowly. When he is confident that the program contains no errors, the programmer can tell the interpreter to compile and assemble it. A complete, correct program is now ready to run, and the microprocessor won't have to waste time translating it any more.

BASIC and LISP are two interpreted languages. BASIC stands for beginner's all-purpose symbolic instruction code, and LISP stands for list processor. BASIC is the first programming language most people use, as it is easy to learn. Because it is an interpreted language, errors in programs can be quickly found and corrected. When a programmer is running a BASIC interpreter, he presses the RETURN key at the end of each statement. This causes the interpreter to translate and execute the statement. If the statement is preceded by a number, the interpreter stores the statement in memory to be executed later. The RUN statement causes the interpreter to execute the program in memory. Here is a BASIC program that prints a message, sums the numbers from 1 to 100, and prints the sum.

```
100 print "The sum of the numbers from 1 to 100 is"
105 sum = 0
110 for i = 1 to 100
120      sum = sum + i
130 next i
140 print sum
150 end
```

Here is a LISP program that prints a message, sums the numbers from 1 to 100, and prints the sum.

```
(defun example ()
    (print "The sum of the numbers from 1 to 100 is")
    (calc-sum 100))
(defun calc-sum (start)
    (if (eq start 0)
        0
```

```
                    (+ start (calc-sum (1- start)))))))
(example)
```

As you can see, LISP programs have many parentheses. Every LISP statement must have as many open parentheses (as closed parentheses) . When a programmer is running a LISP interpreter, the interpreter counts the number of times the programmer types parentheses. The interpreter can tell when the programmer has finished typing a statement by counting the number of open and closed parentheses. When the programmer types the last closed parenthesis and presses RETURN, the interpreter translates and executes the statement.

VARIABLES

In a high-level language, a *variable* is a symbol that stands for a memory address. It is called a variable because the contents of that memory location can vary. Suppose a program puts data at an address that is represented by a variable. We say that the data is "put into" the variable, or "assigned to" the variable. We say that the variable "contains" the data. For example, the following C statement assigns the value 32 to the variable **var**:

```
var = 32;
```

We don't know what address **var** stands for. The compiler picks a location in memory that is not being used. It decides that **var** should stand for this location's address. The programmer can use the symbol and let the compiler worry about exactly what address it will represent. This means there is one less thing for the programmer to deal with.

Once data is put into a variable, the variable can be used in place of the data. For example, the first of the following C statements assigns 32 to the variable **var**. The second assigns **var** to the variable **var2**. The result is that 32 is assigned to both **var** and **var2**.

```
var = 32;
var2 = var;
```

Sometimes, data takes up more than one location in memory. For example, a number that is several bits long might not fit in one location. It will have to be stored in consecutive locations. In such a case, the variable will represent the address of the first location where the number is stored.

OPERATORS, EXPRESSIONS, AND TYPES

An arithmetic *operator* is a symbol that tells us what to do with numbers. The + ("plus") arithmetic operator tells us to add the numbers on either side of it. The - ("minus") arithmetic operator tells us to subtract the number to its right from the number to its left. The * ("times") arithmetic operator tells us to multiply the numbers on either side of it. The / ("divided by") arithmetic operator tells us to divide the number to its left by the number to its right. To *apply* an operator means to perform the indicated operation.

An arithmetic *expression* is a collection of variables, numbers, operators, and other symbols. Together, the symbols in an expression stand for a number. The number that an arithmetic expression stands for is called its value. To *evaluate* an arithmetic expression means to find its value. An expression is evaluated by applying the operators to the numbers. An expression is said to "evaluate to" its value. A variable evaluates to the number it contains. For example, if the variable **num** contains four, then the following expression evaluates to 27:

```
((13 * num) + 2) / 2
```

This expression includes the following smaller arithmetic expressions. Each of them is a collection of numbers, variables, and operators that evaluate to some value:

```
13
num
2
(13 * num)
(13 * num) + 2
```

Parentheses tell us which operators to apply first. In the previous expression, * was applied first, then +, and finally /. In the following expression, + is applied first, then /, and finally *.

```
13 * ((num + 2) / 2)
```

The expression evaluates to 39. As you can see, the placement of parentheses is important in evaluating an expression.

Arithmetic operators are applied to number values. *Boolean* operators are applied to the Boolean values, TRUE and FALSE. The | ("or") Boolean operator checks whether *one* of the values on either side of it is TRUE. The & ("and") Boolean operator checks whether *both* of the values on either side of it are TRUE. A Boolean expression is a collection of variables, values, and operators that evaluate to a Boolean value. The following Boolean expressions all evaluate to TRUE:

```
TRUE & TRUE
```

```
TRUE | TRUE
```

```
TRUE | FALSE
```

```
FALSE | TRUE
```

The following Boolean expressions all evaluate to FALSE:

```
TRUE & FALSE
```

```
FALSE & TRUE
```

```
FALSE & FALSE
```

```
FALSE | FALSE
```

Some special operators are applied to numbers, but expressions containing these operators evaluate to Boolean values. The < ("less than") operator checks whether the value to its left is less than the value to its right. The > ("greater than") operator checks whether the value to its left is greater than the value to its right. The following Boolean expressions evaluate to TRUE:

```
32 < 64
```

```
(9–10) > (12–14)
```

The following Boolean expressions evaluate to FALSE:

```
18.3 < 17.2
```

```
–.001 > .001
```

All the operators we have looked at are applied to two values. They are called binary operators. *Unary* operators are applied to just one value. The ++ ("increment") unary arithmetic operator adds one to the value to its left. The -- ("decrement") unary arithmetic operator subtracts one from the value to its left. The following expressions both evaluate to four:

```
3++
```

```
5.0--
```

The ~ ("not") unary Boolean operator changes the value to its right. ~TRUE evaluates to FALSE. ~FALSE evaluates to TRUE.

One type of operator cannot be applied to a different type of value. For example, the following expressions make no sense.

```
TRUE + FALSE
```

```
26 | 32.3
```

The + arithmetic operator cannot be applied to Boolean values. And, the | Boolean operator cannot be applied to arithmetic values.

Why have I been talking about expressions so much? Expressions are a convenient way to instruct a computer to process data. All high-level languages allow a programmer to use expressions. It is easy for a compiler to check whether an expression makes sense. It is also easy for a compiler to translate an expression into instructions that evaluate the expression. For example, the following C statements instruct the computer to put −3 in the variable **result**, and to put the Boolean value FALSE in the variable **check_positive**:

```
first_value = 10;
second_value = first_value * 2;
result = (first_value + second_value) / (first_value -
second_value);
check_positive = (result > 0);
```

A computer stores all types of values as binary numbers, represented by high and low voltages. Whole numbers are stored as binary numbers. Character values are stored as ASCII numbers. Floating-point numbers are stored as binary numbers using a special code. The two Boolean values, TRUE and FALSE, are usually stored as a binary 1 and a binary 0. This creates a problem, though. Suppose a programmer types the following sequence of statements:

```
first_value = TRUE;
second_value = first_value * 2;
```

The expression in the second statement really makes no sense. The * is an arithmetic operator, and **first_value** contains a Boolean value. However, if the microprocessor executes the first statement, it would store a binary 1 in the location for **first_value**. If it executes the second statement, it would interpret this 1 as an arithmetic value. So it would multiply 1 by 2, and store the result in the location for **second_value**.

Most programming languages have a way to prevent this kind of confusion. They require the programmer to *declare* the type of value that he wants to store in a variable. A statement that declares the type of a variable is called a *declaration*. (The declaration also tells the compiler to find unoccupied memory for the variable.) The compiler needs to know the type of every variable to make sure it is used in expressions correctly. So it usually prints an error message if the programmer uses a variable without first declaring it.

Suppose the programmer typed the statements of the previous example in a program. If he attempted to compile the program, the compiler would print an error message saying that **first_value** is an undeclared variable. The programmer would then modify the program to look like this:

```
boolean first_value;
integer second_value;
first_value = TRUE;
second_value = first_value * 2;
```

The first statement declares **first_value** as a Boolean variable, a variable that can store TRUE or FALSE. The second statement declares **second_value** as an integer variable, a variable that can store whole numbers. Now, suppose the compiler tries to interpret the fourth statement. It will detect that an arithmetic operator (*) is being used to operate on a Boolean value (**first_value**). It will print an error message, and the programmer will have to modify the program to remove the confusion.

DATA STRUCTURES

P eople have been programming computers for many years. Programmers have found that it is useful to arrange data in memory in certain ways. An arrangement of data in memory is called a *data structure.* Most high-level programming languages support data structures: they help a programmer arrange data in useful ways. When we talk about data structures, we are talking about both the data itself and the manner in which it is arranged. By choosing a good data structure over a poor one, a programmer can make a program run faster and use less memory.

Arrays

When consecutive memory locations contain similar data, the memory locations together form an *array.* Each number in the array is called an *element* of the array. The position of an element in the array is called its *index.* The programmer can access each element of an array by specifying

- the first location of the array, and

- the index of the element.

Most high-level languages allow a programmer to declare array type variables. The variable stands for the address of the first element in the array.

For example, suppose the number of inches of rain that fell in your city during the years 1980 to 1989 was stored in memory locations 20000 to 20009. This is shown in the illustration here. Suppose that the array was assigned to the variable **rain**. So **rain** is a symbol that represents the address 20000. To access the first element of the array, you would write **rain[0]**. This tells the compiler to access the location 0 locations after 20000. To access the tenth element of the array, you would write **rain[9]**. This tells the compiler to access the location 9 locations after 20000. **rain[0]** and **rain[9]** can be considered symbols for the *contents* of addresses 20000 and 20009.

Address	Content	
		rain
20000	70	rain [0]
20001	67	
20002	54	
20003	60	
20004	61	
20005	67	
20006	73	
20007	69	
20008	66	
20009	62	rain [9]

Records

It is convenient to store related data items together, especially if they are to be processed as a group. For example, suppose a program processes data about a company's employees. Information about an employee might be stored in consecutive memory locations. The first locations might hold the ASCII numbers for the name of the employee. This might be followed by the employee's salary and phone number. Such a group of related data items is called a *record*. A record is illustrated here. (The actual characters are shown instead of their ASCII numbers.) Each item in a record is called a *field*. An array of employee records could be stored in alphabetical order (by employee name) in the memory of the computer. The microprocessor could quickly find the information about an employee by searching through the first field of every record. When the correct record was found, the microprocessor could read the next few locations to find the other fields. If this sounds familiar, it's because an assembler's symbol table is often an array of records.

Most high-level languages allow a programmer to declare record type variables. The variable stands for the address of the first of the locations that holds the record. The programmer can also name the fields in a record to access them individually.

Field name	Memory content
employee_name	L. M. Fraely
salary	28000
phone	5035551212

Pointers

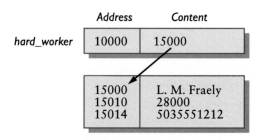

Address	Content
hard_worker 10000	15000
15000	L. M. Fraely
15010	28000
15014	5035551212

A pointer is a variable that contains the address of another data structure. For example, suppose the address of an employee record is stored in the variable **hard_worker**. This is illustrated here. **hard_worker** is a symbol that represents an address. Stored at that address in memory is *another* address. This second address is actually the address of the first location of an employee record.

Linked Lists

One problem with an array is that you cannot add an element between two elements. For example, suppose that the scores a class of students got on a test are stored in an array, as shown in Figure 17-3. There is one element

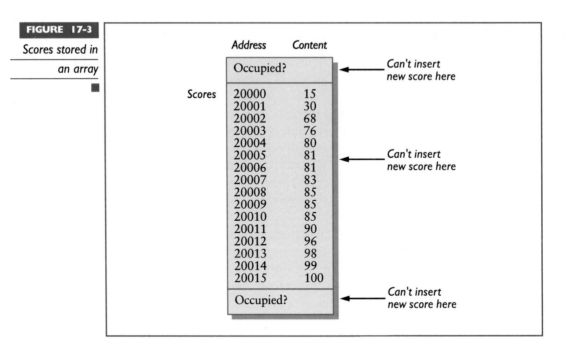

FIGURE 17-3

Scores stored in

an array

■

for each student. The elements are sorted from lowest to highest. The lowest score that any student got is stored in the first element. The highest score that any student got is stored in the last element. This array is assigned to the variable **scores**.

Now, suppose a new student takes the same test. If the new student's score is lower than the lowest score, then where should it be stored? It can't be stored in the memory location before the first element, because that location might be occupied by another variable. If the new student's score is higher than the highest score, it can't be stored in the memory location following the last element, because that location might be occupied by another variable. If the new student's score is between the highest and lowest score, it can't be stored in any of the memory locations in the array, because they are all occupied. The only solution is to find enough unused consecutive memory locations to store the old array as well as the new element. The new array, including the new element, could be stored in these locations. This is not easy to do in most programming languages. So the number of elements in an array is almost always fixed.

A better solution is to store each score in a record. Each record has two fields: **score** and **next_record**. The first field contains the score. The second field is a pointer containing the address of the next record. **scores** is a pointer variable that contains the address of the first record. So **scores** stands for an address. Stored at that address is the address of the first record. The first record contains the first score and the address of the second record. The second record contains the second score and the address of the third record, and so on. In the last record, the **next_record** field contains 0. This means there are no more records. Such a data structure is called a *linked list*. It is a collection of records. Each record includes a score and a pointer, or link, to the next record. The scores in the array of Figure 17-3 are shown in a linked list in Figure 17-4.

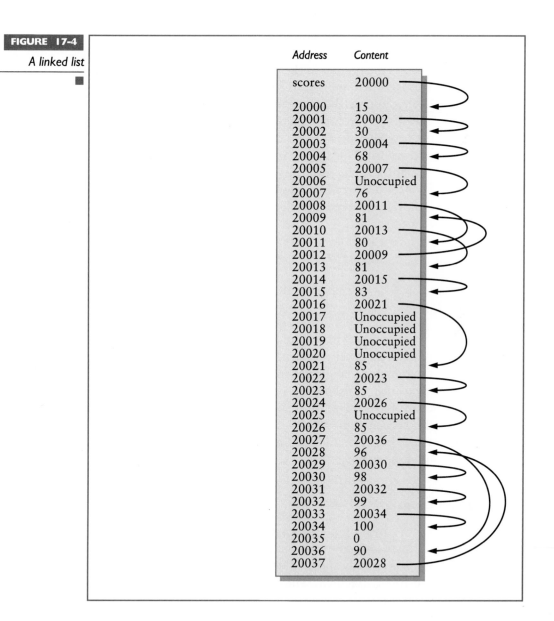

Address	Content
scores	20000
20000	15
20001	20002
20002	30
20003	20004
20004	68
20005	20007
20006	Unoccupied
20007	76
20008	20011
20009	81
20010	20013
20011	80
20012	20009
20013	81
20014	20015
20015	83
20016	20021
20017	Unoccupied
20018	Unoccupied
20019	Unoccupied
20020	Unoccupied
20021	85
20022	20023
20023	85
20024	20026
20025	Unoccupied
20026	85
20027	20036
20028	96
20029	20030
20030	98
20031	20032
20032	99
20033	20034
20034	100
20035	0
20036	90
20037	20028

As you can see, the records do not need to be stored in consecutive memory locations. You can always find one of the records by following the pointers, starting with the pointer in **scores**.

When a new student takes the test, the program only needs to find enough unused consecutive memory locations to store one new record. The new student's score is stored in the first location of the record. Suppose the new student's score is 110, higher than the highest score. The program changes the pointer in the last record to point to the new record, and changes the pointer in the new record to 0. This is shown in Figure 17-5.

Or, suppose the new student's score is 10, lower than the lowest score. The program changes the value in **scores** to point to the new record, and changes the pointer in the new record to point to what was the first record. This is shown in Figure 17-6.

Or, suppose the new student's score is 84, between the highest and the lowest. The program changes the pointer in one of the records to point to the new record, and changes the pointer in the new record to point to the next record. This is shown in Figure 17-7.

In this manner, elements can be inserted in the middle of a linked list. This involves less trouble than inserting an element in the middle of an array. However, a linked list takes up more memory to store the same number of elements.

CONTROL STRUCTURES

Programmers have found that certain sequences of instructions are useful. A useful sequence of instructions is called a *control structure*. Most high-level programming languages support control structures: they have special statements that translate into useful instruction sequences. When we talk about control structures, we are talking about both the instructions themselves and the sequence in which they are executed. By choosing a good control structure over a poor one, a programmer can make a program run faster and use less memory.

FOR Loops

It is often useful for a set of statements to be executed a certain number of times. One control structure that allows this is the *FOR loop*. Every FOR loop has a body and an index variable. The body is the set of statements that are to be executed. The index variable stores the number of times the

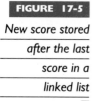

FIGURE 17-5

New score stored after the last score in a linked list

■

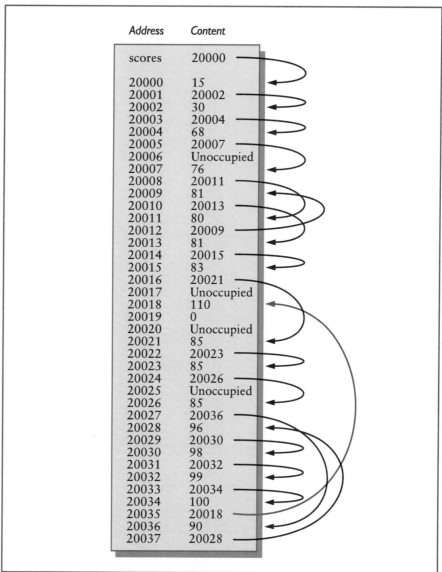

statement has been executed. The following C statements include a FOR loop. The FOR loop specifies that its body should be executed ten times. The statements add up the numbers in a ten-element array and print the result.

```
int index, sum, array[10];
sum = 0;
for (index = 0;  index < 10;  index++)  {
```

FIGURE 17-6

New score inserted before the first score in a linked list

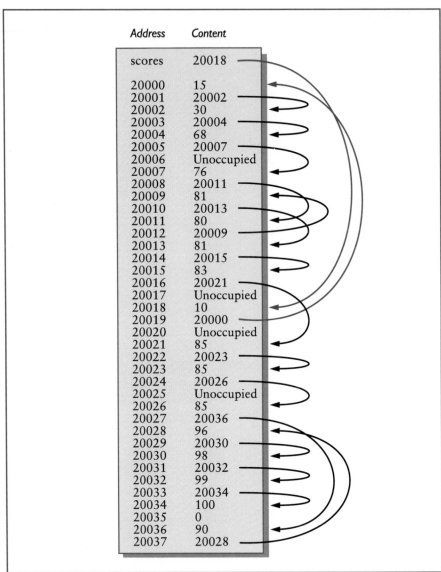

```
        sum = sum + array[index];
}
printf("Sum of elements in array is %d.\n", sum);
```

The programmer specifies the body by putting it between braces { }. The FOR statement does three things:

Address	Content
scores	20000
20000	15
20001	20002
20002	30
20003	20004
20004	68
20005	20007
20006	Unoccupied
20007	76
20008	20011
20009	81
20010	20013
20011	80
20012	20009
20013	81
20014	20015
20015	83
20016	20018
20017	Unoccupied
20018	84
20019	20021
20020	Unoccupied
20021	85
20022	20023
20023	85
20024	20026
20025	Unoccupied
20026	85
20027	20036
20028	96
20029	20030
20030	98
20031	20032
20032	99
20033	20034
20034	100
20035	0
20036	90
20037	20028

1. It sets the initial value of the index variable:

```
(index = 0;
```

2. It specifies that the index variable should be incremented every
   time the body is executed:

```
index++)  {
```

3. It says that the body should be executed while the index variable is less than ten.

```
index < 10;
```

As you can see, the index variable is used

■ to count the number of times the body has been executed, and

■ to access the elements of the array, one at a time.

WHILE Loops

It is often useful for a set of statements to be executed for as long as a certain condition is true. One control structure that allows this is the *WHILE loop*. Every WHILE loop has a body and a Boolean expression. If the expression evaluates to TRUE, then the body is executed, and the expression is evaluated again. This continues until the expression evaluates to FALSE. The following C statements examine the elements of an array until a number less than zero is found.

```
int element_number;
int array[10];
boolean found;
element_number = 0;
found = FALSE;
while ((element_number < 10) && ~found)
{
    found = (array[element_number] < 0);
    element_number = element_number++;
}
```

Again, the programmer specifies the body by putting it between braces. The WHILE statement specifies that the body should be executed while a certain expression evaluates to TRUE. The statements in the body of a WHILE loop must change a variable that is used in the Boolean expression. Otherwise, the expression will never evaluate to FALSE. The statements will get executed over and over again.

DO Loops

It is often useful for a set of statements to be executed repeatedly until a certain condition is no longer true. One control structure that allows this is the *DO loop*. Every DO loop has a body and a Boolean expression. The body is executed once. If the expression evaluates to TRUE, then the body is executed again. This continues until the expression evaluates to FALSE. The following C statements also examine the elements of an array until a number less than zero is found.

```
int element_number;
int array[10];
boolean found;
element_number = 0;
found = FALSE;
do  {
    found = (array[element_number] < 0);
    element_number = element_number++;
} while ((element_number < 10) && ~found);
```

The body of a WHILE loop may never get executed if the Boolean expression evaluates to FALSE initially. However, the body of a DO loop always gets executed at least once.

IF-THEN and IF-THEN-ELSE Structures

Often, the programmer wants some statements to be executed just once if a certain condition is true. One high-level language control structure that allows this is the *IF-THEN structure*. Every IF-THEN structure has a body and a Boolean expression. If the expression evaluates to TRUE, then the body is executed; otherwise, it is not. A related control structure is the IF-THEN-ELSE structure. Every *IF-THEN-ELSE* structure has a Boolean expression and *two* bodies. If the expression evaluates to TRUE, then the first body is executed. If the expression evaluates to FALSE, then the second body is executed.

The following C statements print "Less than zero." if the variable **var** is less than zero; "Greater than zero." if the variable **var** is greater than zero; and "Equal to zero." if it is equal to zero.

```
if (var < 0) {
    printf("Less than zero.");
} else {
```

```
if (var > 0) {
    printf("Greater than zero.");
} else {
    if (var == 0) {
        printf("Equal to zero.");
    }
}
}
```

You might have noticed that the second body of the first IF statement is a second IF statement. The second body of the second IF statement is a third IF statement. When the body of one control structure contains a second control structure of the same kind, the second control structure is said to be *nested* in the first.

SWITCH-CASE Structure

Often, the programmer wants several different things to happen, depending on the value of a variable. One high-level language control structure that allows this is the SWITCH-CASE structure. Every SWITCH-CASE structure has a SWITCH variable and a number of CASE statements. Every CASE statement has a possible value for the variable and a body of statements. If the value of the SWITCH variable matches the value of one of the CASE statements, then the body of that CASE statement is executed. A default CASE can also be specified. If the value of the SWITCH variable doesn't match any of the values of the other CASE statements, then the body of the default CASE statement is executed.

In the following C statement, the variable **hour** is supposed to contain a number from 0 to 23. The statement prints a message if **hour** contains some special values. Otherwise, it just prints the variable.

```
switch (hour) {
    case 8: {
        printf("Breakfast time.");
        break
    }
    case 12: {
        printf("Lunch time.");
        break;
    }
    case 18: {
        printf("Dinner time.");
```

```
        break;
    }
    case 0: {
        printf("Midnight.");
        break;
    }
    default: {
        printf("%d hundred hours.", hour);
        break;
    }
}
```

The word break means that the execution of the SWITCH statement is finished, and execution should continue with the next statement.

Review

- It is difficult for a programmer to write a program in a low-level language like machine language.

- It is easier for a programmer to write a program in an intermediate- or high-level language. The computer can do the work of translating the program into machine language.

- A statement is a group of words that instructs the computer to do something.

- A directive is a group of words that tells the computer how to interpret other statements.

- Each intermediate-level language statement translates to one machine language instruction. Each high-level language statement may translate to several machine language instructions.

- Mnemonics are assembly language words that correspond to machine language operations. An assembler knows how to translate mnemonics into machine language op-codes.

- Symbols are assembly language words that stand for numbers. A programmer must use directives to tell an assembler how to translate symbols into numbers.

- The input to an assembler is a text file containing an assembly language program. The output of an assembler is a file containing a machine language program.

- A cross-assembler runs on one microprocessor but produces machine language instructions for a different microprocessor.

- The input to a compiler is a text file containing a high-level language

Review (continued)

program. The output of a compiler is a text file containing an assembly language program.

■ A compile-time error occurs when a high-level language program doesn't make sense to the compiler. A compiler detects compile-time errors and prints error messages.

■ A run-time error occurs when a program is compiled and run but produces unexpected output. A compiler cannot detect run-time errors.

■ Interpreted languages don't require a separate editor, compiler, and assembler.

■ An interpreter can translate and execute a statement immediately after the programmer types it.

■ An interpreter can store a program in memory or on disk. When the program is run, the interpreter translates and executes each stored statement.

■ Most interpreters can compile a program after the programmer has corrected errors.

■ A variable is a symbol that stands for an address.

■ An expression is a collection of variables, numbers, operators, and other symbols that together stand for a value. Expressions are a convenient way to instruct a computer to perform operations on variables.

■ Most programming languages require the programmer to declare the type of a variable. This prevents confusion when the compiler translates expressions.

■ A data structure is an arrangement of data in memory. By choosing a good data structure, a programmer can make a program run faster and use less memory.

■ A control structure is a useful sequence of instructions. By choosing a good control structure, a programmer can make a program run faster and use less memory.

18

What Operating Systems Do

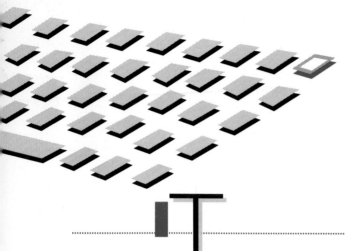

T H E operating system is the most important program that runs on every computer. It starts all other programs that the computer runs. There are some tasks that almost all programs need to perform. The operating system makes a programmer's job easier by doing these tasks for a program. There are some tasks that can be dangerous to the computer. The operating system makes the programmer's job less accident-prone by doing these tasks safely. In this chapter, I am going to discuss the important tasks performed by the operating system. I'll start by describing how programs are assisted by the operating system. Then, I'll describe how operating systems control programs and manage files.

ASSISTING PROGRAMS

There are certain things that almost every program must do. For example, almost all programs must get input from the keyboard and must read and write files. The operating system can include instructions on exactly how to do these things. So, every program doesn't need a separate copy of these instructions. The programs can just ask the operating system to execute its instructions.

In some computers, certain files, devices, registers, and memory locations contain important information. These are important resources that the computer needs if it is to function correctly. The operating system protects these resources, making it difficult for the user to damage or crash the computer (on purpose or by accident). A programmer can write a program without worrying that it might damage the computer. If something risky needs to be done, the operating system does it carefully and safely. If the program must access a protected resource, it can ask the operating system to access it safely on the program's behalf.

How does a program ask the operating system to perform common tasks or access protected resources? By calling *system service routines*, which are part of the operating system. Some system service routines perform actions that almost all programs need to do. For example, suppose a program needs to get input from the keyboard or needs to read or write a file. It simply executes a system call instruction with the correct system call number, and the system service routine performs the task for the program. The instructions are written in just one place, the system service routine, instead of in every program.

Other system service routines access protected resources carefully and safely. Protected resources are only accessible using protected instructions. For example, protected instructions can access any address. Unprotected instructions may not be allowed to access some addressess. Suppose I/O devices are activated by accesses to these addresses. Then these I/O devices will be inaccessible to the microprocessor if the mode bit is cleared.

User programs cannot contain protected instructions, so they cannot directly access protected resources. System service routines can contain protected instructions. The operating system is written by experienced programmers who know the computer well. So system service routines take all necessary precautions before accessing protected resources. When a user program must access a protected resource, it just executes a system call instruction with the correct system call number. The system service routine makes sure that the access is safe.

RUNNING PROGRAMS AND MANAGING FILES

For a computer to do anything useful, it must run a program. To write a program, a programmer must run an editor or an interpreter. To compile and assemble a program, he must run compilers and assemblers on the computer.

In Chapter 13, I discussed the startup program. This is the first program that the microprocessor executes. You might be wondering how the computer moves from one program to another. When one program has completed its job, how does the computer find out which program to run next? How does the computer actually run the next program? The answer to these questions is by using the operating system. The operating system always includes a program that starts other programs. When other programs complete their jobs, the operating system starts running again.

In some computers, the operating system is stored in ROM. When the startup program has completed its tasks, it jumps to the operating system in ROM. But, there is a problem with this. If errors in the operating system need to be fixed, or if the operating system is to be improved, then old ROM chips must be removed from the computer and replaced with new ones.

It is more convenient for the operating system to be stored on disk, and executed from RAM. In this case, the startup program reads the operating system into RAM and then jumps to its starting address. Updating the operating system is now easy. If the operating system is normally read from a floppy disk, the user simply inserts a different disk into the disk drive. If the operating system is normally read from a hard disk, the user replaces the old operating system file on the hard disk.

The operating system on a personal computer takes input from the user through the keyboard or mouse. Every operating system accepts a command to load the directory sector of a disk into memory. Then, it can display information about the files stored on the disk. The operating system normally displays the name, size, type, and date of creation of the file.

Every operating system allows the user to choose a program file that is stored on the disk. The operating system reads the file from the disk and puts it in a section of memory that is not being used. One way to start the program is for the operating system to *call* the program as if it were a subroutine. There must be a return instruction at the end of the program. (The compiler that translated the program can make sure this is so.) When the program is finished, the return instruction causes the microprocessor to start executing operating system instructions again. Now, the operating system can let the user select another program to run.

Operating systems can also accept commands to copy files from one disk to another, change the names of files, and erase files.

EARLY OPERATING SYSTEMS

Simple computer systems usually have minimal operating systems. For example, the first personal computers just ran a BASIC interpreter as an operating system. This interpreter would accept keyboard input from the user and display output on the screen. The BASIC interpreter could execute BASIC commands and store and run BASIC programs. It could also load BASIC and machine language programs from disk or tape.

For people who wanted to learn about programming computers in BASIC, this kind of operating system was fine. However, others were interested in running programs that were already written. To accommodate these people, computers were supplied with a disk operating system (DOS). A *disk operating system* helps to run programs stored on disks and to manage disk files. The startup program checks whether there is a disk in the disk drive. If so, it checks whether a DOS is stored on that disk. Then, it loads the DOS into memory and begins executing it. If there is no DOS on the disk, or if there is no disk in the disk drive, the startup program starts a BASIC interpreter stored in ROM.

MODERN OPERATING SYSTEMS

You might remember from Chapter 16 that a microprocessor can execute millions of instructions in a second (MIPS). In early computers, the microprocessor would run a single program for a single user; however, computer scientists and engineers discovered that the microprocessor wasted a lot of time. For example, when running an editor, a microprocessor spends most of its time just waiting for user input and much less time doing useful things, such as saving files. Early computers were very expensive; therefore, it was important that a microprocessor spend most its time doing useful things.

Time-Sharing

If many users access the computer simultaneously, the microprocessor always has something to do. While the microprocessor is waiting for input from one user, it can do something useful for another. Modern mainframe computers use operating systems that are *time-sharing*—the operating system makes sure that the microprocessor's time is shared by multiple users. The microprocessor runs one user's program for a brief period of time. Then, it runs the next user's program, then the third user's, and so on for all the users. It then goes back to the first user's program, continuing where it left off. By doing a bit of work for each user in turn, the microprocessor eventually runs all of the programs from start to finish.

Figure 18-1 shows how two types of operating systems run programs for three users. The first type is not time-sharing. It runs the first user's program from start to finish. Other users have to wait for the first user's program to

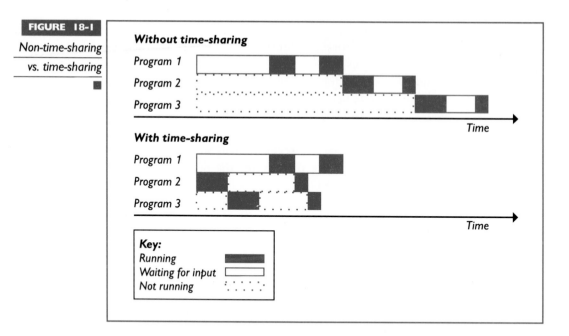

FIGURE 18-1

Non-time-sharing
vs. time-sharing

■

Without time-sharing

Program 1
Program 2
Program 3

Time

With time-sharing

Program 1
Program 2
Program 3

Time

Key:
Running
Waiting for input
Not running

complete. The longer the first user takes to provide input, the longer the other users must wait.

The second type of operating system is time-sharing. As you can see, while it is waiting for user input to the first program, the microprocessor is running the other users' programs. Eventually, all three programs get completed more quickly than with a non-time-sharing operating system.

Processes and Process Context

The concept of a process makes time-sharing possible. A *process* is a program that is being executed. If a program is being executed, then certain things about the computer must be true. For example:

■ The program and its variables must be in memory.

■ The microprocessor's program counter (PC) must point to one of the program instructions.

■ The program status word (PSW) must reflect instructions that have already been executed.

Together, the things that must be true when a program is running are called the *process context*. For the computer to be running the program, the process context must be "in place." If a process context is not in place, the program is not running. However, there can be a record of the process context in memory. The computer can put the process context back in place by examining this record. This is called *restoring* a process context. When a process context is restored, the program starts running.

Things that have no effect on the execution of a program are not part of the process context. For example, if a certain memory location is never accessed by a program, then that location is not part of the program's process context. The contents of that location make no difference to the program.

Context Swaps

For an operating system to be time-sharing, it must be able to perform a *context swap*. It must be able to stop one process, save its process context, and restore a second process context. Since the second process context is in place, the second program starts running.

To summarize, if the microprocessor is running a program, the operating system should be able to interrupt the process. It should save a record of the program, its variables, and the contents of microprocessor registers. It should then examine the process context of another program. It should load new values in the microprocessor registers, and load the new program and variables into memory. The microprocessor will now run the new program. This is called a context swap because the context of one process is traded for the context of another. To continue the first program where it left off, the operating system must stop the current process. It must save its context, and restore the saved context of the first process. Now, the first program begins to run as if it had never been interrupted. A context swap is illustrated in Figure 18-2.

The process context is always saved in the process table. This is an array of records that the operating system maintains in memory. Each record contains the process context for a process that has been stopped.

When the computer is first turned on and a time-sharing operating system begins running, the process table is empty. This is because there is only one process, the operating system, and it is not stopped.

When a user asks the operating system to run the first program, the operating system brings the program into memory. Just before beginning execution of the first program, the operating system stores its own context in one of the process table entries. The first program executes for some time. Then a context swap occurs. While the operating system is running again, a user has a chance to start running a second program. Now, three processes take turns executing on the computer: the operating system and two programs. In this manner, the computer can run several programs for several users.

FIGURE 18-2

Context swap

■

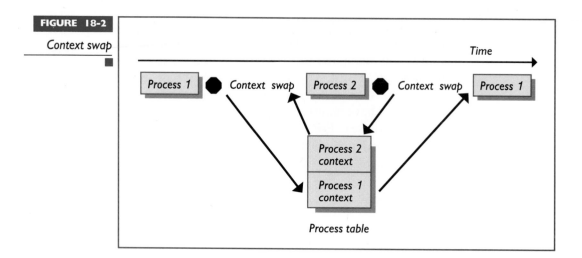

A context swap is not as difficult as it might seem. There are two ways to perform one.

YIELD SYSTEM SERVICE ROUTINES   The first way to perform a context swap is for a program itself to ask for one. A program does this when it contains a *yield* system call. When the microprocessor executes a yield system call, it sets the mode bit and calls the yield system service routine. This service routine saves the current process context in the process table. Then, the yield system service routine goes to the next record in the process table. This record contains the context of another process. The yield system service routine restores this context and a program that was previously stopped, continues. When the microprocessor executes the yield system call in this program, the yield system service routine performs another context swap. Eventually, the yield system service routine restores the context for the first process again. The first program continues where it left off.

There is a problem with doing a context swap inside a yield system service routine. The routine is called only if the microprocessor executes a yield system call in a program. If a program contains no yield system calls, then other processes won't be allowed to finish. Even if the program does contain some yield system calls, they may never actually be executed. Again, other processes won't be allowed to finish. All processes will be allowed to execute and finish only if all programs contain yield system calls that are executed.

TIMER INTERRUPT SERVICE ROUTINES   Another way to do a context swap, one that doesn't require yield instructions, is inside a timer interrupt service routine. Almost all computers contain a simple I/O device called a *timer*. Often, this device is built right into the microprocessor. The microprocessor can program the timer by writing a number to one of its registers. This number is called the *countdown value*. The microprocessor can start the timer by writing to another register. When the timer is started, it starts counting down from the countdown value to zero. Every cycle, it counts the next number. When the timer reaches zero, it makes one of the microprocessor's interrupt lines go to high voltage. Then, it makes the interrupt line go to low voltage and starts counting again. By programming the timer, the microprocessor can arrange to have one of its interrupt lines go to high voltage at regular intervals.

As you learned in Chapter 13, whenever one of the interrupt lines goes to high voltage, the microprocessor executes an interrupt service routine. The task that the timer interrupt service routine performs will happen at regular intervals. If the interrupt service routine does a context swap, then a context swap will occur at regular intervals. It doesn't matter whether the programs running on the microprocessor contain any yield instructions or not. At regular intervals, the timer interrupt line will go to high voltage, the microprocessor will execute the interrupt service routine, and this routine will cause a context swap. Then, all processes will get a fair chance to run to completion.

Virtual Memory

Believe it or not, no matter how much memory a computer has, it always seems to run out. Programs use more and more memory until all of it is occupied by important data. Also, in computers with time-sharing operating systems, many programs can compete for memory simultaneously. *Virtual memory* is a way to make a microprocessor think it has more memory than it really has. The term *virtual* is used to describe something that does not really exist, but which seems to.

If you remember from Chapter 12, the address space of a microprocessor is the range of numbers, including zero, that the microprocessor can put on the address bus. The size of the address bus determines the size of the address space. Virtual memory is used when the address space of the microprocessor is larger than the amount of memory it actually has. The range of addresses that the computer actually has memory for is called the *physical address space*. It depends on the number of memory chips in the computer and the number of address lines those chips have. When discussing virtual memory, the address space of the microprocessor is called the *virtual address space*.

The virtual address space of a microprocessor with a 16-bit address bus extends from 0 to $(2^{16} - 1)$ or 0 to 65,535. The address bus is not big enough to put an address greater than 65,535 on it. We say that the microprocessor can address up to 65,536 bytes, or 64 kilobytes. Since most computers have a least 64KB of RAM, the virtual address space of a microprocessor with a

16-bit address bus is usually not larger than the physical address space of the computer. Many modern microprocessors, however, have 24- or 32-bit address buses. This allows them to put over four billion addresses on the address bus. Even very large workstations have only 256 megabytes of RAM. So the virtual address space of a microprocessor with a 24- or 32-bit address bus is always much larger than the physical address space of the computer.

What happens if the microprocessor puts an address on the address bus that is larger than the physical address space of the computer? Suppose we have a computer with a 22-bit physical address space. Its memory would then have 2^{22} or 4,194,304 locations. Suppose also that the microprocessor has a 32-bit address bus. What if the microprocessor puts the address $(2^{22} + 1)$ on the address bus?

The computer could be built so that the uppermost bits on the address bus are ignored. For example, a four megabyte memory requires 22 address lines (a 22-bit address bus). When a microprocessor with a 32-bit address bus is connected directly to such a memory, the ten leftmost bits of the address bus could be left unconnected. This is shown in Figure 18-3. Now suppose the microprocessor put on the address bus a virtual address that was larger than the physical address space of the computer. The ten leftmost bits of this virtual address would be ignored. The other bits would activate an address that was in the physical address space of the computer. In such a computer, the microprocessor would access the exact same memory location at multiple addresses in its virtual address space. For example, all of the following binary addresses would access the exact same location in memory, since the ten leftmost bits of each address would be ignored:

00000000001111111111111111111111

00000000101111111111111111111111

00000001101111111111111111111111

11111111111111111111111111111111

This is only a few of the 2^{10} virtual addresses that would access the exact same physical address. This is not an acceptable way to build a computer. The microprocessor can put any address on the address bus, but it really doesn't have more than four megabytes of storage for data or programs. The program may instruct the microprocessor to write to a large address; however, this may overwrite a smaller address that is being used. Or, the program may instruct the microprocessor to read from a large address, but it may instead read from a smaller address that contains the wrong data.

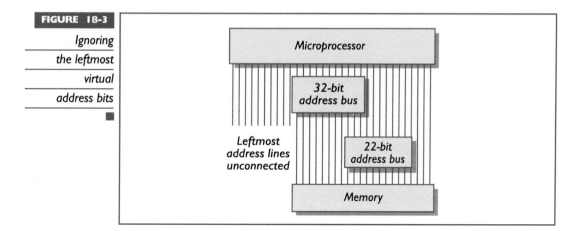

There is a better solution to this problem. In this case, the virtual address space extends from 0 to $2^{32}-1$. The physical address space extends from 0 to $2^{22}-1$. If the microprocessor generates an address that is smaller than 2^{22}, it can read or write a physical memory location. If the microprocessor generates an address that is larger than $2^{22}-1$, there is no location to access. However, the computer can *recognize this and read from or write to the hard-disk drive instead.*

This is the basic principle behind virtual memory. The contents of some virtual addresses are stored in physical memory, and the contents of other virtual addresses are stored on the hard disk. The computer keeps track of which addresses are stored where. Suppose the microprocessor generates a virtual address whose contents are stored in physical memory. Then, the access takes place as usual. Suppose the microprocessor generates a virtual address whose contents are stored on the hard disk. Then, the computer reads data from or writes data to the disk. Either way makes no difference to the microprocessor. Virtual memory makes the entire virtual address space available to the microprocessor for storage. Disk accesses are much slower than the memory accesses, but the illusion of a huge memory is worth the delay.

In order to have virtual memory, a microprocessor must have a *memory management unit* (MMU). This is a circuit that keeps track of whether the contents of addresses are stored in physical memory or on disk. The MMU is sometimes built into the microprocessor, and is sometimes sold on a separate chip.

Pages

In a computer with virtual memory, the virtual address space of the microprocessor is divided into ranges of memory. Each range is called a *page*.

A page is large enough to hold plenty of useful information, yet it is also small enough so that its contents can be written to or read from the hard disk very quickly. Pages are typically 1 to 4KBs in size. The physical address space is also divided into physical pages. Virtual pages are the same size as physical pages. However, since the virtual address space is larger than the physical address space, there are more virtual pages than physical pages. This is illustrated in Figure 18-4.

The most significant bits of an address determine which page it is on. The least significant bits are called the *offset* into the page. They determine the location within the page. For example, if pages are 4KB, or 4,096 bytes, in length, then it is the lower 12 bits of an address that determine the offset. A virtual address can be thought of as a virtual page number and an offset. A physical address can be thought of as a physical page number and an offset. A computer with a 32-bit virtual address space and a 12-bit page size would have 20 bits of virtual pages. It would have $2^{20} = 1,048,576$ virtual pages. A computer with a 22-bit physical address space and a 12-bit page size would have 10 bits of physical pages. It would have $2^{10} = 1,024$ physical pages. This is illustrated here.

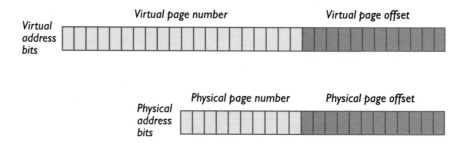

Since there are more virtual pages than physical pages, virtual pages can be resident or non-resident. If a virtual page is *resident,* then its contents are being stored in a physical page. In other words, a page of physical memory is being used to store the virtual page. That physical page is said to be *occupied.* If a virtual page is *non-resident,* then its contents are being stored on the disk. The virtual pages containing exception handlers are always resident. (You'll see why in a moment.) These pages are said to be *locked down.*

One of the purposes of the MMU is to store the following information about each virtual page:

■ Whether it is resident or non-resident, and

■ If it is resident, the number of the physical page it is stored in.

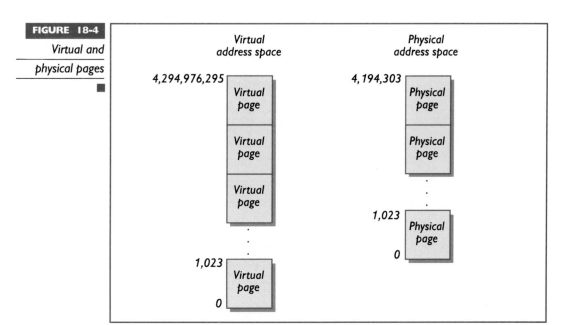

FIGURE 18-4

Virtual and physical pages ■

As you know, the microprocessor puts a virtual address on its address bus whenever it accesses memory. It could be retrieving an instruction from memory, retrieving data from memory, or storing data in memory. When the microprocessor puts a virtual address on the virtual address bus, the MMU sees it as a virtual page number and an offset. It checks whether the virtual page is resident. If it is resident, then it determines its physical page number. The MMU puts a physical address on the physical address bus that is a physical page number and the same offset. In this manner, a virtual memory access gets turned into physical memory access. This is shown in Figure 18-5.

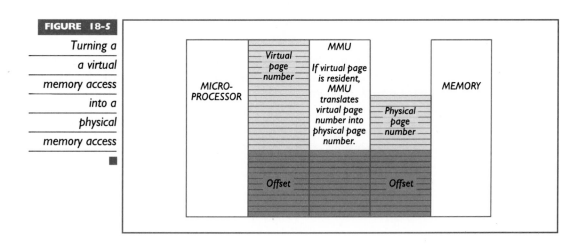

FIGURE 18-5

Turning a a virtual memory access into a physical memory access ■

If the virtual page is non-resident, it must be brought into memory from the disk and made resident.

1. The MMU causes an exceptional condition called a *page fault*.

2. When a page fault occurs, the microprocessor stops whatever it was doing and executes the page fault exception handler. (The page fault exception handler is stored on a page that is locked down. So executing it can't cause another page fault.)

3. The page fault handler checks whether any physical memory pages are unoccupied. If so, it loads the desired virtual page from disk into an unoccupied physical page.

4. The page fault handler updates the information in the MMU. Now, the MMU knows that this virtual page is resident. It also knows which physical page it is stored in.

If all physical pages are already occupied by virtual pages, then the page fault handler must *evict* one of the virtual pages. This means it must make room for the new page by making one of the resident pages non-resident.

1. The page fault handler selects one of the physical pages. (Locked-down pages are never selected.)

2. The page fault handler writes this physical page to the disk.

3. It brings the desired virtual page from disk into the now-unoccupied physical page.

4. It updates the information in the MMU. Now, the MMU knows that the evicted virtual page is non-resident and that the desired virtual page is resident. It also knows which physical page it is stored in.

Once the page fault handler has been executed, the access that caused the page fault exception can complete normally. This is because the desired virtual page is now resident.

Review

- System service routines are part of the operating system of a computer. System service routines can do useful things that almost all programs need done.

- System service routines can contain protected instructions. They can access protected resources. They can do dangerous things for other programs after taking necessary precautions.

- On a personal computer, the operating system allows the user to choose a program to run. The operating system can call the program as if it is a subroutine. When the program completes, the operating system continues running.

- The operating system allows a user to copy, erase, and rename disk files.

- On a computer with a time-sharing operating system, the micro-processor's time is shared by multiple programs and multiple users.

- A process is a program that is running.

- A process context is the set of conditions that must be true about the computer for a program to be running.

- For an operating system to be time-sharing, it must be able to stop a process, save its context, and restore the context of another process. This is called a context swap.

- If the microprocessor executes a yield system call, a context swap occurs.

- The timer interrupt handler can perform a context swap. Then, a context swap will occur periodically.

- Virtual memory is a way to make a microprocessor think it has more memory than it really has.

- Virtual memory is used when the virtual address space of a microprocessor is larger than its physical address space.

- Virtual and physical address spaces are divided into memory ranges called pages.

- An address can be thought of as a page number and an offset into the page.

- If a virtual page is resident, then its contents are being stored in a physical page.

- If a virtual page is non-resident, then its contents are being stored on a hard disk.

- A memory management unit (MMU) stores information about each virtual page, including whether the virtual page is resident. If it is resident, it stores the number of the physical page it resides in. Using this information, the MMU can translate a virtual address into a physical address.

- If the microprocessor accesses a virtual page that is non-resident, the MMU causes a page fault. The page fault handler makes the page resident and updates the information in the MMU.

- If all physical pages are occupied, the page fault handler must make one unoccupied by evicting a virtual page.

19

From Electrons to Artificial Intelligence

I N the previous 18 chapters, I've described how computers work. I started at a basic level, describing the simplest components of a computer. You learned about fundamental principles of electricity, and how transistors can act as switches. You learned how transistors can be used in gates and logic blocks to perform logical and mathematical operations. You saw how memories can store high and low voltages which can represent numbers— numbers that can be instructions to a microprocessor, or data to be processed by it. I discussed how devices could be controlled by a microprocessor and how operating systems manage and assist programs.

With the right program, a computer can perform difficult calculations and make complicated decisions quickly. A computer can do some things much faster than a human being can. This has made computers important and powerful tools in our daily lives. Human beings, however, do certain things easily that even very powerful computers have great difficulty doing. This is because computers haven't been programmed to think and move the way human beings do. Many scientists and engineers believe that computers *are* powerful enough to model human thought processes and behaviors, and they are trying to program computers to think and act like human beings. In this chapter, I will describe their attempts.

WHAT IS ARTIFICIAL INTELLIGENCE?

A computer can do many difficult things correctly and quickly, but there are also a lot of things it cannot do. No computer can drive a car in traffic on the freeway. No computer can land an airplane. No computer can compose a symphony. No computer can "get" a joke. No computer can learn to speak and understand a human language. These are tasks that we believe require intelligence. Scientists and engineers have had great difficulty programming computers to do these tasks. Why?

We perform tasks that require intelligence even though we may not know, down to the smallest detail, exactly how we're able to do them. When we do these tasks, we cannot predict every possible situation that will occur. Thus, we encounter new situations and problems, and we figure out ways to solve them by learning new ways to behave. Sometimes we make mistakes, and learn from them as well. These are some of the reasons we consider the tasks *intelligent*. Driving a car, landing an airplane, composing a symphony, and understanding a language are all intelligent tasks.

When a programmer writes a program, he must anticipate all situations that might occur and be able to predict all possible inputs to the program. He must then write instructions for the computer to deal with all these inputs. If the programmer doesn't predict inputs accurately, the computer will not be able to deal with them. The programmer must also write detailed instructions for the computer to generate all necessary outputs. Otherwise, the computer will not be able to do certain things. Intelligent tasks, however, usually require the ability to deal with unexpected information. They require the ability to learn to do new things. This is why it is difficult to program computers to perform intelligent tasks.

Computers cannot do things that they are not programmed to do. Some people say that computers will never be intelligent, because they just run programs. Because of this, they say that computers can't "think." They say that no program can deal with as much information as a human being can deal with, nor can it learn to do as many different things as a human being can.

People have tried very hard to program computers to perform intelligent tasks. For many years, people thought that playing chess was an intelligent task. Today, there are computers that can beat all but the best chess players in the world. We still don't consider them intelligent. Why? One reason is that all they can do is play chess. Even though they play chess very well, they cannot do the other things that human beings normally do. They can't even talk about playing chess. For many years, people thought that solving algebraic equations was an intelligent task. Today, there are computers that can solve very complicated algebraic equations. We still don't consider them intelligent. Why? One reason is that they don't *learn* to solve algebraic equations. They don't know what algebraic equations really mean. All they do is move the symbols in an algebraic equation according to certain rules. Even though they do so correctly and quickly, they don't seem to do so in the way human beings normally do.

Whenever we program a computer to perform a task, we end up having to understand the task completely. We must know precisely how it is done, down to the smallest detail. We end up instructing the computer exactly how to deal with every new situation and problem. Sometimes, we manage to program a computer to perform an intelligent task. However, we have programmed the computer to deal with every situation and problem. So even though the computer can perform the task, we don't feel that we have made it intelligent.

It is difficult to know for sure whether or not a task requires intelligence. No one knows exactly what it means to "think" or be "intelligent." So no one can say for sure whether or not computers are intelligent, or if they ever will be.

Most computer scientists and engineers believe that computers could think and reason like human beings. They believe that it's just a matter of writing the correct program. If the correct program were running on a computer, it *would* drive a car in traffic or land an airplane. It would do many things, including play chess, learn to solve algebraic equations, and understand English. Such a computer would be intelligent. Unlike human beings, however, it would not have *natural* intelligence. It would have man-made, or *artificial intelligence (AI)*. AI is the field in which people look for programs that make a computer intelligent.

The people who study AI can program a computer to do difficult things. As we have seen, when a computer can do these things, they don't seem to require intelligence after all. On the other hand, we don't know exactly what intelligence is. For these reasons, many people are annoyed and frustrated with the field of AI. They don't like to keep hearing that people who study AI will someday make computers intelligent. They like to say that people who study AI just write programs that make a computer do things it hasn't done before.

In the following sections, I am going to talk about the different approaches people have taken in the field of AI. They all overlap each other quite a bit. However, each approach focuses on what some scientists think is the most important aspect of intelligence.

MACHINE LEARNING

Some scientists believe that the ability to learn is the most important aspect of intelligence. They try to program computers to learn things in different ways. Their subject is called *machine learning*. Most people would agree that learning is knowing something you didn't know before. Perhaps, one way to make a computer learn is to put something in its memory that wasn't there before. However, it is not enough that some information be in a computer's memory. For example, suppose the following sentence was in a computer's memory in the form of ASCII characters, "The earth's diameter is 25,000 miles." Can we say that the computer has learned something? Not really. That would be like writing those words down and saying that the paper had learned something!

What does it mean to know something? This is a very difficult question. However, we must try to answer it in order to program a computer to know something it didn't know before. One answer is that when you know something, you can answer questions about it. If a computer can answer questions about something, it must know that thing. To answer questions about something in its memory, a computer must run a program. It must be able to accept a question from the user, interpret it, and answer it. If it doesn't have the answer, it must be able to say "I don't know." These are all very difficult tasks. So when you really think about it, knowing something means much more than just having a sentence stored in memory.

In Chapter 17, I said that the choice of a good data structure could make a program run faster and use less memory. The choice of a good data structure is even more important in AI. If the wrong data structure is used, the computer may not even be able to complete its task. Scientists have studied effective ways to represent statements about the world in a computer. Their subject is called *knowledge representation*. For example, if the computer stores a fact as a string of ASCII characters, it may have difficulty finding related facts. But by representing the knowledge differently, a computer may be able to access related knowledge quickly and be able to draw interesting conclusions more easily. It may be able to act on what it knows more quickly and may be able to tell when it *doesn't* know something. And, it may be able to learn new things easily.

There are different kinds of learning:

■ A person can learn about something by seeing examples of it.

■ A person can learn from his mistakes.

■ A person can learn by being taught.

■ A person can even learn new ways of learning.

Scientists have written programs that allow a computer to learn a few things in each of these ways.

Some scientists believe that a computer that learns and learns will eventually run out of memory. Its memory will be full of information that might be useless. These scientists are studying ways to make a computer forget information that is useless, in order to make room for new information.

PROBLEM-SOLVING AND SEARCH

Some scientists believe that the ability to solve problems is the most important aspect of intelligence. One way to represent a problem is by describing a starting state and a solution state. The *starting state* is a description of the current situation and the *solution state* is a description of the desired situation. For example, suppose you are in Portland and you want to get to Los Angeles. This problem could be represented by saying that the starting state is that you are in Portland. The solution state is that you are in Los Angeles. A problem represented in this manner is solved by changing the current state until it matches the solution state.

When you want to change your current situation, you take some kind of action. This action is represented in the computer by a *state operator*. If the current state is that you are in Portland, then some operators would be

- Drive north 20 miles.

- Walk east 1 mile.

- Take a taxi south 10 miles.

- Fly west 200 miles.

These operators represent actions that change the current state. Some operators bring the current state closer to the solution state. Other operators take the current state further from the solution state. The collection of all possible states is called the *problem space*. (Just as the range of possible numbers on an address bus is called the address space.)

One way to find the solution to a problem is to try different operators and change the current state until it matches the solution state. In this manner, problem solving is represented in the computer as a search through a problem space.

Game Trees

Computers can use search through a problem space to play games. For example, in tic-tac-toe, the starting state is an empty board like the one

Memory:
000000000

shown here. A tic-tac-toe board could be represented in the computer as an array of nine numbers, one for each board position. When there is an X in a position, the computer could put a 1 in the array. When there is an O in a position, the computer could put a 2 in the array. When the position is empty, the computer could put a 0 in the array. Initially, the array contains all 0's.

Two people who play tic-tac-toe have different sets of solution states. Each person knows several arrangements of X's and O's that represet a winning board for him. The computer can be programmed to "play" imaginary games "against itself." It can put 1's and 2's in the array according to the rules of tic-tac-toe. By doing this, the computer can play all possible games of tic-tac-toe. Two of these games are shown in Figure 19-1. The set of all games together looks like a tree. Each branch of the tree represents a different move by one of the players. Together, these representations of the game board are called a *game tree*.

FIGURE 19-1

Part of the

tic-tac-toe game

tree

■

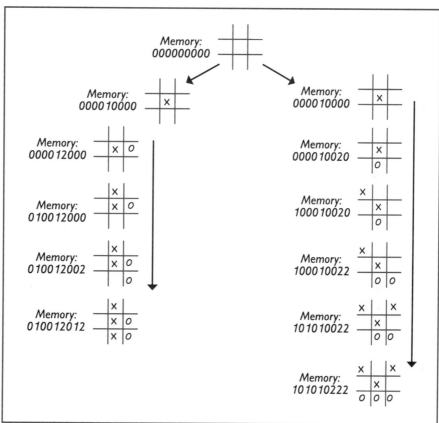

The computer could be programmed to play against a user. Instead of playing both sides of the game, the computer would play one side and let the user play the other. The computer would look at the current board and find it in the game tree. It would make a move that led toward a winning board. Such a computer would never lose a game. It would know all possible ways that a game could end. It would look several moves ahead in the tree. It could play in such a way that it would always win or tie with the user.

In a game tree, the number of branches depends on the number of possible moves that a player can make. The game tree for tic-tac-toe is quite small. This is because the largest number of possible moves a player can make is nine, when the board is completely empty. As squares of the board are filled in, the number of possible moves a player can make gets smaller. In contrast, the game tree for checkers is much larger, and the game tree for chess is many times bigger than the one for checkers. This is because, at every turn, a player can make hundreds of possible moves. It is estimated that the complete game tree for chess, including all possible games, would have 10^{120} boards. Suppose a computer could generate one billion (10^9) boards every second. To generate the whole game tree would require 10^{111} seconds. This is more than 10^{102} years. The number of years it would take for a computer to generate the complete tree is 1 with 102 zeros after it!

Obviously, a computer cannot generate the complete game tree for chess, as it can for tic-tac-toe. A computer that plays chess doesn't generate boards to the end of the game. It generates boards for the next few turns. By examining the possible boards that could exist in the next few turns, the computer decides what move to make. The best chess computers are also programmed with other strategies. Games played previously by other people are stored in a convenient representation in the computer's memory. The computer can check whether the game it is currently playing matches one of the previously played ones. From this, the computer can make good moves made previously by other people and avoid their mistakes.

LOGIC AND PROLOG

Some scientists used to think that logical reasoning was the most important aspect of intelligence. As you may recall from Chapter 3, logic means drawing a correct conclusion from facts. The facts are often called axioms. *Axioms* are statements that are assumed to be true. The following is an example of logical reasoning:

Axiom: Socrates is a man.

Axiom: All men are mortal.

Conclusion: Socrates is mortal.

The first axiom could be represented in the computer as a record with two fields containing two ASCII-character words, "Socrates" and "man." This is shown in the following illustration:

Field Name	Content
Thing	Socrates
Is_A	Man

The second axiom could be represented as a set of instructions. The instructions would look for records in which the second field contains "man." If such a record were found, the instructions would create a new record. The new record would contain the first field of the old record and "mortal" in its second field. This is shown in the following illustration:

Field Name	Content
Thing	Socrates
Is_A	Man

Field Name	Content
Thing	Socrates
Is_A	Mortal

In this manner, the computer would generate a correct conclusion based on facts. Suppose another axiom were added:

Axiom: All mortals are Earth-dwellers.

This axiom would cause another record to be added in the computer's memory, as shown here.

Field Name	Content
Thing	Socrates
Is_A	Man

Field Name	Content
Thing	Socrates
Is_A	Mortal

Field Name	Content
Thing	Socrates
Is_A	Earth-Dweller

Scientists have programmed computers to do this kind of reasoning. In fact, they have even created a special language in which computers can be programmed to solve problems using logic. This language is called *Prolog*. Many people thought that with the invention of Prolog, the problems of artificial intelligence were solved.

However, there are many problems with logical reasoning. For example, facts like "things with wings can fly" can be represented easily. Exceptions, like "penguins have wings but cannot fly" are more difficult. Even if they can be represented, it is difficult for a computer to take them into account while reasoning.

When a computer uses logical reasoning, it is difficult to teach it new facts. This is because every fact has hundreds of other facts associated with it. All of them must be programmed into the computer. Otherwise, the computer will be unable to draw interesting conclusions.

Axioms can be represented easily in the computer. However, facts that are true now may become false later. For example, "The year is 1993." Likewise, facts that are false now may become true later. Such facts are difficult to represent in the computer. Even if they are represented, it is difficult to make sure that false facts are never in the computer's memory.

EXPERT SYSTEMS

One kind of program that was developed by AI scientists has become widely used. It is called an expert, or rule-based system. An *expert system* is supposed to contain the knowledge of an expert in a particular subject. There are three parts to an expert system: *working memory, rules,* and an *inference engine.* Working memory is just the memory that the expert system works with. It contains data structures called *working memory elements,* or *WMEs.* Each WME contains a bit of useful information. An example of a WME is

```
(THING TYPE=MAN NAME=SOCRATES)
```

(Exactly how this WME is represented in memory doesn't really matter.)

Rules are very much like IF-THEN statements. The purpose of the rules is to manipulate WMEs. Each rule has a condition and an action. The *condition* contains

- A particular WME, or

- A particular *type* of WME, or

- A *set* of WMEs.

The *action* contains instructions to:

- Add a WME to working memory,

- Modify a WME, or

- Remove a WME from working memory.

Whenever the conditions of some rules match WMEs that are in working memory, those rules are said to be *triggered*. One of the triggered rules is selected to be *fired*. When a rule is fired, its action is performed. In this manner, new WMEs get put in working memory, WMEs in working memory are modified, and WMEs are removed from working memory. Here is a rule that adds a WME to working memory:

```
(if (THING TYPE=MAN NAME=?1)
-->
(THING TYPE=MORTAL NAME=?1))
```

The ?1 variable can stand for any value. This variable allows the condition to match several different WMEs. This rule's condition would match the WME that I showed you before. In this case, the variable should be made to stand for SOCRATES. Whatever the variable stands for gets used in the action. If this rule were fired, its action would create the following new WME:

```
(THING TYPE=MORTAL NAME=SOCRATES)
```

The inference engine does all the work in an expert system. It compares the conditions of rules with the contents of working memory. It determines which rules should be triggered. It selects which of the triggered rules should be fired. And it carries out the actions of the fired rule. The input to a rule-based system is a set of rules and WMEs. The output is another set of WMEs. The output WMEs contain decisions or new information that is generated from the input WMEs and the rules.

An expert system has been successfully used to diagnose illnesses. WMEs describing the symptoms that a patient has can be written. Based on these WMEs, the expert system generates new WMEs. The new WMEs can tell the doctor what disease the patient probably has. Or, they can tell the doctor which tests should be conducted for more useful information. Another expert system has been successfully used to configure large computer systems. A salesperson can write WMEs describing what a customer needs. Based on these WMEs, the expert system generates new WMEs. The new WMEs tell the salesperson exactly what hardware and software the customer should purchase, and how much everything will cost. A third expert system has been successfully used to design computer systems. A designer can write WMEs describing the kind of computer to be built. He can specify that he wants the fastest computer possible, or the cheapest computer possible. Based on these WMEs, the expert system generates new WMEs. The new WMEs tell the designer which chips and devices to buy and exactly how to connect them together.

CONNECTIONISM

Some scientists believe that the way the human brain is built is what gives us our intelligence. The brain is a collection of nerve cells, or *neurons*. Our senses send electrical impulses to the brain over neurons. The brain sends electrical impulses to our muscles over neurons, which causes the muscles to move. This is illustrated in Figure 19-2.

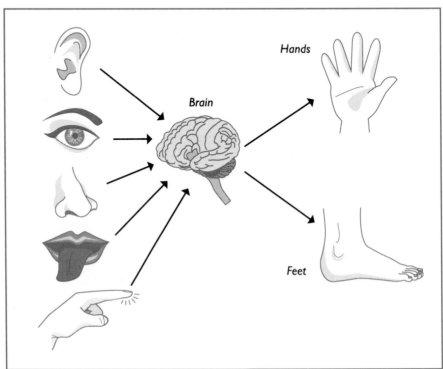

Within the brain, each neuron can be connected to several other neurons. This is illustrated in Figure 19-3. Sometimes, if an impulse travels over a neuron, it will cause impulses to travel over all the other neurons connected to the first neuron. Sometimes, an impulse travels over a neuron only if impulses arrive over many or all of the connected neurons. Neurologists have discovered that when we learn things, the connections between neurons become stronger. This means that an impulse traveling over one is more likely to cause an impulse to travel over the other.

The speed at which electrical signals travel over neurons is much less than the speed at which they travel in computers. This suggests that computers should be able to model neurons, and think and reason the way neurons allow us to. The idea that the connections between neurons are what make us intelligent is called *connectionism*. Scientists believe that by modeling neurons and the connections between them, we can make a computer intelligent. Models of the connected neurons are called *neural networks*. However, there is one major difference between the brain and a computer. In a computer, a few very fast devices work together simultaneously. When we think, on the other hand, thousands of relatively slow neurons work together simultaneously. Before we can program a computer to model the brain, we must understand how neurons work together.

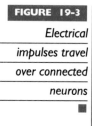

FIGURE 19-3

Electrical impulses travel over connected neurons

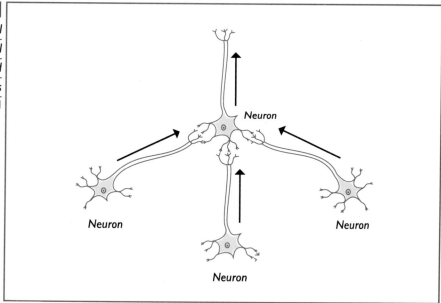

Neuron

Neuron

Neuron

Neuron

VISION

V

ision is the field in which scientists study how to make computers see and recognize objects in pictures and movies. A movie is represented in a computer's memory as a series of pictures. Each picture is represented as an array of pixels. Vision programs must analyze these pixels to recognize objects.

Recognizing the boundaries between objects is one important task that all vision programs must perform. This is called *edge detection*. For example, suppose that a picture contains a light object on a dark background. The light object is represented by pixels with large values. The dark background is represented by pixels with small values. A computer can examine small sections of the picture. If the pixels go from light to dark suddenly in a small section, then the computer knows the edge of the object passes through the section. This is illustrated in Figure 19-4.

It is very difficult for a computer to differentiate various objects from each other. It helps if the computer knows something about the objects: their shapes, sizes, or colors. However, this creates a difficult problem of knowledge representation. The knowledge must be represented in such a way that the computer can use it to differentiate objects in a picture.

Even the best vision program are unable to pick out objects if the picture

- shows them from an unusual angle,

- shows them in an unusual size,

- shows them under unusual lighting, or

- is blurred or distorted.

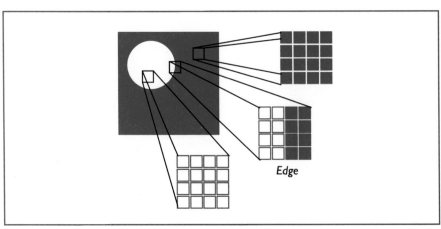

FIGURE 19-4

Edge detection

Edge

ROBOTICS

Robotics is the field in which scientists study how to make computers interact physically with the world. Robotics researchers write programs that allow computers to control robot arms and fingers, or even the wheels of toy cars. A computer controlling a robot must be able to see and recognize objects. Only then can it control a robot arm effectively, or move a car around obstacles. So robotics and vision researchers work together to help computers see and manipulate objects in the real world.

Some scientists don't believe we can build computers and robots that think and act like human beings yet. They believe that we don't know enough about how human beings think. On the other hand, we do know a lot about how some animals with lesser intelligence think. Some scientists believe we should make computers think like animals instead of trying to make them think like human beings. They believe this will eventually teach us enough to make computers and robots think and act like human beings. These scientists have built insect-like robots with legs and antennae. These robots run simple programs, but they have learned to walk, climb over obstacles, chase each other, stalk people, and retrieve objects.

Simple insect robots could be very useful even if they can't think and act like human beings yet. For example, a small robot could wander through your house vacuuming the carpet. Insect robots could also explore other planets. The Viking spacecraft that landed on Mars was actually a large, complicated, expensive robot which helped gather a lot of valuable information. However, it stayed in just one place. Some parts of the robot failed after a while and stopped sending information. Some scientists want to send hundreds of simple, cheap insect robots to Mars. Each one would crawl over the landscape and send back information. Even if many of the robots failed, the others could still send back valuable information. In this manner, we would spend less money and get more information.

COGNITIVE ARCHITECTURES

As you can see, there is a lot of overlap between the fields within AI. A robotics researcher must use vision techniques so that the robot can see. A vision researcher must represent knowledge in such a way that it can be used to recognize objects. All researchers must know about machine learning, otherwise their programs will never learn to do new, interesting things.

Some scientists believe that a wide range of abilities is required for a computer to think like a human being. They are looking for ways to give a computer all of these abilities simultaneously. These scientists are studying cognitive architectures. A *cognitive architecture* is a framework or system for accumulating and using knowledge. Scientists studying cognitive architectures are looking for:

- A small set of ways to represent all knowledge.

- A small set of flexible learning methods.

- A small set of problem-solving methods.

- A small set of ways to get input from the real world. This input could include sights, sounds, and even textures, tastes, and smells.

- A small set of ways to produce behaviors. This "output" could include moving about, speaking, and manipulating objects.

Researchers in cognitive architectures hope these methods will allow computers to do everything human beings can do.

Review

- AI is the field in which scientists look for programs that make a computer intelligent. No one, however, is exactly sure what it means to be intelligent.

- It is difficult to program a computer to perform intelligent tasks. These tasks require a computer to deal constantly with new situations and learn new behaviors.

- Some people don't think computers will ever be intelligent. Once computers have been programmed to perform tasks that are considered intelligent, those tasks no longer seem to require intelligence.

- Most computer scientists and engineers believe that a computer could be intelligent if only the right program were created for it.

- Scientists who study machine learning try to program computers to learn things in different ways.

- Scientists who study knowledge representation try to represent facts about the real world in effective ways.

Review (continued)

- In a computer, a problem can be described as

  A starting state,

  A solution state, and

  A collection of state operators.

- Problem solving can be represented as a search for a solution state within a problem space.

- The problem space for a board game can be represented by a game tree. A game tree can help a computer play against a human being.

- Logical reasoning means drawing conclusions from axioms.

- Prolog is a special language that allows computers to solve problems using logical reasoning.

- Expert systems include an inference engine, working memory, and rules. The inference engine uses the rules to manipulate working memory elements (WMEs). The resulting WMEs represent decisions and results based on the input WMEs.

- Scientists who study connectionism try to model, on computers, neurons and the connections between them.

- Scientists who study vision try to make computers see and recognize objects in pictures and movies.

- Scientists who study robotics try to make computers interact physically with the real world.

- Scientists who build insect robots believe they will eventually teach us about how humans think and behave.

- Scientists who study cognitive architectures look for ways to give a computer a wide range of abilities at once.

20

The Computers of the Future

C

OMPUTERS already play important roles in our daily lives. In this chapter, I'm going to talk about what computers will be like in the future. I'll describe how fast, powerful computers will transform our lives in the years to come.

MULTIMEDIA

Increasingly, computers are being used for multimedia. Media means "methods of communciation." Radio and television are examples of media. *Multimedia*, then, means "multiple methods of communication."

Multimedia computers communicate information by using several different kinds of output devices. Typically, they are connected to compact disc (CD) players, high-quality stereo systems, and videodisc players, as well as monitors and printers. They control these devices and use them in combination to teach and entertain users. For example, a multimedia computer might teach a user about Tchaikovsky by displaying an encyclopedia entry about him, reading it aloud, showing a short documentary about his life, and then playing an excerpt from the *Nutcracker Suite*. In the future, you can expect multimedia computers to play an increasingly important role in education and entertainment.

Multimedia computers make a tremendous amount of information available to a user. Often, this information is stored on CD-ROMs. A *CD-ROM* is an ordinary compact disc that is used to store computer files instead of music. You learned in Chapter 15 that a tape recorder can be connected to a computer, allowing it to retrieve information from tapes. Similarly, a special kind of CD player can be connected to a computer, allowing it to retrieve information from CD-ROMs. Unfortunately, computers cannot record information on CDs. That's what makes CD-ROMs like read-only memories. A single CD-ROM, however, can store up to 600 megabytes of data. So, a single CD-ROM can store the entire *Encyclopedia Britannica* and still have plenty of storage space available!

**WHAT MAKES
SUPERCOMPUTERS
SUPER**

Some problems require even more processing speed and power than workstations or mainframe computers have. These problems include weather prediction, analysis of airflow around airplanes, and analysis of underground water flow. Some of these problems are so important that solving them is worth a lot of money and effort. Supercomputers are computers especially built to solve such problems. Supercomputers have the fastest and most powerful processors of all computers.

Instead of using different kinds of silicon, transistors can be built with a substance called *gallium arsenide*. Processors built using gallium arsenide are faster than ones built using silicon. However, gallium arsenide devices are more expensive and more difficult to make than silicon devices. Also, if the processor is faster, other devices in the computer must be faster, too. That's why supercomputers have the fastest memories and storage devices of all computers.

Recently, engineers have started building computers containing hundreds of processors. To solve a large and difficult problem, each processor is assigned a part of it. Working together, the processors can solve the problem in a fraction of the time one would require alone. The processors are said to work in *parallel*. Computers with many processors are called *massively parallel processors*, or *MPPs*. Today, the fastest supercomputer in the world can perform 35 gigaflops, or 35 billion floating-point operations per second. The next goal of supercomputer engineers is to build one that can perform 1 teraflop, or 1 trillion floating-point operations per second.

There are special problems with building and programming MPPs. The processors in the supercomputer must communicate with each other to exchange data and results. If this communication does not take place quickly and efficiently, the whole computer is slowed down. Programmers must also be careful that the processors don't interfere with each other. One must not be allowed to overwrite a memory location that is being used by another. Most importantly, many problems simply can't be divided in a way that allows an MPP to solve it quickly. Each part of the problem might depend on the results of another part. Then, it is of no use for different processors to work on the parts together. They end up having to wait for each other.

NETWORKS

've already briefly discussed computer networks in Chapter 16. Networks allow computers to quickly exchange files of information. Computers can also be connected with each other over phone lines. In this manner, computers all over the world can exchange information with each other. Exchanging information over phone lines is slower than exchanging information over wires, but it is still very fast.

Today, there are networks over which computers around the world can exchange information. Suppose I need a file that is stored on a computer in Europe. If my computer is connected to one of the networks, I can ask my computer to contact the other computer and have it send mine the file. I can send ASCII files to other people who have computers on the network. When they use their computer, they can read messages I have sent them.

Scientists are working on ways to make communication between computers faster, cheaper, and more reliable. There may come a time when there is just one big virtual computer. You will feel like the computer on your desk is amazingly fast and powerful. Whenever you need some information or want to run a program, your computer will automatically access it for you from wherever in the world it is stored. If your computer is not powerful enough to run the program, it will ask a supercomputer to run it and give you the results. You may not even notice that this communication has happened.

VIRTUAL REALITY

n Chapter 16, I talked about simulation, and explained how the operation of an airplane could be simulated on a computer. The computer showed you pictures of things that exist in the real world. The computer knew about the sizes, shapes, and colors of these things. It calculated how they would look from the cockpit of an airplane and displayed them on the screen. Using input devices, you could move controls in the cockpit, and look in different directions. This is the basis of virtual reality. *Virtual reality* is the simulation of an entire world. The world may be similar to the real world, or it may be completely imaginary. Like virtual memory, virtual reality is reality that seems to exist, but doesn't.

Special input and output devices make virtual reality different from other simulations. One virtual reality output device is a special pair of glasses that contain TV screens. When a person wears these glasses, he sees a three-dimensional view of the virtual world. He feels like he is really inside this world instead of just seeing it on a video screen. The glasses may also allow the computer to detect the motion of the person's head. If the computer detects head movements, it changes the view shown in the glasses. Another output device is a special pair of headphones. Sounds that the wearer hears in the headphones seem to come from different directions in the virtual world. One virtual reality input device is a glove that allows the computer to detect hand and finger movements. The computer may show the image of a floating hand. If the computer detects hand or finger movements, it changes the image of the hand. The person can point in different directions to move around in the virtual world. He can pick up and move virtual objects using his virtual hand.

It can be a lot of fun to explore an imaginary world using virtual reality. However, virtual reality can also be very useful. With virtual reality, people can clearly see and experience things that may be difficult to imagine. They can learn things by experience, instead of by reading books or watching other people. Flight simulation is just one example of how virtual reality helps people learn new skills. Another example is from the field of chemistry. Chemists have always found that plastic models help them to understand the shape and structure of molecules. This is important because the shapes and structures of molecules affect how they will interact with other molecules. Virtual reality allows chemists to build and view models of highly complex molecules. The computer can even accurately simulate the interaction of molecules. Virtual reality will also allow doctors to practice operations on virtual patients. This will train doctors to operate on real patients. By communicating over networks, computers could help people all over the world meet in virtual conference rooms.

Computer systems for virtual reality are still very expensive. Many calculations are required to display images that are colored and shaded accurately and realistically. However, the prices of powerful microprocessors are always going down. Soon, more and more people will be able to experience virtual reality and benefit from it.

PEN-BASED COMPUTERS

Computers have gotten smaller and smaller in the past few years. This book was written on what is called a notebook computer. It is about the size of a small phone book and runs on a rechargable battery. It has a keyboard and a flip-up screen. The screen can display 16 shades of gray. This notebook computer has a built-in 1.4 megabyte 3 1/2-inch floppy-disk drive. It has an 80 megabyte hard-disk drive that is about the size of a deck of cards. It fits in my briefcase, so I can take it anywhere I want to go.

Recently, engineers have been trying to make computers even more portable and easy to use. *Pen-based computers,* such as the one shown in Figure 20-1, don't even need a keyboard. The input device is a special pen and screen. Whenever the pen touches the screen, a dot appears under it.

If you recall from Chapter 14, a video circuit takes the values in memory locations and uses them to draw pixels on the screen. A pen-based computer has a circuit that does the exact opposite. It dectects when you draw pixels on the screen and puts values in memory locations. In this manner, the circuit can tell the computer whenever you touch the screen with the pen. You can draw lines and curves on the screen. The computer can also draw items on the screen. Then, you can select them by touching them with the pen.

However, there is only so much you can do by selecting objects on the screen. There must be a way to give the computer word commands. When you write words on the screen, pixels get recorded in the computer's memory. The computer needs a way to translate these pixels into ASCII characters that it can interpret. So, a pen-based computer runs a special operating system that can understand written words. It can translate the pixels that you draw into ASCII characters for letters and numbers. You might have

FIGURE 20-1

A typical

pen-based

computer

guessed from reading Chapter 19 that vision researchers wrote the programs to recognize letters and numbers in "pictures."

You may have noticed that cellular phones have gotten so small that they can fit in your pocket. Companies that make computers are working on ways to make portable computers with built-in cellular phones. A computer with a cellular phone will always be able to communicate with other computers all over the world. If you had such a computer with you, you would never get lost. No matter where you were, your portable computer would be able to retrieve a map and show it to you. Satellites orbiting the earth would be able to detect a signal from your computer and pinpoint your location to within a few feet.

MICRO-MACHINES

By designing and building computers, scientists and engineers have learned skills and methods that are useful in other areas. The masking process for VLSI has taught them to make tiny parts on silicon wafers. By extending the masking process, some scientists have constructed tiny gears, mechanical switches, and motors on a silicon chip. They are so small that several of them could fit in the dot of an *i* or in the period at the end of a sentence. These are called *micromachines*. One advantage of micromachines is that hundreds of them can be produced on a single wafer, just as VLSI chips are. If a machine does not need to be very large, then a micromachine could be built more cheaply than a larger one. Another advantage is that micromachines can be built right into the microprocessors that control them.

Micromachines have another advantage: the motors in micromachines are so tiny that they require very little power to run. However, it is hard to give them the little power they do need. Scientists are working on different ways to produce electricity to power micromachines. Because micromachines require so little, the electricity can be generated in unusual ways. Most of the motors that have been built are powered by static electricity. Static electricity is what gives you a shock when you rub your feet on a carpet on a dry day.

Scientists have just started building micromachines. People like to speculate on what might be possible if microscopic robots were built using micromachines. For example, millions of solar-powered microrobots could be spread out on your lawn. When a blade of grass got too long, a micromachine would cut it. Your lawn would never need to be mowed!

Microrobots could be injected into human beings to perform delicate surgery. They could remove cholesterol from clogged arteries.

CONCLUSION

Computers make many people nervous. This is because computers that have been built in the past few years can do some amazing things. People are not yet used to machines that can do such things, and it is difficult to understand how computers can possibly do them.

It seems like computers are used everywhere, for everything. People who are not used to computers feel like their lives are being invaded. I have worked with computers since I was a teenager. Still, when I think of a single virtual computer that circles the earth, even I get nervous! However, I know that there is nothing magic about computers. They can do amazing things because people have built them to do amazing things. Computers are tools and are meant to help us. Sometimes they confuse and frustrate us. But we should be patient. By learning about computers and understanding how they really work, we can make them help us in wonderful ways we never imagined.

Glossary

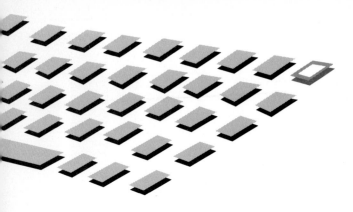

Absolute   An addressing mode in which the data is in a memory location whose address is in the instruction itself.

Action   The part of a rule that adds, removes, or modifies working memory elements (WMEs).

Addend   A number that is being added to another.

Adder   A logic block that can give the sum of two numbers in binary number representation.

Address   The number of a memory location.

Address bus   The conductors used to connect a microprocessor to a memory's address lines.

Addressing mode   The method for obtaining from memory any data an instruction may require. *See also* Absolute, Immediate, Predecrement, Postincrement, Register direct, *and* Register indirect.

Address registers   Microprocessor registers used to store addresses.

Address space   See Virtual address space.

Alt key   A keyboard key that, when pressed in combination with another key, gives that other key an alternative meaning.

AND gate   A gate whose output is at high voltage only if both of its inputs are at high voltage.

Apply (an operator)   To perform the indicated operation on numbers.

Arithmetic and logic unit (ALU)   Part of a microprocessor that performs arithmetic and logical operations on data.

Array   Consecutive memory locations containing similar data. *See also* Logic array.

Arrow keys   Keyboard keys normally used to move a cursor on the monitor screen.

Artificial intelligence (AI)   The field in which people try to write programs to make computers intelligent.

ASCII   American Standard Code for Information Interchange. A code which represents commonly used characters using seven-bit binary numbers.

Assembler   A program which translates assembly language instructions into machine language.

Assembly language   An intermediate-level language that uses mnemonics to specify machine language op-codes, and symbols to represent numbers.

Atoms   The microscopic particles out of which everything is made.

Axiom   In logic, a statement that is assumed to be true.

Binary number representation   Representation of any number by means of two symbols.

Bit   Binary digit. A symbol used for binary number representation.

Boolean   A type of operator that operates on the values TRUE and FALSE.

Branch   A type of instruction that causes a jump to a branch address if certain program status word (PSW) bits are set.

Bus   A group of conductors that are used together.

Byte   Eight bits.

Cache   A small, fast memory that ranks between registers and main memory in the storage hierarchy of a computer.

Cache hit   When the microprocessor accesses data that is stored in the cache.

Cache miss   When the microprocessor accesses data that is not already stored in the cache.

Call   A type of instruction that pushes the return address on the stack and then jumps to a subroutine.

Cathode-ray tube (CRT)   A device inside a monitor which fires a beam of electrons at a phosphor-coated screen.

CD-ROM   A compact disc used to store computer files instead of music.

Character   A letter, number, or other written symbol.

Chip   A small piece of silicon.

Circuit   A circular path for electrons.

Client   A computer that uses the services of other computers in a network.

Clocked D flip-flop   A flip-flop that stores its D input at its output when its CLK input goes to high voltage.

CMOS technology   A method of building gates and other devices using complementary transistors. CMOS stands for complementary metal-oxide semiconductor.

Cognitive architecture   A framework for accumulating and using knowledge.

Compare   A type of instruction that sets bits in the program status word (PSW) based on the values of numbers.

Compiler   A program which translates high-level language programs into assembly language or machine language.

Compile-time error   A mistake in a high-level language program that is detected by a compiler.

Complementary transistors   Transistors that do the same thing but with opposite voltages.

Computer-aided design (CAD)   The use of a computer to help describe how something should be built.

Condition   The part of a rule that must match working memory elements for the rule to be triggered.

Conductors (electrical)   Substances through which electrons can move easily.

Connectionism   The idea that it is connections between neurons that produces intelligence.

Contact cuts   Holes in the protective layer of silicon dioxide that allow transistors on a chip to be connected to each other.

Context swap   Saving a record of the current process context and restoring a different process context.

Control key   A keyboard key used in combination with other keys to alter their function.

Control structure   A useful sequence of instructions in a program.

Control unit   A kind of finite state machine that controls all other parts of a microprocessor.

Countdown value   The value that determines how often a timer interrupts the microprocessor.

Counter   An arrangement of flip-flops that counts the number of times its input goes from low to high voltage.

Cross-assembler   An assembler which is run by one microprocessor but which generates machine language instructions for a different microprocessor.

Cursor   A flashing line or square on the monitor screen that an editor uses to show where typed characters will appear.

Daisy wheel   A print head that consists of a wheel with raised letters on blocks at the ends of the spokes.

Data   Information.

Data bus   The conductors that connect a microprocessor to a memory's data lines.

Data path   The path that data can take between parts of a microprocessor.

Data processing   The storage, movement, and utilization of data.

Data registers   Registers used to store data in a microprocessor.

Data structure   A useful arrangement of data in memory.

Decimal number representation   Representation of any number using ten symbols (digits).

Declaration   A statement which tells a compiler the type of value that will be stored in a variable.

Decoder   A logic block which puts one of its outputs at high voltage when the number of that output is at its inputs.

Decrement   Opposite of increment. To reduce a number, usually by one.

Device   Any working part of a computer.

Digit   A symbol used for decimal number representation.

Directive   A statement which tells a compiler or assembler how to interpret other statements.

Directory   Information that tells a computer where the data on a disk is stored.

Disk crash   When a head of a hard-disk drive crashes into a platter.

Disk operating system (DOS)   A type of operating system specialized to run programs stored on disks and to manage disk files.

DO loop   A control structure which instructs that a body of instructions be executed at least once, and repeatedly until a Boolean expression evaluates to FALSE.

Dot-matrix   A print head that consists of pins that move in and out of a block.

Edge detection   Recognition of the boundaries between objects.

Editing keys   Keyboard keys used especially to give instructions to an editor.

Editor   A program which allows the user to create and modify text files.

Electron-beam lithography   Use of a controlled beam of electrons instead of ultraviolet light to polymerize photoresist in the masking process.

Electrons   Microscopic particles found inside atoms.

Element   One of the data items stored in an array.

Encoder   A circuit whose output lines indicate the number of the input line that is at low voltage.

Endless loop   A set of instructions that are executed repeatedly, forever.

Error message   A message produced by a compiler or assembler indicating why a program could not be compiled or assembled.

Escape key   A key normally found on computer keyboards that can be assigned a variety of functions depending on which program or operating system is running.

Evaluate   To find the value of an expression.

Evict   To make a virtual page non-resident by saving it on a disk.

Exceptional condition   An unusual microprocessor condition that requires the execution of an exception handler.

Exception handler   A kind of subroutine that is automatically called when an exceptional condition occurs.

Execute   To follow an instruction.

Expert system   See Rule-based system.

Expression   A collection of variables, numbers, operators, and other symbols that represents a value.

Field   A data item in a record.

Filament   The piece of metal inside a light bulb that glows when electrons move through it.

File   A gathering of information on a particular subject.

Finite state machine   A device with a finite number of states which can help a computer perform step-by-step operations.

Fire   To execute the action of a rule.

Firmware   Software stored in hardware, i.e., programs and data stored in read-only memory (ROM).

Flip-flop   An arrangement of gates that can store a high or low voltage.

Floating-point number   A number that includes a fractional part.

Floppy disk   A round, flexible disk used to store information.

Floppy-disk controller   The part of a computer that controls a floppy-disk drive.

Floppy-disk drive   A device which stores information on and retrieves information from floppy disks.

FLOPS   Floating-point operations per second.

Flush   To force a write-back cache to update main memory with the new data it contains.

FOR loop   A control structure which instructs that a body of instructions be executed a certain number of times.

Formatting   The preparation of a floppy or hard disk for the storage of information.

Free block   A set of consecutive, unused memory locations.

Freeze   A system crash.

Function keys   Keys on a keyboard in addition to letter and number keys used for special input to programs.

Gallium arsenide   A substance used in place of silicon to make transistors with very small switching times.

Game tree   A representation of configurations that are possible during the play of a board game.

Gate An arrangement of transistors whose output can be predicted from its input(s).

Generator A machine that can move electrons over long distances through wires.

Gigabyte (GB) Approximately one billion (1,073,741,824) bytes.

Hang A system crash.

Hard-disk drive A fast, large storage device that ranks between main memory and other storage devices in the storage hierarchy of a computer.

Hardware The physical components of a computer.

Hertz (Hz) Cycles per second. Referring to how often the CLK input to a computer's microprocessor alternates from high to low voltage.

High-level language A language in which one statement can translate into multiple machine language instructions.

High-voltage terminal The metal part on a battery that draws electrons in.

Immediate An addressing mode in which the data is in the instruction itself.

Increment Opposite of decrement. To increase a number, usually by one.

Index The position of an element in an array.

Inference engine The part of a rule-based system that determines which rules are triggered and which rules are fired.

Ink-jet A print head that consists of tubes in a block that squirt ink onto the paper.

Input Information you give to a device.

Input/Output (I/O) devices Devices that provide input from a user to a computer and that display output from a computer to a user.

Instruction length How many numbers there are in a machine language instruction.

Instruction set   The set of numbers that are valid instructions to a microprocessor.

Insulators (electrical)   Substances through which electrons cannot move easily.

Intelligence   Roughly, the natural human ability to acquire and act upon large amounts of knowledge.

Intermediate-level language   A language in which one statement translates into a single machine language instruction.

Interpreter   A program which combines an editor and a compiler, allowing users to execute statements immediately after typing them.

Interrupt line   A microprocessor input line that allows devices to interrupt its execution.

Interrupt request   When a device puts one of a microprocessor's interrupt lines at high voltage.

Interrupt service routine   A kind of subroutine that is automatically called as a result of an interrupt request.

Interrupt vector   The address of the interrupt service routine for a particular interrupt line.

Iron oxide   Rust. Used to store information on cassette tape.

JK flip-flop   A flip-flop whose output can be set, reset, or toggled by its inputs.

Joystick   A movable stick in a base used in conjunction with a button to provide input to a computer.

Jump   An instruction that tells the microprocessor to begin retrieving instructions for execution from a new address.

Keyboard   An input device consisting of a group of buttons labeled with letters, numbers, and other characters.

Kilobyte (KB)   Approximately one thousand (1,024) bytes.

Knowledge representation   The field in which people try to find effective ways to store statements about the world.

Large-scale integration (LSI)   The placement of up to 5,000 transistors on a single chip.

Least significant bit (LSB)   The rightmost bit in a binary number.

Linked list   A collection of records where, in each record, one field is a pointer to the next record.

Locked down   Referring to a virtual page whose contents are permanently stored in a computer's memory.

Logic   Taking something you know and drawing a valid conclusion from it.

Logic array   An arrangement of input and output lines, horizontal and vertical NOR gates.

Logic block   A collection of gates connected together to do one thing.

Loop   A type of instruction that causes a microprocessor to execute instructions it has previously executed.

Low-level language   A language which can be directly interpreted by a microprocessor.

Low-voltage terminal   The metal part on a battery that pushes electrons out.

Machine language instruction   A number that tells a microprocessor's control unit which microprogram to execute.

Machine learning   The field in which people try to make computers learn things in different ways.

Mainframe   A large computer that can be used by many people simultaneously.

Mask   A dark pattern on a clear plate used during the masking process.

Masking   The process that allows placement of tiny pieces of substances on a chip.

Massively parallel processor (MPP)   A type of supercomputer with hundreds or thousands of processors working together.

Media   Methods of communication.

Megabyte (MB)   Approximately one million (1,048,576) bytes.

Memory   A device that a computer uses to store numbers in binary number representation.

Memory location   In a memory, a set of transistors or flip-flops that stores one number.

Memory management unit (MMU)   A device that tells the computer which virtual page is stored in each physical page.

MFLOPS   Megaflop. One million floating-point operations per second.

Microinstruction   One state of a microprocessor's control unit.

Micromachine   A tiny machine constructed on a silicon chip using the masking process.

Microprocessor   A small device that processes data.

Microprogram   A set of microinstructions.

Minuend   A number from which another is being subtracted.

MIPS   Millions of instructions per second.

Mnemonic   In assembly language, an easy-to-remember word that specifies a machine language operation.

Mode bit   A program status word (PSW) bit that determines whether the microprocessor can execute protected instructions.

Monitor   An output device similar to a television.

Most significant bit (MSB)   The leftmost bit in a binary number.

Mouse   An input device that allows a user to point to and choose objects displayed on the screen.

Multiple-input gates   NAND and NOR gates with more than two inputs.

Return A type of instruction that pops the return address off the stack and stores it in the PC, returning execution to the instruction following the call instruction.

Return address The value in the PC pushed on the stack by a call instruction.

Robotics The field in which scientists study how to make computers interact physically with the world.

RS flip-flop An arrangement of gates whose output can be set or reset.

Rule-based system A type of AI program that stores the knowledge of an expert in the form of rules.

Rules Statements which match working memory elements (WMEs) and, if fired, add, remove, or modify WMEs.

Run To follow the instructions in a program.

Run-time error A mistake in a program that is not detected until the program is run.

Schematic diagram Also simply "schematic." A picture consisting of schematic symbols.

Schematic symbols Simple pictures of devices.

Sector Sections that a floppy-disk track is divided into.

Sector map Part of the directory that tells a computer which disk sectors contain data and which are empty.

Sector size The amount of data that can be stored in a disk sector.

Selector See Two-line selector.

Selenium A substance used on the cylinder in a laser printer.

Semiconductors Substances that are conductors sometimes and insulators at other times.

Server (dedicated) A computer which does nothing but provide a service to other computers in a network.

Silicon   A type of atom out of which glass, sand, and transistors are made.

Silicon dioxide   A chemical whose formula is SiO_2.

Simulation   A computer model of something in the real world.

Small-scale integration (SSI)   The placement of up to 100 transistors on a single chip.

Software   The programs and data used by a computer.

Solution state   A computer representation of the solution to a problem.

Stack   A free block of memory accessed using a stack pointer.

Stack overflow   When the value of the stack pointer exceeds the address space of a microprocessor.

Stack pointer (SP)   An address register that always contains the address of the first location in a free block of memory.

Stack underflow   When the value of the stack pointer is decremented below zero.

Starting state   A computer representation of the initial state of a problem.

Startup   The alternation of a CLK line between high and low voltage that begins when the computer is turned on.

Startup program   The program that is automatically run when the computer is first turned on.

State   The condition of a device, especially whether its outputs are at high or low voltage.

State diagram   A picture that shows the states that a finite state machine transitions through.

State operator   An action that changes the current state of a problem.

Storage hierarchy   An arrangement of methods for storing data.

Subroutine   A single useful set of instructions that might be executed from anywhere in a program.

Substrate   Base.

Subtracter   A logic block that finds the difference of two numbers in binary number representation.

Subtrahend   A number that is being subtracted from another.

Supercomputer   A large, expensive computer with one or more extremely fast, powerful processors for solving difficult problems.

Switch array   A circuit that could be placed under a set of keys on a keyboard to indicate which one is pressed.

Switching time   The time it takes for a change in voltage to travel across the bottom layer of a transistor.

Symbol   In assembly language, a word that stands for a number.

Symbol table   Memory that an assembler uses to store symbols and the numbers they stand for.

System call   An instruction that puts the microprocessor in protected mode and calls a system service routine.

System call vector   The address of a system service routine.

System crash   When something goes wrong and the computer stops accepting input or displaying output.

System service routine   A kind of subroutine that contains protected instructions and is called by a system call instruction.

T flip-flop   A flip-flop whose output toggles when its input goes briefly from low to high voltage.

Terminal   A metal part on a battery. *See also* High-voltage terminal *or* Low-voltage terminal. Also, a simple I/O device that can be used to communicate with computers.

Text file   A file containing ASCII-coded characters.

Thin oxide   A special type of silicon that is always an insulator.

Timer   A device that can periodically interrupt the microprocessor.

Time-sharing Division of a microprocessor's execution time among several programs.

Timing diagram A picture that shows what voltage different conductors are at over time.

Toner A substance that a laser printer uses to mark paper.

Tracks Concentric rings that a formatted floppy disk is divided into.

Transistor The simplest, smallest, and most important device in a computer. *See also* PNP transistor *or* NPN transistor.

Transition The change of a finite state machine from one state to another.

Triggered Referring to a rule whose condition matches working memory elements (WMEs) in working memory.

Truth table A table showing the output of a gate or logic block for every possible input.

Two-line selector A device that allows one of two inputs to be selected for output.

Ultraviolet A color of light that is invisible to the human eye but which can be produced by special light bulbs.

Unary A type of operator that is applied to just one value.

Underflow When the answer of a subtraction is less than zero.

User A person operating a computer.

Vaccuum tube A device that was used, prior to the development of transistors, in early computers.

Variable A symbol that stands for an address.

Vector scanning Creating pictures on a monitor screen by drawing lines of glowing phosphor at various lengths and angles.

Very-large-scale integration (VLSI) The placement of up to 50,000 transistors on a single chip.

Video circuit   A circuit which reads numbers from video memory and uses them to control a cathode-ray tube (CRT).

Video memory   The section of memory from which a video circuit reads numbers to draw pictures on the screen.

Virtual   Seeming to exist when actually nonexistent.

Virtual address space   The range of addresses that a microprocessor can place on its address bus.

Virtual memory   Making a computer behave as if it has more memory than it really has.

Virtual reality   The simulation of an entire world on a computer.

Vision   The field in which scientists study how to make computers see and recognize objects.

Wafer   A circular sheet of n-silicon.

WHILE loop   A control structure which instructs that a body of instructions be executed repeatedly as long as a Boolean expression is true.

Wire   A thin piece of metal surrounded by plastic that forms a tunnel for electrons to travel through.

Working memory   The memory used by a rule-based system.

Working memory elements (WMEs)   Bits of information stored by a rule-based system.

Workstations   Computers in a network.

Write-back cache   A type of cache which does not update memory when the microprocessor writes data if the old data is stored in the cache.

Write-through cache   A type of cache which updates memory whenever the microprocessor writes data.

Yield   A type of system call that causes a record of the current process context to be saved and a different process context to be restored.

INDEX